DIMENSION

FYI

2nd Edition

For Teams™

Based on the Team Architect®

FOR TEAM MEMBERS, TEAM LEADERS,
AND TEAM COACHES

Cara C. Capretta, Robert W. Eichinger,
Michael M. Lombardo & Victoria V. Swisher

FYI For Teams™

Tel. +1 952-345-3610
Tel. +1 877-345-3610 (US/Canada)
Fax. +1 952-345-3601
www.kornferry.com
www.lominger.com

Leadership Architect® is the exclusive registered trademark of
Lominger International: A Korn/Ferry Company.

ISBN 978-1-933578-18-7

Item number 21024

FYI For Teams™ 2nd Edition Printings:
version 09.1a 1st—06/09
version 09.1a 2nd—02/10
version 09.1a 3rd—04/11

Table of Contents

Factor V: TASK SKILLS

The Effort Necessary to Execute Successfully

Factor VI: TEAM SUPPORT FROM THE ORGANIZATION

How Well the Leadership of the Organization Enables the Team to Perform

Factor VII: TEAM LEADER FIT

How Well-Matched the Team Leader Is with the Needs of the Team

Appendix A:

Appendix B:

Appendix C:

Introduction

Who is this book for?

This book was designed for any motivated team, team member, or team leader with a need at any level in the organization. The suggestions provided for diagnosing and remedying team development needs will also help anyone who is serving as a team facilitator or team coach.

Any team member or team who has not yet accepted a need or limitation or weakness or developmental opportunity will not be helped by what's in this book. If the team, team member, or team leader is in denial, rationalizing, confused, or being defensive about having needs, nothing in this book will help.

Teams and team members who do accept that they have a need but do not have the motivation, drive, urgency, or energy to do anything about it also won't be helped by what's in this book.

So, this book is intended for teams and team members who believe they have a need and want to do something about it. Additionally, this book references other developmental resources. Many times a team, team member, or team leader will have a vague notion of what's wrong but can't quite define it. This book contains hundreds of very specific needs to choose from.

What does it mean when you say a team has a need?

When it is said that the team has a weakness, there are a number of possibilities:

1. The entire team is weak on something—like setting priorities. In that case, the whole team should work on how to set priorities.
2. Some team members are not good at setting priorities and therefore cause problems for the rest of the team. In that case, those particular team members should work on priority setting with help provided by those team members who are already skilled.
3. One member of the team is bad at setting priorities and that one person is preventing the entire team from being effective. In that case, that one person needs to work on the need with support from the rest of the team.
4. The entire team is stumbling but the causes are many. Most members have a need or two that are contributing to the less-than-stellar performance.

In that case, each member would have a development plan on his/her specific need(s).

Use of this book will drive the creation of one or more of a wide variety of development plans to improve one or more team competencies and to impact individuals, subgroups, and the entire team.

The 200 tips in this book will help any team, team member, or team leader who recognizes specific needs and is motivated to do something about them. If that's you or your team, read on.

Where did these 20 dimensions come from?

The 20 effectiveness dimensions that represent the main chapters of *FYI for Teams*™ come from the Team Architect®. These dimensions are based on the extensive research that has identified the key behaviors imperative for high-performance teams. The Team Architect® measures seven factors of team functioning. These seven factors compose the T7 Team Effectiveness Model. These seven factors include:

I.   THRUST – A common mind-set about what needs to be accomplished.
II. TRUST – Trusting others to do what's right for the team and for each other.
III. TALENT – The necessary collective skills to get the job done.
IV. TEAMING SKILLS – Operating the team's business efficiently and effectively.
V.   TASK SKILLS – The effort necessary to execute successfully.
VI. TEAM SUPPORT FROM THE ORGANIZATION – How well the leadership of the organization enables the team to perform.
VII. TEAM LEADER FIT – How well-matched the team leader is with the needs of the team.

The first five factors assess conditions, skills, and processes *inside* the team. The last two factors measure issues *outside* the team. Factor VI examines the degree of support an organization provides the team. Factor VII diagnoses the match (or fit) between the team members and the team leader. Embedded in these seven factors are 20 dimensions of team functioning that the T7 Model suggests are critical for successful team performance.

Where did the remedies in *FYI for Teams*™ come from?

FYI for Teams™ contains 200 direct tips for developing team performance. A rich array of research exists on high-performing teams—what effective teams do well, what stumbling teams have trouble with, what experiences teach the effective skills, what the experiences look like, and what the key drivers are. The content of the remedies is based on this research. You'll also see references to the best books that we've seen on the various topics in the pages that follow.

Additionally, the authors have been researchers and practitioners in the team development business for a combined 75 years. We've heard hundreds of teams and team members describe their difficulties during meetings and team-building sessions, worked with them to figure out what's getting in their way, and have tested ideas for fixing things with them. We know from experience and research what tips are most likely to work.

The structure of this book:

Each of the 20 chapters addresses one of the 20 team effectiveness dimensions and includes the following sections:

- **Definition** – To clearly describe the dimension.
- **Quotes** – To inspire thinking about the dimension.
- **Items** – A list of the Team Architect® items contained in that particular dimension. Note that these items are numbered in the order they occur in the survey. When the survey is administered electronically, as is typical, the eTeam™ Online Survey items are presented in a randomized order.
- **Unskilled** – A list of descriptors that applies to teams that do not demonstrate strength in the dimension.
- **Skilled** – A list of descriptors that applies to teams that demonstrate exceptional strength in the dimension.
- **Overused** – A list of descriptors that applies to teams that demonstrate strength that is used too much or too singly in the dimension. We have also listed Compensating Dimensions and Compensating Competencies to use when a team needs to compensate for overused strengths.
- **Some Causes of Poor Performance** – A list of some of the root causes that can explain why your team is weak in the dimension.
- **The Map** – A description of the dimension to provide a broad context. The map explains key elements of the dimension and their importance.
- **Some Remedies** – Suggestions for actions that teams can take to increase effectiveness in each dimension. Based on our research and experience, these are the tips that are most likely to work. Choose a few to include in your development plan.
- **Suggested Readings** – A reference list of resources we've found useful in learning about and further exploring issues related to each dimension.
- **Translation to the Leadership Architect® Competency Library** – A list of the Leadership Architect® competencies that would most likely be in play for each Team Architect® item.

What's new for the 2nd Edition?

While maintaining the integrity of the book, we've introduced new content to make it easier for your team or team members to identify what goes well and where to focus team development. New or updated content includes:

A *Work Team Effectiveness* chapter details our view on team effectiveness, introduces the T7 Team Effectiveness Model, and offers a comparative review of other well-known team effectiveness models.

Quotes provide food for thought and inspiration.

Suggested Readings were selected from hundreds of research studies, articles, and books to ensure we stay current and have good sources to recommend, sources you can readily transfer into your team development plan.

Updated Remedies in each dimension provide suggestions for actions that teams can take to enhance effectiveness in each dimension. We looked at the most current literature on team effectiveness and updated where appropriate.

An added focus on *Virtual Teams* is included in this edition. As organizations become increasingly global, the presence and impact of virtual teams has also increased. In the United States alone, two-thirds of all companies rely on virtual teams to perform everyday work. Each Dimension chapter addresses the special conditions required for virtual team effectiveness.

The *Development Plan* in Appendix A has a new template where you can record your team's development needs and action plan. Two examples illustrate ways to maximize the plan's effectiveness when you are addressing unskilled and overused development needs.

Guiding principles behind the remedies:

- **Brief.** Most readers, being motivated people with needs, want to get started right away. They want the low-hanging fruit. They want quick help. The tips were designed to help teams get started quickly and see results as soon as they begin executing the tips.

- **A focus on ease of application.** While there are many complex and involved methods available to increase proficiency on team skills, most are not included here. In *FYI for Teams*™, we assume that the team is not very good at whatever need they are trying to address and would appreciate tips that don't assume they are practiced or proficient. This book is for teams that want to get started and do something.

- **Just the 10 key tips.** Hard as it was to hold ourselves to 10 topics per dimension, we believe the 10 most likely or 10 most common topics to deal with will do you the most good. Where the topic is quite complex, we recommended a book as well.

- **Quick results.** While some of our topics involve longer-term effort, most are things teams can do tomorrow and hopefully see some quick improvement.

Guiding principles behind the suggested readings:

Each dimension in *FYI for Teams*™ has 10 to 18 sources for further reading.

In selecting the readings, we used these criteria:

- **ROI** – Is there a significant and immediate payoff for reading this book? Are there developmental suggestions busy people can implement?

- **Organization** – Is the book well-laid-out? Is it easy to find what you are looking for?

- **Ease** – Is it well-written?

- **Solid** – Is the advice more than opinion?

- **Prolific** – Are there lots of tips and examples?

- **Available** – Is the book available?

How do I use this book?

1. **Determine the need.** From regular feedback or use of the Team Architect® cards or the eTeams™ Online Survey, try to determine what the need is and which needs to work on. Sometimes even excellent feedback can identify the wrong need. Even if everyone agrees that the team is having problems with open communication, the question is why? Maybe the real problem is due to Trust in Truthful Communication (Dimension 4). It could also be any of the other Trust dimensions, Conflict Resolution (Dimension 12), or even Focusing (Dimension 15). So if none or only a few of the tips for the team's identified need seem to make sense, check other likely dimensions to see if the need is more likely one of these.

   There are four conditions under which some development might be called for:

   – The team or one or more team members are average in a skill that needs to be higher.

   – The team or one or more team members are weak (unskilled) in an important area.

   – The team or one or more team members are untested (maybe unskilled) in an important area.

   – The team or one or more team members overuse or overdo a strength to the point that it is causing problems for the team.

2. **Read the unskilled definition for the need.** Which bullet points describe the need best? Look to the skilled definition. What would the team like to be able to do when it is done working on this need? This is the before and after picture.

3. **Check the causes that might apply.** Many developmental efforts have floundered because the plan attacked the wrong problem. Write down the team's specific need—what it looks like, what causes it, who it plays out with, and in what situations.

4. **Read the map for the dimension.** The map gives the lay of the land. It reviews the general case of the behavior, how it operates, and why it's important. The map sets context and helps clarify what the dimension is all about.

5. **Look at the general plan.** Appendix A lists 10 ways to develop in any area. Pick any of those that seem to fit. This general, or universal, plan can be used as a basic core for any plan.

6. **Look at the remedies and pick the specific ones that apply.** Each topic is written against a specific manifestation of being unskilled at the dimension. It is unlikely that all of the topics or remedies will apply to any team or person. Pick a few that apply. Start small. Think back to the causes the team checked and the "why it's important" noted from the map.

7. **Look at the suggested readings listed.** They might also be helpful to deepen your understanding on your needs and to help put together the action plan.

8. **Look at the Leadership Architect® Competencies associated with the need.** Each competency has a complete development plan associated with it in *FYI For Your Improvement*™ or the *Career Architect® Development Planner*. It may be that one or more team members will need to build or modify their personal development plan(s) to improve their effectiveness in the team.

9. **Lay out a plan and a schedule.** The plan should include at least three items the team will work on immediately. Use the development plan in Appendix A. The team should measure the number of times they did this or didn't do that and record these efforts so they can track improvement. Set a specific time frame of no more than a month to try these items repeatedly. If the time frame is longer or indefinite, the team will be less likely to do anything. Start today.

FYI for Teams™ **contains numerous resources:**

- Tips for the 20 team effectiveness dimensions are listed in each corresponding chapter of this book.
- Appendix A contains a general, or universal, plan for attacking any developmental need—anything you or your team wants to get better at doing—along with sample templates to use when creating a plan.
- Appendix B contains the 80 Team Architect® Sort Card Items by Factor and Dimension.
- Appendix C contains the Competency Summary: A listing of the 23 Leadership Architect® Competencies that are most associated with the 20 Team Architect® Dimensions—the 23 key characteristics (competencies) most likely to drive overall team effectiveness; mapping to the Leadership Architect® Competency Library; developmental difficulty for team dimensions based on mapping to the Leadership Architect® Competencies; and a complete list of the 67 Leadership Architect® Competencies.

Additional references:

This book can be used as a stand-alone assessment and development source, in conjunction with the Team Architect® or eTeams™ Online Survey, or in conjunction with *FYI For Your Improvement*™—a comprehensive book for individual development that includes a full library of leadership competencies and tips. *FYI For Your Improvement*™ contains 10 tips for each of the 67 Leadership Architect® Competencies and the 19 Career Stallers and Stoppers identified in research over the decades. More extensive developmental recommendations on the same material are contained in the *Career Architect® Development Planner*. A subset of the 67 Leadership Architect® Competencies most closely linked to a particular dimension appears at the end of each chapter.

About the Authors

Cara C. Capretta

Cara Capretta is a former Senior Partner of Korn/Ferry Leadership and Talent Consulting. Prior to Korn/Ferry's acquisition of Lominger International in 2006, she was President and Chief Operating Officer at Lominger. She is the coauthor of *FYI for Talent Management*™, a book for developing learning agility—a concept that is strongly connected to being a "high potential," and coauthor of *The Interview Architect*®, a book for developing competency-based interview guides. Cara has over 15 years of practical experience working with leaders, teams, and organizations on development. Prior to joining Lominger, she was the Director of Executive Development for Nationwide, a Fortune 500 insurance company, where she designed and implemented a succession planning system to identify, develop, and place global talent in an organization with over 30,000 employees. She currently resides in Columbus, Ohio.

Robert W. Eichinger

Bob Eichinger is Vice Chairman of the Korn/Ferry Institute for Korn/Ferry International. Prior to Korn/Ferry's acquisition of Lominger International, he was cofounder and CEO of Lominger Limited, Inc. and cocreator of the Leadership Architect® Suite of management, executive, and organizational development tools. During his 40+ year career, he has worked inside companies such as PepsiCo and Pillsbury, and as a consultant in Fortune 500 companies in the United States, Europe, Japan, Canada, and Australia. Dr. Eichinger lectures extensively on the topic of executive and management development and has served on the Board of the Human Resource Planning Society. He has worked as a coach with more than 1,000 managers and executives. Some of his books include *The Leadership Machine*, written with Mike Lombardo, *100 Things You Need to Know: Best People Practices for Managers & HR*, written with Mike Lombardo and Dave Ulrich, and *FYI for Strategic Effectiveness*™, written with Kim Ruyle and Dave Ulrich.

Michael M. Lombardo

Mike Lombardo has over 30 years experience in executive and management research and in executive coaching. He is one of the founders of Lominger Limited, Inc., publishers of the Leadership Architect® Suite. With Bob Eichinger, Mike has authored 40 products for the suite, including *The Leadership Machine, FYI For Your Improvement*™, the *Career Architect*®, *Choices Architect*®, and VOICES®. During his 15 years at the Center for Creative Leadership, Mike was a coauthor of *The Lessons of Experience*, which detailed which learnings from experience can teach the competencies needed to be successful. He also coauthored the research on executive derailment revealing how personal flaws and overdone strengths caused otherwise effective executives to get into career trouble, Benchmarks®, a 360° feedback instrument, and the Looking Glass® simulation. Mike has won four national awards for research on managerial and executive development.

Victoria V. Swisher

Vicki Swisher is an Intellectual Property Development Consultant of Korn/Ferry Leadership and Talent Consulting. Vicki has a broad range of experience in human resource development, with much of her work centered in the areas of change leadership, performance management and improvement consulting, instructional design, and training. Prior to joining Korn/Ferry, she was in an organizational effectiveness leadership role with Hartford Life. While at Hartford Life, Vicki rolled out a comprehensive change management methodology and provided internal consulting to client partners in the areas of performance management and leadership development. Previously, Vicki spent 15 years in the hospitality sector with Marriott International and the Ritz-Carlton Hotel Company. During her time in the hotel industry, she held leadership positions in group sales and catering, worked in public relations, and managed a sales training function.

Acknowledgements

We are indebted to a number of people who contributed ideas and assistance in the preparation of this book.

King Yii (Lulu) Tang did an outstanding job conducting a thorough literature review and combed through hundreds of research studies, articles, and books to ensure we were current and had good sources to recommend. Lulu contributed significant content to the new remedies and helped shape our point of view on virtual teams.

Evelyn Orr was instrumental in updating the appendices, including creating a new, more user-friendly team development plan template and sample plans which make it easier for teams to work on a need.

Ken De Meuse and Kim Ruyle served as reviewers and made great suggestions to improve the book. Ken also did much of the heavy lifting in developing the new Work Team Effectiveness chapter.

Lesley Kurke, Diane Hoffman, and Zach Schaap did an excellent job of design, layout, and production.

Bonnie Parks, as always, did an outstanding job of proofreading and editing our manuscript.

We appreciate the contributions of all.

Work Team Effectiveness

Corporate America is having a hot love affair with teams. And why not?
When teams work, there's nothing like them for turbocharging productivity.
Brian Dumaine – Author

We're no strangers to groups. We've all been members. We've been active participants. Perhaps we played trombone in a high school band. Pitched on our Little League baseball team. Served on the manufacturing plant's safety committee. Sung in the church choir. Loved and served our families. We can't escape groups. We carpool together. Eat together. Play together. Work together. Groups united by a purpose and interrelated activities—*teams*—have become an ongoing part of our everyday life. Most of us have participated in highly successful teams and also in teams that failed to meet expectations. Given this wealth of experience, we know quite a bit about how teams operate. Or, do we?

Which of the following five statements about teams are true?

1. Large teams perform better than small ones because they have more—more diversity, more resources, more muscle, and more intellectual horsepower.
2. Teams whose members like each other and work together harmoniously outperform those teams that have conflict and members who don't like each other.
3. Although virtual teams are popular today, they simply do not perform very well—they have problems communicating, they cannot agree on team objectives, and they have lots of turnover.
4. Performance on teams which remain intact for a long time gradually deteriorates because members become complacent, are careless, receive insufficient supervision, and are too forgiving of each other's mistakes and oversights.
5. The primary influencer of team behavior and dynamics is the managerial style of the team leader, particularly as it relates to dictatorial or democratic approaches.

Actually, none of these five statements are true (Hackman, 2002; Gibson & Cohen, 2003; Hunsaker & Hunsaker, 2008; Kozlowski & Ilgen, 2006). The way things *may appear* to function in groups is not necessarily how they *actually operate.*

Teams have been one of the most researched topics in the behavioral sciences. Sociologists, political scientists, industrial/organizational psychologists, and economists have studied group dynamics for over 75 years. A recent Google search for "team" registered 192,000,000 hits. We know a lot about what makes teams tick. For example, we know teams evolve over time and progress through various stages of development. We know that communication is critical to team success, but not sufficient. We know that having a common goal influences performance. We know that talent is important. In this chapter, we will do the following five things:

1. Identify the characteristics of a team and review the four basic types of teams.
2. Investigate why teams are so important in today's workplace.
3. Examine the various stages through which a team progresses as it evolves.
4. Present the T7 Team Effectiveness Model.
5. Review other team effectiveness models in the literature and highlight similarities and differences with the T7 Model.

What is a team anyway?

Fans at a college football game. A jazz quartet. Professors in the university biology department. Shoppers at the local mall. Soldiers in an army unit. An airplane flight crew. Employees in the marketing department. Drivers waiting on the freeway during rush hour. Which are examples of teams? Which are simply a collection of individuals, just a group of people? A simple gathering of individuals in one space and time does not denote a team (McGourty & De Meuse, 2001).

A work team is a group of individuals whose work is interdependent and who are collectively responsible for accomplishing a performance outcome (Hackman, 2002). The work might involve designing a car, sailing a ship, analyzing a problem, or implementing a quality-improvement program. Teams come in all shapes, sizes, and compositions. Teams vary according to their purpose, function, duration, member location, complexity of tasks, skill requirements, stability of membership, leadership, and collaborative intensity. Regardless of the work performed, all teams are characterized by the following features:

- Tasks are coordinated among individuals on the team.
- There is a high level of interdependence among members.
- A dynamic exchange of information and resources occurs among members.

- Ongoing adjustments to both team and individual task demands take place.
- There is a mutual accountability for performance and team outcomes.

Thus, a team can be characterized as *a defined number of people with complementary skills who are committed to a common purpose, work interdependently toward performance goals, and share accountability for outcomes.*

Overall, there appear to be four fundamentally different types of work teams. They are:

1. Functional teams. Functional teams consist of a group of employees from the same unit or department that work together to accomplish a shared goal. A functional team is composed of a manager and direct reports from a particular business function. These teams can have varying levels of independence and interdependence. Typically, someone remains a member of a functional team until transferred, promoted, or terminated.

2. Cross-functional teams or project teams. Cross-functional teams consist of team members from varied areas in a company who work together to solve mutual problems. Cross-functional teams (or project teams) tend to be temporary. Such teams are formed for a variety of reasons, including to (a) solve problems that impact multiple parts of the organization, (b) improve work processes that cross departmental lines, (c) coordinate processes or activities that cross organizational boundaries, and (d) perform tasks that require breadth and depth of knowledge, skills, and experience.

3. Self-directed teams. Self-directed work teams operate without formal managers and are responsible to complete work processes or segments. Most decisions are made through consensus. Employee empowerment often is an important component of such a team. Some self-directed teams may be empowered to set their own work schedules, train new hires, and even make hire and fire decisions. Others have much more restricted authority to make decisions. These teams can be independent or interdependent (Bergmann & De Meuse, 1996; Wellins, Byham, & Wilson, 1991).

4. Virtual teams. Virtual teams are formed when a group of people work together across time, space, and geographical boundaries with the assistance of technology. Recent enhancements in technology, transportation, and communication have spurred rapid growth in the application of virtual teams. The organizational structure tends to be horizontal, and human resources are geographically distributed in virtual teams. The increasing globalization of trade and corporate activities has

stimulated the formation of virtual teams to encompass a broader labor pool and reduce travel expenses (Bowers, Salas, & Jentsch, 2006; Hoefling, 2003).

Why teams are important today:

"Not finance. Not strategy. Not technology. It is teamwork that remains the ultimate competitive advantage, both because it is so powerful and so rare." This is the way Patrick Lencioni opened his best-selling book (p. vii) entitled *The Five Dysfunctions of a Team* (2002). It has been estimated that nearly all of the Fortune 500 companies employ teams of some form or type in their businesses (see Dumaine, 1994; Joinson, 1999; Kirkman, Gibson, & Shapiro, 2001). Increasingly, teams are being used in a variety of applications by a wide range of organizations (e.g., project teams, task forces, quality circles, self-directed work teams, standing committees). The importance of work teams appears to be gaining in strength as jobs get bigger, organizational structures get more complex, and more and more companies become multinational in scope (Naquin & Tynan, 2003). In today's corporate environment, it seems as though the team—not the individual—holds the key to business success.

Teams add a powerful dimension to the workforce. Teamwork integrates the competencies and the creativity of a diverse number of employees to produce an effective outcome. At virtually every level of the organization—from manufacturing on the plant floor to decision making in executive boardrooms—teams, not individuals, are doing the work. Consequently, more and more businesses are searching for new recruits who possess not only critical technical skills but also the ability to work effectively in a self-directed, collaborative environment inherent in teaming.

As companies restructure, downsize, and reinvent themselves, the new roles being created tend to be team oriented. Organizations are becoming flatter, leaner, and more agile to more effectively address continuously escalating customer expectations. Many jobs and projects are becoming increasingly complex, less time-bound, and global in scope. All these factors collectively are making it increasingly difficult for one person to perform a single job. The contemporary workplace uses teams as the basic work unit (e.g., surgical units, airplane crews, research and development teams, and production crews).

With such a heightened emphasis on teams, one might expect that organizations would be highly skilled in team management and performance. Ironically, this is not the case. For example:

- Up to half of the leaders in any organization do not build cohesive teams (Hughes, Ginnett, & Curphy, 2008).
- A study of the effectiveness of senior leadership teams found 79% perform at a poor or mediocre level (Wageman, Nunes, Burruss, & Hackman, 2008).
- In a recent Center for Creative Leadership (CCL) study, less than half of executives surveyed believe leaders in their organizations are highly skilled in collaboration (Criswell & Martin, 2007).
- Based on interviewing members from hundreds of teams in multinational companies, the "average" team member perceived that his or her team was at a 5.8 level of effectiveness, but needed to be at an 8.7 level—based on a 10-point rating scale (Goldsmith & Morgan, 2000).
- According to one study, 9 out of 10 teams fail ("The Team-Based Organization," 1994).
- Another study conducted by Mendzela (1997) found that 60% of teams fail.

Although teams are ubiquitous in organizations, most employee-related functions are individualized (e.g., selecting, training, evaluating, rewarding). Such misalignment between an organization's need to foster teamwork and its natural tendency to focus on the individual employees can create many problems. In addition, some research suggests a key reason why some teams fail is that employees are ill-prepared to make the transition from individual contributor to team member. Bergmann and De Meuse (1996) investigated the implementation of self-managed work teams in a large food-processing plant. They observed that employees lacked the basic team skills of problem solving, dealing with conflict, conducting effective meetings, and interpersonal communication. Eventually, the employees resisted the movement to self-managed work teams to such an extent that management returned to the old system of production after 10 months.

It takes considerable time and effort to develop a successful, high-performing team. It takes proper guidance and support from the team leader. Development is not easy, automatic, or quick. In fact, many teams never reach full maturity. It's helpful to know how teams form and evolve and to understand the stages of team development.

Stages of team development:

At a basic level, teams are composed of individuals—individuals that not only look different but are different. Just as team members differ in terms of physical characteristics such as race, age, gender, height, and weight, they likewise differ in terms of personal values, motives, goals, personalities, preferences, sensitivities, leadership styles, responses to stress, and so on. Individual differences that you can see are not nearly as important as those differences you cannot see.

Those individual differences can significantly contribute to ineffectiveness when there are conflicting personal agendas, misdirection, or poor leadership. As a team evolves from a collection of disparate individuals (see Stage 1 below) into a highly cohesive team (see Stage 4 below), members recognize how to capitalize on these differences rather than have them hinder performance. In many ways, the maturation of a team is similar to an infant growing into an adult. An effective leader, like a wise parent, recognizes that the needs of a team (or child) change over time and modify guidance accordingly. Effective team members, likewise, know what to expect. They understand what's going on as the team matures, why certain issues emerge at certain developmental stages, and how to respond accordingly.

It's generally acknowledged that there are five stages or phases of team development (Forsyth, 2009; Tuckman, 1965). These five stages are predictable and fairly observable to knowledgeable team members.

Stage 1: Forming – The Formative Stage. This stage involves the transformation of a group of individuals into the beginnings of a team. Members naturally struggle at this stage with (a) defining the nature of the tasks to be completed; (b) knowing each other's personalities, values, motives, work styles, etc.; (c) determining acceptable and unacceptable individual and group behavior; (d) deciding what information and resources are needed to perform the given objectives; and (e) simply trying to determine when, where, and how to begin. Conversation among members tends to be polite but guarded. The team is quite passive and dependent on the leader to tell them what to do. As an infant who requires structure and proper nurturing from a parent, the team in Stage 1 depends upon the leader to learn what to do and to obtain guidance on how to accomplish it. Unfortunately, team leaders often fail to provide the proper structure and guidance to forming teams and then wonder why they stumble in early stages.

Stage 2: Storming – The Conflict Stage. As the team progresses, it transitions into a stage similar to adolescence. In this stage, members often vie for control over the group, much like teenagers attempt to gain control of their own lives. Members begin to think they know more than they really do, set unrealistic expectations regarding their performance capabilities, and typically argue openly among themselves. By this point, the team has experienced some success and now believes it is ready "to take on the world." It can be an emotionally charged time. On one hand, there is high energy, enthusiasm, and optimism. On the other hand, there can be anger, resentment, and restlessness. Polarization and blaming can occur as the team seeks to define itself, to find its identity. When this happens, it's not uncommon for misfit or unhappy team members to leave—voluntarily or involuntarily. Stage 2 is a very challenging time for the team and the team leader. Nevertheless, it is a necessary condition for the team as it matures to the next stage of development.

Stage 3: Norming – The Structure Stage. During the norming stage, team members resolve basic differences and begin to work together effectively. While some members may have left the team, those that remain are far more accepting of each other, their roles, and the team's goals and processes. A culture of friendliness, cooperation, and mutual respect characterizes this stage. Individuals share information willingly, communicate openly, and solve problems as they arise. Individuals begin to understand the differing strengths and weaknesses of various team members and consider those strengths and weaknesses in task assignment. Members begin to identify strongly as a group. They become cohesive. Develop bonds. They may frequently socialize outside of the work setting and begin to become close friends as well as colleagues. As the name of this stage suggests, the team develops behavioral and performance norms to ensure that the members respond accordingly. Team leaders must recognize that their role changes as individuals monitor their own effectiveness in the team.

Stage 4: Performing – The Work Stage. Eventually, team members feel an intimacy with each other and gain a great deal of satisfaction from the exchanges that occur within the team. There is no issue of power, control, or status. When problems arise, members accept them as part of the interpersonal dynamics of the team and openly work through them. Individuals are comfortable with their roles and with each other. They work as a unit to accomplish assignments. The team is productive, efficient, highly focused, and energized. Credit for success is shared. The members recognize a synergy when working together.

Stage 5: Adjourning – The Dissolution Stage. The last stage of team development is adjourning. This stage may or may not occur during a team's life cycle. In some instances, a team will achieve its mission and disband. In other cases, teams continue for years and years—members come and go but the team structure, dynamic, and identity remain intact. When a highly functioning team dissolves, there is a period of letting go and moving on with individual lives. Members realize that their time as a group is over. No matter how committed the individuals are to keeping in contact, their journey as a team has ended. Most members experience a sense of loss. There may be much sadness and grieving. On the other hand, it also can be a joyous occasion because the team is proud of what they accomplished and members recognize they were part of a special group in a moment in time. As a whole, this stage is characterized as a period of mixed emotions.

A basic knowledge of these five stages of team development will enhance your understanding of the interpersonal dynamics of work teams. Your awareness of these stages as a natural evolution of team maturity will enable you to better perform in that environment. As a team leader, it is imperative that you manage the team differently as it evolves. You would not parent a five-year-old the same way as a seventeen-year-old or a thirty-five-year-old. Likewise, you should not manage a newly formed team the same as you would manage a mature one. As a team member, someone is more likely to contribute to the effectiveness of the team when he/she understands the emotional and behavioral dynamics in the various stages of development.

Overall, you should realize that a team gradually performs at a higher level as it becomes cohesive and matures (see figure 1). Possessing this knowledge should prepare you to lead the group through the beginning stages of team formation more quickly and efficiently. Your behavior can make a huge difference leading the team effectively through the various stages.

FIGURE 1 – PERFORMANCE INCREASES AS TEAM MATURES

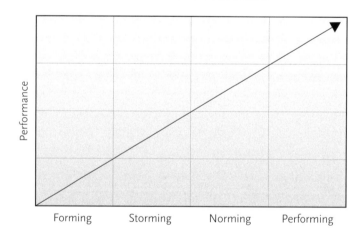

Source: Adapted from McGourty and De Meuse (2001).

THE T7 TEAM EFFECTIVENESS MODEL

Michael Lombardo and Robert Eichinger originally developed the T7 Team Effectiveness Model in 1995 to represent the key facets that influence the performance of work teams. Based upon their review of the research literature, they identified five factors *inside* the team and two factors *outside* the team which impact team effectiveness. Each one of the factors was named to begin with the letter "T." Hence, the name T7 Model (see figure 2).

FIGURE 2 – THE T7 TEAM EFFECTIVENESS MODEL

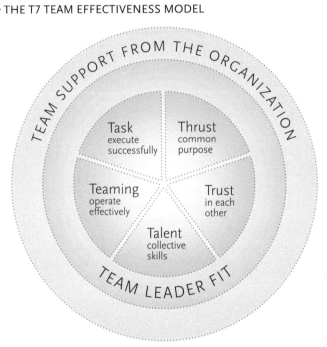

The five internal team factors include:

- Thrust – a common purpose about what needs to be accomplished or team goal(s).
- Trust – in each other as teammates.
- Talent – the collective skills of the team members to get the job done.
- Teaming Skills – operating effectively and efficiently as a team.
- Task Skills – executing successfully or getting the job done.

The two external team factors are:

- Team Support from the Organization – the extent to which the leadership of the organization enables the team to perform.
- Team Leader Fit – the degree to which the team leader satisfies the needs of the team members.

Intro-19

Each of the factors inside the team can be divided into subfactors, or dimensions. For example, Thrust refers to agreed-upon vision, mission, values, and goals among members within a team. Moreover, members employ a common strategy and tactics to accomplish goals. Specifically, Thrust consists of the following three behavioral dimensions: Thrust Management, Thrust Clarity, and Thrust Commitment. In contrast, Trust includes the following dimensions: Trust in Truthful Communication, Trust in Actions, and Trust Inside the Team. In total, the five internal factors consist of 18 dimensions of team effectiveness (see table 1).

TABLE 1 – INSIDE THE TEAM FACTORS AND DIMENSIONS

Internal Factor	Dimension
Thrust	■ Thrust Management ■ Thrust Clarity ■ Thrust Commitment
Trust	■ Trust in Truthful Communication ■ Trust in Actions ■ Trust Inside the Team
Talent	■ Talent Acquisition and Enhancement ■ Talent Allocation and Deployment
Teaming Skills	■ Resource Management ■ Team Learning ■ Decision Making ■ Conflict Resolution ■ Team Atmosphere ■ Managing Process
Task Skills	■ Focusing ■ Assignment Flexibility ■ Measurement ■ Delivering the Goods

All five internal factors have to be present for teams to be high performing. While all are important, Thrust has special significance because it leads to a shared mind-set that is essential for any of the other factors to have a major impact. In other words, team effectiveness starts with Thrust. Further, it's not enough to have the five internally focused factors in play. Teams cannot be high performing unless the necessary organizational support and leadership support are also provided. So, even if a team excels in Thrust, Trust, Talent, Teaming Skills, and Task Skills, it will have difficulty achieving its potential without support from the organization and the right leadership fit (Lombardo & Eichinger, 1995).

The factor and dimension structure of the T7 Team Effectiveness Model recently was validated. A total of 303 teams and 3,328 participants were administered the eTeam™ Online Survey. The teams were employed in 50 organizations across a variety of industry sectors (e.g., manufacturing, health care, telecommunications, finance). The T7 Model was supported, whether data were obtained from the team leader, team members, or were aggregated at the team level (De Meuse, King, & Dai, 2009).

In addition, the literature on teams was examined to determine whether any additional factors and dimensions were required to capture various components of team effectiveness. Based on a comprehensive review of the relevant research, it was found that no additional factors or dimensions were needed (De Meuse, 2007).

Nevertheless, there are several other models of team effectiveness in the literature. Five of the most popular are:

- Rubin, Plovnick, and Fry (1977)
- Katzenbach and Smith (1993)
- LaFasto and Larson (2001)
- Hackman (2002)
- Lencioni (2005)

Each of the above models can be related to the T7 Model.

Other models of team effectiveness in the literature:

RUBIN, PLOVNICK, AND FRY MODEL

This model by Rubin, Plovnick, and Fry (1977) is one of the oldest models of team effectiveness. It is sometimes referred to as the GRPI Model, which stands for Goals, Roles, Processes, and Interpersonal Relationships. The authors present their model in terms of a pyramid similar to Maslow's Hierarchy of Needs theory (1954). However, unlike Maslow's theory, one starts at the top of the pyramid. According to the model, a team always should begin with a team-level goal. After the goal is defined, the roles and responsibilities will become clearer. As individuals work together (processes), they will see that goals and responsibilities often are insufficiently clear. Consequently, team members will need to redefine them. That redefinition enables team members to adjust and readjust team processes such as decision making, conflict resolution, and workflow. While doing all that, they will be developing the interpersonal relationships needed to relate to other team members and the team leader (see figure 3).

FIGURE 3 – THE GRPI MODEL OF TEAM EFFECTIVENESS

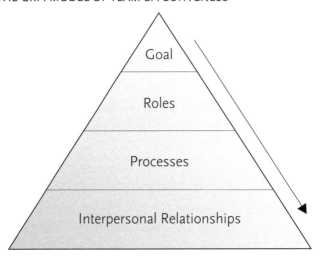

Source: Adapted from Rubin, Plovnick, and Fry (1977).

The authors provide much guidance for defining and clarifying the components of the model.

- Goal definition:
    - Clarity about the main purpose of the team
    - Agreement on the desired results
    - Understanding of the main tasks
    - Agreement on the standards and expectations
    - Clarity of priorities and deadlines
    - Understanding of boundaries

- Role clarification:
  - Acceptance of a team leader
  - Understand all members' roles
  - Individual responsibilities
  - Shared responsibilities
  - Clear boundaries
  - Identify and fill gaps
- Processes and workflow:
  - Team processes (e.g., how decisions are made, how the team solves problems and resolves conflict, communication)
  - Work processes (e.g., procedures and workflow)
- Interpersonal relationships:
  - Relating with the other team members
  - Trust
  - Sensitivity and flexibility with each other
  - Good communication
  - Collaboration in problem solving
  - Effective methods for dealing with conflict

KATZENBACH AND SMITH MODEL

Katzenbach and Smith (1993) assert that most people realize the capabilities of teams, but there is a natural resistance to moving beyond individual roles, responsibilities, and accountabilities. In general, individuals do not easily accept responsibility for the performance of others or embrace others assuming responsibility for them. Overcoming this resistance requires that team members understand, accept, and apply the basics of teamwork. Katzenbach and Smith depict these team basics in the form of a triangle (see figure 4). There are three overarching goals in their model: Collective Work Products, Personal Growth, and Performance Results. These outcomes are presented in the vertices of the triangle and indicate what teams can deliver. In contrast, the sides and center of the triangle describe the team elements required to make it happen—Skills, Accountability, and Commitment.

FIGURE 4 – FOCUSING ON TEAM BASICS MODEL

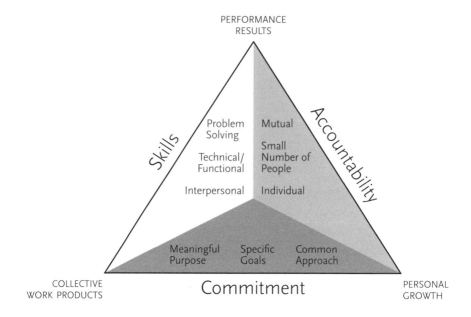

Source: Adapted from Katzenbach and Smith (1993).

The authors contend that successful teams are deeply committed to their goals, approach, and purpose. Members in these teams also are very committed to each other. They understand that the "wisdom of teams comes with a focus on collective work-products, personal growth, and performance results" (Katzenbach & Smith, 1993, p. 9). They assert that successful teams always are a result of pursuing demanding performance goals at the team level.

Katzenbach and Smith pose the following series of six questions to diagnose the functioning of teams and enhance their effectiveness:

1. Is the size of the team appropriate?
2. Do members have sufficient complementary skills?
3. Is the purpose of the team truly meaningful and understood?
4. Are there team-oriented goals—are they clear, realistic, and measurable?
5. Does the team have a well-thought-out, articulated working approach?
6. Is there a sense of mutual accountability?

For teams to be effective, all six questions need to be addressed satisfactorily.

LaFasto and Larson Model

LaFasto and Larson (2001) developed a model of team effectiveness which they refer to as the "Five Dynamics of Teamwork and Collaboration." They based this model upon the insights they gleaned from investigating 600 teams in a variety of industries. They theorize that there are five fundamental elements or components which must be understood and actively managed to increase the likelihood of team effectiveness. These elements are presented in figure 5.

FIGURE 5 – FIVE DYNAMICS OF TEAMWORK AND COLLABORATION MODEL

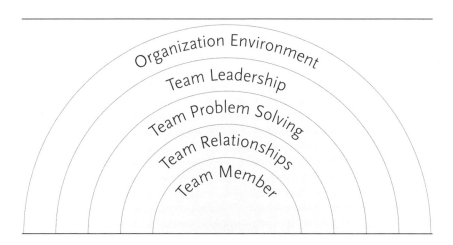

Source: Adapted from LaFasto and Larson (2001).

Similar to other model authors, LaFasto and Larson provide much definition and guidance for each of the components in their model. The authors devote an entire chapter in their book clarifying and offering suggestions as to how to enhance team effectiveness for *each* of these five components (LaFasto & Larson, 2001). For example, the initial element is "team member." A key to team success is to begin with the right people. There are four necessary behaviors for members in a team setting: openness, supportiveness, an action orientation, and a "positive personal style." The model components are addressed in the following manner:

- What makes a good *team member*—the abilities and behaviors that really matter?
- What behaviors in a group foster effective *team member relationships*?
- What are the behaviors of teams—as perceived by their members and leaders—that cause some teams to be more successful than others at *problem solving*?

- What are the behaviors of *team leaders*—as viewed by members of the team—that foster team success or failure?
- What *organizational processes and practices* promote clarity, confidence, and commitment in a team?

HACKMAN MODEL

Hackman (2002) declared that a team is most likely to be effective when the following five conditions are satisfied: (1) it is a *real* team rather than a team in name only, (2) the team has a compelling direction for its work, (3) it has an enabling structure that facilitates teamwork, (4) the team operates within a supportive organizational context, and (5) it has ample expert coaching in teamwork available. According to Hackman, team effectiveness is measured by providing products or services that exceed customer expectations, growing team capabilities over time, and satisfying team member needs. These points are depicted in the model in figure 6.

FIGURE 6 – CONDITIONS FOR TEAM EFFECTIVENESS MODEL

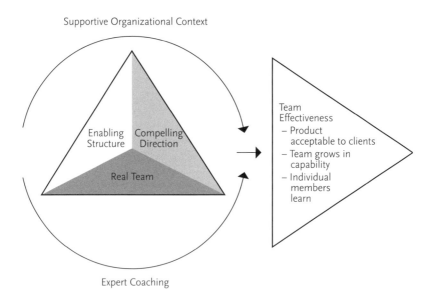

Source: Adapted from Hackman (2002).

Hackman goes on to clarify the five necessary conditions for team effectiveness as follows:

1. A so-called *real team* has these four features: a team task, clear boundaries, clearly assigned authority to make team decisions, and membership stability.

2. Possessing a *compelling direction* refers to whether the team has clear, challenging, and consequential goals that focus on the ends to be accomplished rather than the means the team must use to pursue them.

3. An *enabling structure* refers to whether the team's task, composition, and norms of conduct enable rather than impede teamwork.

4. *Supportive organizational context* refers to whether the team receives adequate resources, a rewards system, information system, education system, intergroup relations, and support that members need to accomplish their tasks.

5. *Expert coaching* refers to the availability of a competent coach to help team members deal with potential issues or existing problems in order to accomplish the team tasks. Expert coaching also helps team members to take advantage of emerging opportunities and improve their coordination and collaboration.

LENCIONI MODEL

One of the most interesting models of team effectiveness was developed by Lencioni (2005). According to him, all teams have the potential to be dysfunctional. To improve the functioning of a team, it is critical to understand the type and level of dysfunction. Again, a pyramid is used to demonstrate the hierarchical progression of team development. Similar to Maslow's Hierarchy of Needs theory (1954), there are five levels, and each must be completed to move on to the next one (see figure 7).

FIGURE 7 – FIVE DYSFUNCTIONS OF A TEAM MODEL

Source: Adapted from Lencioni (2005).

In Lencioni's model, there are five potential dysfunctions of a team:

- **Dysfunction #1:** Absence of Trust
  This outcome occurs when team members are reluctant to be vulnerable with one another and are unwilling to admit their mistakes, weaknesses, or need for help. Without a certain comfort level among team members, a foundation of trust is not possible.

- **Dysfunction #2:** Fear of Conflict
  Teams that are lacking trust are incapable of engaging in unfiltered, passionate debate about key issues. It creates situations where team conflict can easily turn into veiled discussions and back-channel comments. In a work setting where team members do not openly air their opinions, inferior decisions result.

- **Dysfunction #3:** Lack of Commitment
  Without conflict, it is difficult for team members to commit to decisions, fostering an environment where ambiguity prevails. Lack of direction and commitment can make employees, particularly star employees, disgruntled and disenfranchised.

- **Dysfunction #4:** Avoidance of Accountability
  When teams do not commit to a clear plan of action, even the most focused and driven individuals are hesitant to call their peers on actions and behaviors that may seem counterproductive to the overall good of the team.

- **Dysfunction #5:** Inattention to Results
Team members naturally tend to put their own needs (e.g., ego, career development, recognition, and so on) ahead of the collective goals of the team when individuals are not held accountable. If a team has lost sight of the need for achievement, the business ultimately suffers.

Summary of the models of team effectiveness:

Table 2 (below) highlights the similarities and differences among the five models of team effectiveness relative to the T7 Model. Both factor-level and dimension-level comparisons are provided. The most striking observation is the amount of similarity across all the models. For example, all the models examine issues related to thrust, trust, and teaming skills. Four of the five models also identify member talent as an important factor in team effectiveness. Likewise, four of the five models indicate that team leader fit needs to be considered. Perhaps one should not be surprised with the substantial overlap of factors among the models. Goals and goal-setting activities have been recognized as a key ingredient to high performance for decades (see Latham & Locke, 1979). Psychologists have long contended that mutual trust and open communication are the foundation for any successful relationship. It also is logical that how someone resolves conflicts, makes decisions, and deals with resource issues would be highly related to team effectiveness.

The LaFasto and Larson (2001) and Katzenbach and Smith (1993) models most closely mirror the T7 Model. LaFasto and Larson address all seven factors of the T7 Model as well as 17 out of the 20 dimensions. Katzenbach and Smith examine five of the seven factors and 16 of the 20 dimensions. The Lencioni (2005) model has the least correspondence with the T7 Model, with four common factors and 11 common dimensions. Overall, two conclusions are apparent. First, the six models of team effectiveness have much, much similarity in the manner in which they view team functioning. Second, the T7 Model is one of the most (if not the most) comprehensive assessments of team effectiveness in the literature (see table 2).

TABLE 2 – COMPARING THE T7 MODEL WITH OTHER TEAM EFFECTIVENESS MODELS IN THE LITERATURE

Factor / Dimension	Rubin, Plovnick & Fry (1977)	Katzenbach & Smith (1993)	LaFasto & Larson (2001)	Hackman (2002)	Lencioni (2005)	Total
Thrust	■	■	■	■	■	5
1. Thrust Management	o	o	o	o	o	5
2. Thrust Clarity	o	o	o	o	o	5
3. Thrust Commitment	o	o	o		o	4
Trust	■	■	■	■	■	5
4. Trust in Truthful Communication	o	o	o	o	o	5
5. Trust in Actions	o	o	o	o	o	5
6. Trust Inside the Team	o	o	o	o	o	5
Talent	■	■	■	■		4
7. Talent Acquisition and Enhancement	o	o	o	o		4
8. Talent Allocation and Deployment		o	o			2
Teaming Skills	■	■	■	■	■	5
9. Resource Management		o		o		2
10. Team Learning			o			1
11. Decision Making	o	o	o		o	4
12. Conflict Resolution	o	o	o		o	4
13. Team Atmosphere	o	o	o	o	o	5
14. Managing Process	o	o	o	o		4
Task Skills			■		■	2
15. Focusing	o			o	o	3
16. Assignment Flexibility		o				1
17. Measurement		o	o			2
18. Delivering the Goods			o		o	2
Team Support from the Organization			■	■		2
19. Team Support from the Organization			o	o		2
Team Leader Fit	■	■	■	■		4
20. Team Leader Fit	o	o	o	o		4
Total Factors [■]	5	5	7	6	4	
Total Dimensions [o]	13	16	17	12	11	

Intro-30

Final remarks:

Helen Keller once declared that "alone we can do so little, but together we can do so much." It makes little difference whether you are referring to manufacturing a truck in Detroit, assembling a computer in Mumbai, performing open heart surgery in Munich, or creating a new advertising campaign in Tokyo, a highly coordinated team of individuals can outperform one person. However, successful teams learn to work together. They have clear, acceptable goals. The members trust and respect one another. They communicate often and openly. Members have talent—be it building trucks or creating ideas. The team leader is a good fit with the needs of the team. And the support and resources from the wider organization and community are provided.

Teams have the potential to be one of the most powerful drivers of success in an organization today. However, highly performing teams simply don't happen. They take time to evolve and mature. They take proper leadership. In this book, we offer you the opportunity to carefully examine the dynamics of your work team. Depending upon the specific problems and needs of your team, we offer hundreds of suggestions and remedies to enhance skills. The T7 Model provides the framework by which to analyze the operations of your team. The eTeam™ Online Survey enables you to systematically collect the perceptions of your team members as well as obtain the views of relevant others. It is up to you to understand how teams function, and then improve the cohesiveness, chemistry, and productivity of the team. Talent is not enough! After all, as noted major league baseball coach Casey Stengel used to say, "It's easy to get good players. Getting 'em to play together, that's the hard part."

References

Bergmann, T. J., & De Meuse, K. P. (1996). Diagnosing whether an organization is truly ready to empower work teams: A case study. *Human Resource Planning, 19*(1), 38-47.

Bowers, C., Salas, E., & Jentsch, F. (Eds.). (2006). *Creating high-tech teams: Practical guidance on work performance and technology.* Washington, DC: American Psychological Association.

Criswell, C., & Martin, A. (2007). *10 Trends: A study of senior executives' views on the future* [White paper]. Retrieved March 14, 2009, from Center for Creative Leadership: http://www.ccl.org/leadership/pdf/research/TenTrends.pdf.

De Meuse, K. P. (2007). *Summary of the current team literature: How well is the 20-dimension Team Architect® measure supported by research?* Minneapolis, MN: Lominger International: A Korn/Ferry Company.

De Meuse, K. P., King, K. Y., & Dai, G. (2009). *Construct validation of the Lominger T7 team effectiveness model.* Minneapolis, MN: Lominger International: A Korn/Ferry Company.

Dumaine, B. (1994, September). The trouble with teams. *Fortune, 130*(5), 86-92.

Forsyth, D. R. (2009). *Group dynamics* (5th ed.). Pacific Grove, CA: Brooks/Cole Wadsworth.

Gibson, C. B., & Cohen, S. G. (Eds.). (2003). *Virtual teams that work: Creating conditions for virtual team effectiveness.* San Francisco: Jossey-Bass.

Goldsmith, M., & Morgan, H. (2000). Team building without time wasting. In M. Goldsmith, L. Lyons, A. Freas, & R. Witherspoon (Eds.), *Coaching for leadership: How the world's greatest coaches help leaders learn* (pp. 103-109). San Francisco: Jossey-Bass.

Hackman, J. R. (2002). *Leading teams: Setting the stage for great performances.* Boston: Harvard Business School Press.

Hoefling, T. (2003). *Working virtually: Managing people for successful virtual teams and organizations.* Sterling, VA: Stylus.

Hughes, R. L., Ginnett, R. C., & Curphy, G. J. (2008). *Leadership: Enhancing the lessons of experience* (6th ed.). New York: McGraw-Hill/Irwin.

Hunsaker, P. L., & Hunsaker, J. S. (2008). Virtual teams: A leader's guide. *Team Performance Management, 14*(1/2), 86-101.

Joinson, C. (1999). Teams at work. *HR Magazine, 44*(5), 30-37.

Katzenbach, J. R., & Smith, D. K. (1993). *The wisdom of teams.* New York: HarperCollins.

Kirkman, B. L., Gibson, C. B., & Shapiro, D. L. (2001). "Exporting" teams: Enhancing the implementation and effectiveness of work teams in global affiliates. *Organizational Dynamics, 30*(1), 12-29.

Kozlowski, S. W. J., & Ilgen, D. R. (2006). Enhancing the effectiveness of work groups and teams. *Psychological Science in the Public Interest, 7*(3), 77-124.

LaFasto, F., & Larson, C. (2001). *When teams work best*. Thousand Oaks, CA: Sage.

Latham, G. P., & Locke, E. A. (1979). Goal setting: A motivational technique that works. *Organizational Dynamics, 8*(2), 68-80.

Lencioni, P. (2002). *The five dysfunctions of a team: A leadership fable*. San Francisco: Jossey-Bass.

Lencioni, P. (2005). *Overcoming the five dysfunctions of a team: A field guide for leaders, managers, and facilitators*. San Francisco: Jossey-Bass.

Lombardo, M. M., & Eichinger, R. W. (1995). *The Team Architect® user's manual*. Minneapolis, MN: Lominger International: A Korn/Ferry Company.

Maslow, A. H. (1954). *Motivation and personality*. New York: Harper & Row.

McGourty, J., & De Meuse, K. P. (2001). *The team developer: An assessment and skill building program*. New York: John Wiley.

Mendzela, E. (1997). Effective teams. *CPA Journal, 67*(9), 62-63.

Naquin, C. E., & Tynan, R. O. (2003). The team halo effect: Why teams are not blamed for their failures. *Journal of Applied Psychology, 88*(2), 332-340.

Rubin, I. M., Plovnick, M. S., & Fry, R. E. (1977). *Task oriented team development*. New York: McGraw-Hill.

The team-based organization. (1994). Chicago: A. T. Kearney.

Tuckman, B. W. (1965). Developmental sequence in small groups. *Psychological Bulletin, 63*(6), 384-399.

Wageman, R., Nunes, D. A., Burruss, J. A., & Hackman, J. R. (2008). *Senior leadership teams: What it takes to make them great*. Boston: Harvard Business School Press.

Wellins, R. S., Byham, W. C., & Wilson, J. M. (1991). *Empowered teams: Creating self-directed work groups that improve quality, productivity, and participation*. San Francisco: Jossey-Bass.

Dimension 1
Thrust Management

Definition:
Team operates with a common purpose and collaborates to set challenging goals that align with organization objectives.

Addresses the question:
Does the team set its course early and well?

A Dimension in the THRUST Factor
A common mind-set about what needs to be accomplished.

> *All winning teams are goal oriented. Teams like these win consistently because everyone connected with them concentrates on specific objectives. They go about their business with blinders on; nothing will distract them from achieving their aims.*
> Lou Holtz – American author, motivational speaker,
> and former NCAA football coach

Items
1. Team members put disagreements on goals up for discussion and everyone on the team has an opportunity to provide input.
19. Team members look ahead; they scan the environment to see what impact it will have on the work of the team and adjust accordingly.
37. The team has a process that constantly monitors the accuracy of its goals and plans.
55. The team sets challenging goals.

Unskilled
☐ Team does not have a well-defined purpose
☐ A goal-setting process has not been established
☐ Goals are narrowly focused and lack line of sight to organizational goals
☐ Team mishandles conflict around goals
☐ Although team members disagree on goals, individual members hold back opposing viewpoints
☐ Team members are not asked for input on team purpose and goals
☐ Team does not adjust goals to changing demands
☐ Team does not monitor progress toward achieving goals

1

Skilled

- ☐ The team has a process in place to align itself with organization-wide purpose, goals, strategies, and vision
- ☐ There is a free exchange of all points of view within the team about purpose and goals
- ☐ The team sets specific, measurable, clear, stretch goals that are nimble enough to address shifting demands
- ☐ Team members actively participate in setting goals; goal setting is a collaborative process
- ☐ Team members are attuned to the organization and business environment
- ☐ There is a process in place to monitor and measure team members' performance toward the goals
- ☐ Team members openly discuss merit of goals under consideration; all members have an opportunity to provide input
- ☐ The team has a clear mission that provides focus for its efforts and provides clarity on success criteria

Overused

- ☐ The team is so absorbed with goal setting that nothing much else gets done
- ☐ The team is too rigid about its goals
- ☐ The team gets into endless debate without the leader calling time and moving on
- ☐ The team sets goals that are too high and demotivating
- ☐ The team sets its goals in a vacuum, shutting out external input and context

Note on overused strengths: Overused skills and disproportionately used strengths tend to have the negative effects listed above. To decrease those negative consequences, you have two alternatives. You can scale down or use the strength less, or you can compensate for it with another skill or behavior. In practice, it is very difficult to get an individual or a team to use a strength less. In most cases, the best path is to develop compensators. Team Architect® Dimensions that can compensate for overusing this dimension and compensating skills from the Leadership Architect® Library's 67 Competencies are listed below.

(Note: Team Dimension numbers are listed in parentheses. Competencies are listed in numerical order by competency number.)

Compensating Team Dimensions:

☐ Conflict Resolution (12)
☐ Focusing (15)
☐ Delivering the Goods (18)
☐ Team Support from the Organization (19)
☐ Team Leader Fit (20)

Compensating Competencies:

☐ 2. *Dealing with* Ambiguity
☐ 3. Approachability
☐ 9. Command Skills
☐ 42. Peer Relationships
☐ 48. Political Savvy
☐ 53. *Drive for* Results

Some Causes of Poor Performance

☐ The organization in which the team exists may not have goal/objective-setting processes in place
☐ Team goals and objectives may be dictated by the organization or leader without input from members
☐ Team members, leader, or organization may be averse to conflict; members just want to get along
☐ A few team members may dominate/control the team
☐ Team members may be very tactical or non-strategic
☐ Team members may not be able to shift gears rapidly enough
☐ Team members may not buy into the goals and may not be committed to achieve them
☐ Team goals do not include performance measures
☐ Team leader or organization does not monitor team accomplishments
☐ Team goals are too easy, too difficult, or too vague

The Map

If you're not clear about where you're going, you're likely to end up anywhere but the right destination. To become high-performing units, teams must first focus on the basics—a clear definition of purpose and well-defined goals and metrics. Thrust implies a shared purpose, clearly understood direction, common ground, team identity, and unity. Setting specific and challenging goals that are aligned with organizational goals helps improve team performance. Having a common thrust, or mind-set, is essential for all performance-based

3

teams. A shared mind-set is especially important for virtual teams. It helps team members to stay focused on team objectives, regardless of location or amount of direct contact with fellow team members. Team members identify more with goals if they are involved in setting them. They are more committed to attaining the goals if they agree on them. Shared goals shape, guide, and direct behavior. Team members make better decisions when guided by a common thrust. Allocation and alignment of resources is enhanced by thrust. Team members know what to spend time on. Thrust provides a challenge that rallies team members, inspires them, focuses them on success. The best teams spend a lot of time exploring, shaping, and agreeing on a charter that belongs to them collectively and individually. Without thrust, without a clear goal, without embracing a challenge, teams are destined for mediocrity.

Some Remedies

☐ 1. **Get aligned.** In some cases, a team resides in an organization that has a vision, mission, a set of strategies, and measurable goals. In that case, the key is to ensure alignment. The steps are:

– Get a clear understanding of the organization-wide vision, mission, strategies, and goals. Invite someone from the organization who is familiar with the vision, mission, strategies, and goals to come and present them to the team. Encourage the team to ask lots of clarifying questions. Ask about the assumptions that were used to create the vision. Ask about the risks and unknowns. Ask about future scenarios that may affect the vision. Ask what the organization expects from this specific team.

– In a team meeting, ask for suggestions. How can this team support the organization-wide vision? Enhance the mission? Drive strategies? Add value? Ask! Whether it's increased market penetration, better cost management, opening new territories, or being the leader in customer service, most teams will find pieces and parts of the organization-wide thrust they can support.

– With as much specificity as possible, have the team outline the specific subgoals and tactics that support the organization thrust.

– Put all of the goals and tactics together into one plan to see if it works, given the resources of the team.

– Set measures ahead of time that will help the team track its performance against those goals.

– Present the plan back to the person or function that presented the organization thrust to see if they see the plan as aligned and on target.

– Make any adjustments that might be necessary and execute the plan.

☐ **2. Create a team charter.** A charter, which succinctly states the team's purpose, mission, and goals, can serve as a reference point for more detailed plans and for alignment of team member effort and measurement for performance. The best team charters are clear enough to indicate performance expectations, but flexible enough to allow the teams to create their own purpose, goals, and approach. In sum, a charter may:

– Clarify the expectations of the team.

– Provide focus.

– Provide a basis for setting goals and making decisions.

– Help team members visualize their potential by painting a picture that depicts success.

– Communicate the team's purpose to others.

When creating a charter, it is crucial to have all team members participate and provide input. For virtual teams where lack of face-to-face interaction may make it harder to connect, it is critical to ensure buy-in to the charter. The leader or a coach should facilitate the creation of a charter. Some facilitation tips include:

– *Pre-Work.* Ask team members to come to the session with key components for inclusion in the charter.

– *Group Participation.* Ask all members to brainstorm and provide input in a dedicated session.

– *Review and Adjust.* Send the rough draft back to team members and encourage them to make additional suggestions for improvement once they've had a chance to digest the draft.

– *Communicate.* Finalize the charter with the new input and distribute it to the appropriate parties.

☐ **3. Set specific, clear, and measurable goals.** Goal setting is more complex than telling people to do their best. Team members need to understand the goals. Goals need to be specific to communicate precise performance expectations that will guide behavior. Clear goals reduce uncertainty and ambiguity. Measurable goals provide focus, enhance motivation, and enable real-time self-monitoring and course correction. In a virtual team where members don't physically "sit" together, having specific goals is particularly important.

☐ **4. Build stretch into team goals.** Significant performance challenges will energize teams. The research on the value of goals as a motivator generally says that moderately stretching goals motivate the most. Low goals, goals that everyone can reach comfortably, do not motivate nor bring about peak performance. In contrast, goals that are too difficult do not motivate, either. Goals that almost no one can reasonably meet do not cause people to try harder—they cause people to give up and not try at all. Moderately stretching goals are the best. It is vital to challenge the team, yet be realistic. While it's hard to put a metric around what moderate means, try to think about goals that 85% of individuals can reach with peak performance—people working at their best. A common set of demanding performance challenges that the team considers important to achieve will generally lead to both high performance and a more effective team.

☐ **5. Involve the whole team.** Get input and participation from team members. Everyone needs to be on board with the goals for a team to reach peak performance. Research has found that one of the best ways to get people engaged and committed is to ask for their input, especially if goals still need shaping. When forming a team, make sure the team leader and members know where each member stands on the goals or prospective goals of the team. After all, it's likely that not all members are initially enthusiastic volunteers. Some may be apprehensive. Reluctant. Even resistant. The earlier the team leader and other members find out where everyone stands on the goals of the team, the more likely they will be to address and resolve any conflicts. A simple exercise of roundtable bantering can get this started. Have a facilitator post each team goal on a flip chart and then allow team members to spontaneously call out the first thing that comes to mind when they read each goal. The facilitator should post the responses under each goal.

☐ **6. Discuss the undiscussables.** Moving toward consensus on purpose and goals usually involves some conflict. If team members disagree on the team purpose and goals, this issue needs to be surfaced. You also need to find out why there is disagreement. Since many people shy away from direct face-to-face conflict, this may not be an easy task. Have a coach facilitate an "undiscussables" exercise. Research by Chris Argyris has shown that the more issues left unsurfaced, the less well the team will work together. Use a form that looks something like this to gather the information:

Goal	Concern/Disagreement with Goal	Suggested Remedy

The coach should distribute the form to all team members and gather the information ahead of the session to look for common themes. Then the coach can review the results with the group and facilitate a candid discussion around the disagreements and suggestions for moving forward.

It will be important to get the team leader and organization engaged prior to, during, and after this exercise to ensure the results can be acted upon and implemented.

☐ **7. Identify the discipline of goals and measures and the reality of change.** Recent research has shown that truly legendary leaders have two seemingly opposing traits. One is the discipline of executing strongly against a well-thought-out plan, and the other is being adaptable and open to change. This paradox—discipline and adaptability—probably extends to legendary teams. The world is changing faster than most of us are comfortable with. Success means having a plan, sticking to it, and executing the plan efficiently and effectively. At the same time, the team needs to be on the lookout for signs of change that affect the purpose and goals of the team. You can play on this paradox two ways:

- Be proactive. Plan for contingencies. When you set goals, extend the discussion to include what the team might do if things change. Do a change analysis, listing likely changes inside the team, to the organization in which the team resides, and to the world outside the organization. Do change-scenario planning to predetermine likely responses to anticipated changes.

- Be reactive. Wait until something changes. In this scenario, the team will need a scanning discipline to detect internal or external change. When the change is detected, assemble the team of the affected individuals to modify and adjust the plan.

In either case, a good plan will have an element in it that lays out the process for midcourse changes.

☐ **8. Create the measures.** Once the goals are established, have the team work backwards to create the measures, time lines, and accountabilities for achievement. What gets measured usually gets done. Ask the team how they will determine if the goals are accomplished. This process will further clarify goals and ensure understanding by all team members. Focus on what really matters and not just on what sounds impressive. Use the SMART approach to goals and objectives. Are they Specific, Measurable, Actionable, Realistic, and Timely? If they aren't measurable, how can their achievement be determined? Creating the measures will help to keep team members clear on the goals and assignments, which in the long run may prevent some conflict. Here are some sample questions for the team leader or coach to ask to get the process started:

- What are our real objectives and goals?
- How can we track our progress against the objectives and goals?
- How often should we measure?

FACTOR I: THRUST

1

– Who else should we involve in our measurement efforts?

– What data do we need to implement the metrics? Where does the information reside? How do we access it? What are the constraints?

☐ **9. Review the goals over time.** Business demands are constantly in flux. Economic trends, market forces, technology upgrades, customer demographics—all these factors make it crucial for team goals to be flexible. Constantly monitor and evaluate the relevance of the team's goals and plans related to the business environment. If the goal appears obsolete and won't move the business forward, adapt it or eliminate it. Being too rigid in a fast-changing environment will be counterproductive to team performance. The team needs to be flexible and open to change. When creating goals, emphasize the need to constantly scan the business landscape. Encourage team members to actively question the continued relevance of goals and do a gut check: will accomplishing this goal achieve the business results we're looking for? When goals are on track, make sure to monitor progress consistently. All team members should participate in this process because their input is crucial. Giving and getting meaningful feedback on performance against goals allows team members to know where they stand and whether they are on the right path.

☐ **10. Include team improvement goals.** It's usually a good idea to include some team improvement goals along with the business goals. High-performing teams are ones that continually build new skills. Base the selection of skill-building goals on the performance of the team's previous year or reporting period. Ask everyone to contribute opinions about what the team could have done better. Using the content from Team Architect®, discuss which items or dimensions are most connected to improving performance. Put a plan in place to improve in those areas. For newly formed teams, look at the aggregate strengths and weaknesses of individual team members. Focus development goals on those competencies that are critical to performance but are not in high supply on the team.

Suggested Readings

Bell, B. S., & Kozlowski, S. W. J. (2002). A typology of virtual teams: Implications for effective leadership. *Group and Organization Management, 27*(1), 14-49.

Bergiel, B. J., Bergiel, E. B., & Balsmeier, P. W. (2008). Nature of virtual teams: A summary of their advantages and disadvantages. *Management Research News, 31*(2), 99-110.

Beyerlein, M. M., Freedman, S., McGee, C., & Moran, L. (2003). *Beyond teams: Building the collaborative organization.* San Francisco: Jossey-Bass/Pfeiffer.

Cascio, W. F. (2000). Managing a virtual workplace. *Academy of Management Executive, 14*(3), 81-90.

Duarte, D. L., & Snyder, N. T. (2006). *Mastering virtual teams: Strategies, tools, and techniques that succeed* (3rd ed.). San Francisco: Jossey-Bass.

Forester, G. L., Thoms, P., & Pinto, J. K. (2007). Importance of goal setting in virtual project teams. *Psychological Reports, 100*(1), 270-274.

Hackman, J. R. (2002). *Leading teams: Setting the stage for great performances.* Boston: Harvard Business School Press.

Herrenkohl, R. C. (2004). *Becoming a team, achieving a goal.* Mason, OH: South-Western.

Katzenbach, J. R., & Smith, D. K. (2005). The discipline of teams. *Harvard Business Review, 83*(7/8), 162-171.

Shane, S. L., & Von Glinow, M. A. (2008). *Organizational behavior: Emerging realities for the workplace revolution* (4th ed.). New York: McGraw-Hill.

Yeh, E., Smith, C., Jennings, C., & Castro, N. (2006). Team building: A 3-dimensional teamwork model. *Team Performance Management, 12*(5/6), 192-197.

Translation to the Leadership Architect® Competency Library

In order for a team or individuals on a team to perform well in this area, these are the competencies that would most likely be in play. Aside from a team improvement plan where everybody works on the same thing, some individual team members may need to work on some of these competencies. A critical number (but not necessarily all) of team members need to be good at:

Mission Critical:	Important:	Nice to Have:
2. *Dealing with Ambiguity*	5. Business Acumen	15. Customer Focus
35. Managing and Measuring Work	12. Conflict Management	32. Learning on the Fly
50. Priority Setting	51. Problem Solving	33. Listening
53. *Drive for* Results		34. Managerial Courage
57. Standing Alone		37. Negotiating
		46. Perspective
		52. Process Management
		58. Strategic Agility

In addition to the 10 tips listed for this dimension, there are some tips that may apply from *FYI For Your Improvement*™. Below are the four items from the Team Architect® that make up this dimension. The item number appears to the left of each item. Immediately below the text of each item are competency and tip numbers from *FYI*. The competency is listed first (from 1 to 67), followed by the tip number (1 to 10). For example, 33-4 refers to competency 33 (Listening), tip number 4. The tips are generally written for individual development, so some adaptation might be needed in the team context.

1. Team members put disagreements on goals up for discussion and everyone on the team has an opportunity to provide input.
12-1,2,5; 33-3,6; 34-1,3; 42-1; 57-2,3

19. Team members look ahead; they scan the environment to see what impact it will have on the work of the team and adjust accordingly.
2-1,5; 15-1,3,6; 32-2,4; 46-1,3,4

37. The team has a process that constantly monitors the accuracy of its goals and plans.
35-1,2,3,4,7; 50-2; 52-3,8; 53-3; 63-3

55. The team sets challenging goals.
5-6; 35-1,3,4; 36-2,3,10; 53-1,7; 57-1

Dimension 2
Thrust Clarity

Definition:
Team members know how their work aligns with team and organizational goals and can articulate team purpose and success measures to others.

Addresses the question:
Are the goals and objectives of the team clear to everyone on the team?

A Dimension in the THRUST Factor
A common mind-set about what needs to be accomplished.

> *So in order to achieve clarity and be fully and positively engaged in what you're doing, you must (1) know the goal or outcome you're intending, and (2) decide and take the next physical move to propel you in that direction.*
> David Allen – American author, speaker, and consultant

Items
2. Team members understand team goals.
20. Team members can clearly describe their mission and vision.
38. Team members can clearly state their measures of success (what it will take to achieve each goal).
56. All team members know how the goals align with their work.

Unskilled
- ☐ Goals exist but are not clearly communicated to team members
- ☐ Poorly crafted goals and unclear direction create confusion for team members about priorities and decisions
- ☐ There is a lack of clarity about team mission, vision, strategies, and tactics
- ☐ Success metrics are not established or may be vague; achievement is difficult to determine; there is disagreement on what constitutes success
- ☐ Team members cannot describe the steps, route, or process needed to achieve their goals
- ☐ Actual work is disconnected from goals; individual goals do not support those of the team
- ☐ It is not clear how the goals of this team fit into the larger picture
- ☐ There is a lack of alignment and integration of the mission, vision, objectives, goals, and metrics

Skilled

- ☐ Goals are well-defined and include tangible business measures
- ☐ All team members can credibly communicate the mission, objectives, goals, and metrics of the team to others outside the team
- ☐ Any team member can quickly bring a new team member up to speed on the team vision, goals, and metrics
- ☐ Any team member can explain how the output of the team creates value for the broader organization
- ☐ Goals are well understood and accepted by team members
- ☐ Team members can identify specific performance metrics for each goal
- ☐ Team members understand and can articulate what it takes to achieve goals
- ☐ All team members know how their daily work contributes to team and organizational goals

Overused

- ☐ The team, in an attempt to make the mission and goals crystal clear, oversimplifies things
- ☐ The team spends so much time being certain about goals and measures that the work doesn't all get done
- ☐ The team locks everything it does to specific goals and measures to such an extent that it loses flexibility and adaptability
- ☐ The team spends more time creating measures than doing the work
- ☐ Team members do not calibrate their level of goal clarity regularly because they assume too much

Note on overused strengths: Overused skills and disproportionately used strengths tend to have the negative effects listed above. To decrease those negative consequences, you have two alternatives. You can scale down or use the strength less, or you can compensate for it with another skill or behavior. In practice, it is very difficult to get an individual or a team to use a strength less. In most cases, the best path is to develop compensators. Team Architect® Dimensions that can compensate for overusing this dimension and compensating skills from the Leadership Architect® Library's 67 Competencies are listed below.

(Note: Team Dimension numbers are listed in parentheses. Competencies are listed in numerical order by competency number.)

Compensating Team Dimensions:
- ☐ Thrust Management (1)
- ☐ Team Learning (10)
- ☐ Managing Process (14)
- ☐ Delivering the Goods (18)

Compensating Competencies:
- ☐ 2. *Dealing with* Ambiguity
- ☐ 50. Priority Setting
- ☐ 53. *Drive for* Results
- ☐ 65. *Managing* Vision and Purpose

Some Causes of Poor Performance
- ☐ Entire organization lacks a clear goal-setting and/or communication process
- ☐ Objectives, goals, and measures are not specified, expected, or supported
- ☐ Lack of communication to the team around goal setting; organizational goals are not fully disclosed to all
- ☐ Lack of communication within the team around goal setting; goals are not fully discussed
- ☐ Team members have competing work priorities, perhaps because of a matrix reporting structure that splits responsibilities between multiple functions or units
- ☐ Lack of participation by team members in setting goals
- ☐ Team or organization is not goal- or results-oriented
- ☐ Team members don't fully comprehend what it takes to get the job done
- ☐ Team goals are not really measurable
- ☐ Team goals are not perceived as attainable

The Map
A clean and clear template of mission and goals in enough detail makes priority setting easier, resource allocation more equitable, decision making faster, and measurement of success open and understandable. When team members do not work at the same time and/or location and rely heavily on communication technology, thrust clarity is critical. To have a chance at success, team mission and goals should connect the work of each team member to the team. And each person on the team should know how his/her work contributes to achieving overall organizational goals and objectives. A clear path showing

how the work of the team contributes to the organization as a whole helps build commitment and understanding. It also helps team members articulate to others how team goals align with organizational priorities. A team cannot function effectively if team members do not understand and agree with the team goals. Everyone needs to be on the same page and have a common mind-set.

Some Remedies

☐ 1. **Define team goals.** One of the first requirements of any successful team is to define its goals and objectives. Define the team goals in terms of activities necessary to achieve them. Team members need to be able to explain and identify the nature and qualities of the team's goals. For virtual or remotely located team members who likely will be working independently, clear, well-defined goals are critical to guide their work efforts. A team can define their goals by asking these questions:

- What is the team's goal?
- Is it aligned with the organizational goals?
- What are the leader's responsibilities?
- What are the roles and responsibilities of each team member?
- How will the team make decisions?
- What decisions does the team have the authority to make?

☐ 2. **Check for total charter clarity.** Every team should have the charter talked about in Dimension #1 (Thrust Management). The charter should be a written document recording the strategy and goals of the total organization, how this team's goals support that, the tactics and work processes the team will use to reach its goals, the specific products and services the team will deliver to its customers, the resource allocation within the team, and the measures the team will use to gauge its success. Have the team leader or a facilitator spend a few hours with the team to make sure the mission or purpose is clear to everyone. By simply flipcharting the following questions, the leader or coach can gauge and improve clarity among team members:

- Do the goals of this team support the goals of the organization?
- Can you tie the goals of this team into your job?
- When we do our job well, what difference does it make to our customers? To the organization?
- Do we all agree that the measures of success specified in the charter are a fair measure of success?
- Is there anything missing?
- How can we as a team improve ourselves to accomplish the goals?

14

☐ **3. Drive for goal clarity and alignment.** Team goals and purpose need to be aligned with the organization's goals and translated into the team's activities. The clearer the line of sight, the easier it is for the team to stay aligned. A clear line of sight is especially critical for virtual teams since they are more at risk to drift from the team focus and become fragmented. Aside from having a charter that is well understood by all on the team, making sure the mission and charter are translatable into day-to-day work is a key. Don't leave anything to the imagination. The mission should be easily interpreted and translated into how the team does its daily work. One exercise that can help ensure thrust clarity: have each team member write down and present to the rest of the team what the goals mean for that person's job.

☐ **4. Drive for measurement clarity and alignment.** People love to have something to measure against. Metrics shape expectations for team members. They are the yardsticks against which performance is measured. So it's very important that performance metrics be clear, transparent, and easily understood by all. Facilitate a session in which metrics are explained and discussed. Ask team members to present what they will do in their specific job to achieve the goals. Gain agreement from everyone about the best way to measure success. Establish norms for regular check-ins about progress on performance metrics. Make sure that all team members, whether collocated or geographically dispersed, participate in this process.

☐ **5. Validate the goals and metrics.** Since the mission of the team is generally directed by the organization, or at least is in the context of the organization's goals, it makes good political sense to feed the goals and measures back to the sponsor(s) or area(s) that chartered the team. What are the expected deliverables from the team? What work needs to be accomplished to create those deliverables? How do individual accomplishments contribute to the team's deliverables? How is the organization's mission served by team accomplishments? How is success defined? Have team members figure this out sooner rather than later and include in the charter. Visualize the deliverables. Visualize success. Bring the team's charter to life. Use it to drive accountability. Ensure the goals and metrics are fully reviewed and approved before publishing and communicating to the rest of the organization.

☐ **6. Make the goals and metrics transparent.** As simple as it may seem, you need to get the team goals from the charter down on paper so that they become a public reference point for the team. Make them short and sweet. Limit published goals to a reasonable number so that priorities are clear. Once written and distributed, it becomes hard to argue that you didn't know

FACTOR I: THRUST

about or understand the goals of the team. Post them in the workplace or on a virtual space so that everyone has access to them. Ever notice how athletes keep their eyes on the clock and the scoreboard? They're checking their progress against time and the competition in order to win the game. Track progress against metrics visually. Post signs or use technology to display team goals, data, and progress toward accomplishment. Straightforward devices like the United Way Thermometer or a posting of key metrics serve as constant reminders of progress. Electronic postings or distribution lists make it easy to get the same information to everyone in a timely manner.

☐ **7. Sell the goals.** It doesn't do anyone any good to write up the goals if you don't share and communicate them for external clarity and understanding. The team leader and team members should present the goals to others who participate in creating and executing the organization's strategy, to those who are impacted by the results. In this way, the team gains credibility by involving stakeholders in the process, and team members get a chance to validate the goals outside the team. By talking through team goals with others, team members increase understanding and commitment to the team mission and charter. One of the best ways to understand something is to have to present it to others. Be receptive to suggestions. Graciously receive criticism. Consider it. Act on it. Use Webcasts or teleconferences to allow virtual team members to participate in presenting goals. Team members working remotely can serve as the voice of the team in their home location, gaining exposure for both the team and themselves.

☐ **8. Constantly monitor progress and clarity.** Talk about the team goals and individual accountabilities on a regular basis in team meetings and other encounters with team members. Ask individuals to discuss their work as part of the team meeting agenda. Schedule discussion around goals to help ensure understanding, correct misunderstanding, and encourage ownership. Encourage face-to-face meetings with virtual team members on a regular basis by using videoconference calls. Set some parameters around how each person presents an update. Create a standard format that might follow something like this:

- Status on assignments from last meeting.
- Status on individual objectives (ahead of target; on target; missing target and why).
- Impact of individual objectives on achieving team goals.
- Individual and team targets on the horizon; new assignments.
- Potential roadblocks or barriers to goals; actions to remove barriers.

☐ **9. Use goal clarity to encourage team improvement.** Engage all team members to improve the clarity of goals. Uncover misconceptions that may impact the team and adversely impact performance. When conducting a postmortem on team performance, use the goals as the foundation for the discussion. Where lack of clarity of any element of the charter leads to less-than-stellar performance, make that a topic at a staff meeting. Turn each success and stumble into a learning opportunity. What went right? What went wrong? How could the charter have been made clearer and more useful to aid in achieving high performance? Apply those lessons to the next period.

☐ **10. Foster cultural understanding.** In a global marketplace, teams are often formed with employees from various geographic areas, many times from different countries. These virtual teams use information technologies to connect people with different expertise across different countries so they can work together effectively. Virtual multicultural teams often have to overcome cultural differences and language barriers. When these differences are not addressed early on, it creates undue noise for the team, which detracts from the mission. To ensure that all team members have a clear understanding and commitment to the goals, virtual team members need to be aware of cultural differences. Take time to develop interpersonal relationships with team members. Slow down. Repeat and clarify when someone does not understand what is being said. Do not use slang or jargon. Regular face-to-face meetings via videoconference calls help build relationships and cultural understanding.

2

Suggested Readings

Beyerlein, M. M., Freedman, S., McGee, C., & Moran, L. (2003). *Beyond teams: Building the collaborative organization.* San Francisco: Jossey-Bass/Pfeiffer.

Brake, T. (2006). Leading global virtual teams. *Industrial & Commercial Training, 38*(3), 116-121.

Cascio, W. F. (2000). Managing a virtual workplace. *Academy of Management Executive, 14*(3), 81-90.

Gibson, C. B., & Cohen, S. G. (2003). The last word: Conclusions and implications. In C. B. Gibson & S. G. Cohen (Eds.), *Virtual teams that work: Creating conditions for virtual team effectiveness* (pp. 403-421). San Francisco: Jossey-Bass.

Hackman, J. R. (2002). *Leading teams: Setting the stage for great performances.* Boston: Harvard Business School Press.

Herrenkohl, R. C. (2004). *Becoming a team, achieving a goal.* Mason, OH: South-Western.

Hinds, P. J., & Weisband, S. P. (2003). Knowledge sharing and shared understanding in virtual teams. In C. B. Gibson & S. G. Cohen (Eds.), *Virtual teams that work: Creating conditions for virtual team effectiveness* (pp. 21-36). San Francisco: Jossey-Bass.

Katzenbach, J. R., & Smith, D. K. (2005). The discipline of teams. *Harvard Business Review, 83*(7/8), 162-171.

Luecke, R. (2004). *Creating teams with an edge: The complete skill set to build powerful and influential teams.* Boston: Harvard Business School Press.

Marquardt, M. J., & Horvath, L. (2001). *Global teams: How top multinationals span boundaries and cultures with high-speed teamwork.* Mountain View, CA: Davies-Black.

Ross, J. A. (2006). Trust makes the team go 'round. *Harvard Management Update, 11*(6), 3-6.

Surplus, S. H. (2004). Motivating the troops: Moving from the power of "me" to the power of "we." *Supervision, 65*(4), 9-12.

Translation to the Leadership Architect® Competency Library

In order for a team or individuals on a team to perform well in this area, these are the competencies that would most likely be in play. Aside from a team improvement plan where everybody works on the same thing, some individual team members may need to work on some of these competencies. A critical number (but not necessarily all) of team members need to be good at:

Mission Critical:	**Important:**	**Nice to Have:**
27. Informing	5. Business Acumen	33. Listening
35. Managing and Measuring Work	15. Customer Focus	47. Planning
	46. Perspective	49. Presentation Skills
	65. *Managing* Vision and Purpose	50. Priority Setting
		52. Process Management
		58. Strategic Agility
		67. Written Communications

In addition to the 10 tips listed for this dimension, there are some tips that may apply from *FYI For Your Improvement*™. Below are the four items from the Team Architect® that make up this dimension. The item number appears to the left of each item. Immediately below the text of each item are competency and tip numbers from *FYI*. The competency is listed first (from 1 to 67), followed by the tip number (1 to 10). For example, 33-4 refers to competency 33 (Listening), tip number 4. The tips are generally written for individual development, so some adaptation might be needed in the team context.

2. Team members understand team goals.
   3-6; 27-1,2,5; 33-3; 35-2,5,7; 36-3; 60-1

20. Team members can clearly describe their mission and vision.
   5-6,10; 15-1,3; 27-1,4; 65-1,2,4,9

38. Team members can clearly state their measures of success (what it will take to achieve each goal).
   27-2,3,6; 35-1,2,5,7; 52-3,8; 65-2

56. All team members know how the goals align with their work.
   27-1,4; 35-1,2,3,4,7; 47-1,7; 50-2

FACTOR I: THRUST

2

Dimension 3
Thrust Commitment

Definition:
Team members feel a common sense of ownership over goals and pull together to collectively achieve team and organization objectives.

Addresses the question:
Is every team member truly committed to the goals and objectives of the team?

A Dimension in the THRUST Factor
A common mind-set about what needs to be accomplished.

> *If you want to build a ship, don't drum up people together to collect wood*
> *and don't assign them tasks and work,*
> *but rather teach them to long for the endless immensity of the sea.*
> Antoine de Saint-Exupery – French aviator and writer

Items
3. There is an observable sense of commitment in the team.
21. Team members are committed to their collective work goals and products—what can only be achieved by all pulling together.
39. All team members feel responsible for customer commitments.
57. Team members are expected to share the values of the team and the organization.

Unskilled
☐ The goals of the team are not equally attractive to all the team members
☐ Team lacks passion for its mission
☐ Some team members are loners and not supportive of the team as a whole
☐ What the team needs to do is not very exciting or motivating
☐ Team members do not have their eyes on the customers
☐ Team members' values don't complement or conflict with those of the rest of the organization
☐ Some team members fail to carry their share of the load

Skilled
☐ The team works well together
☐ There is infectious enthusiasm in the team; members keep each other motivated
☐ Each team member feels like he/she owns the goals of the team
☐ The team celebrates wins together
☐ Team members agree on what the team goals are
☐ Team members put in extra effort to achieve the goals
☐ The team is seen by others as cohesive, determined, and focused

Overused
☐ Commitment to the charter is too much of a litmus test for approval in the team
☐ Team works together so much that individualism is lost
☐ Team spends too much time on being a team and too little time performing
☐ People in the team help others so much that their individual goals are not met

Note on overused strengths: Overused skills and disproportionately used strengths tend to have the negative effects listed above. To decrease those negative consequences, you have two alternatives. You can scale down or use the strength less, or you can compensate for it with another skill or behavior. In practice, it is very difficult to get an individual or a team to use a strength less. In most cases, the best path is to develop compensators. Team Architect® Dimensions that can compensate for overusing this dimension and compensating skills from the Leadership Architect® Library's 67 Competencies are listed below.

(Note: Team Dimension numbers are listed in parentheses. Competencies are listed in numerical order by competency number.)

Compensating Team Dimensions:
☐ Thrust Management (1)
☐ Talent Acquisition and Enhancement (7)
☐ Talent Allocation and Deployment (8)
☐ Focusing (15)
☐ Delivering the Goods (18)

Compensating Competencies:

- ☐ 21. *Managing* Diversity
- ☐ 31. Interpersonal Savvy
- ☐ 36. Motivating Others
- ☐ 53. *Drive for* Results

Some Causes of Poor Performance

- ☐ Lack of buy-in among team members regarding team purpose
- ☐ The nature of the team's work is not inherently interesting or challenging
- ☐ The work the team does is all individual work; there is no reason to act like a team
- ☐ The work of the team is divided in such a way that only a few have interesting and motivating tasks
- ☐ One or a few members of the team are doing most of the work
- ☐ There is insufficient role clarity, accountability, or performance metrics with consequences
- ☐ The team has one bad apple that causes noise for everyone else
- ☐ Lack of incentive or compensation aligned with team performance
- ☐ Company culture doesn't support the energy or focus of the team
- ☐ Lack of customer focus in organization or team
- ☐ There is so much turnover in the team that it is difficult to gel
- ☐ The team and/or organization hasn't clearly identified its values

The Map

It's easy to spot a team that's truly committed to its objectives. The commitment shines through in the way its members "walk their talk." In the way they are personally vested in team outcomes. In the way they interact with each other. In the way they represent the team to external stakeholders. When team members are committed to achieving the goals, they willingly put in extra effort to achieve them. They have a sense of ownership. People do their individual best when they are challenged and motivated by the work itself, when they are personally invested in the products and services produced and the customers served. No group ever becomes a high-performing team until it can hold itself accountable collectively as a team. Creating a high level of commitment in a team is much more difficult without face-to-face interaction. Building commitment in virtual teams requires focused, up-front relationship building. This helps all team members, regardless of their location, to see themselves as working collectively toward achieving goals. High-performing teams are deeply committed to their purpose, goals, and methods. The

23

FACTOR I: THRUST

highest-performing teams also have members who are committed to one another. This double commitment to the charter and to each other is the key to sustained high performance.

Some Remedies

☐ **1. Agree on the goals.** It's tough to be committed when you don't agree. It's tough when team members are dispersed across different functions or locations. But commitment to goals is deepened when team members find agreement, when they believe they're following the same map, when they believe their challenges and successes are truly shared by their fellow team members. Gaining consensus around goals minimizes the tension between individual and team priorities. Open discussions and negotiation are pivotal in reaching consensus on goals by clarifying misunderstanding and promoting ownership. For virtual teams, both formal and informal communication networks can be used to provide constant communication about the team goals and challenges.

☐ **2. Vision the outcomes.** Walk the team through a visioning exercise. Ask them to envision the team finishing its work and reaching all of its goals successfully. Ask what it looks like. How do customers feel? What's in it for the team? How does each member of the team feel? Why was the team successful? What did it do well? What did it avoid doing? What kinds of rewards and consequences are there? Are all of the above elements motivating to the team? To what extent will this depend on the effort of a cohesive team and not just a collection of individuals? If this exercise does not produce excitement in the team, then you need to rethink the goals or lower your expectations.

☐ **3. Plan for small wins.** Break the journey toward the goal into small trips. Small wins are invaluable to building members' commitment as well as overcoming the inevitable obstacles that get in the way of achieving meaningful long-term purpose. Set up benchmarks along the way. Measure success in increments. Celebrate the small wins along the way.

☐ **4. Develop team values, norms, and rules of engagement.** Walk the team through a series of exercises to determine the team values, supporting norms, and rules of engagement statements. These are generally basic attributes that have to do with respect and openness as well as guidelines around timeliness, workload, and contribution to the team. These guiding values and rules help the team to create an environment of open communication and build commitment to high performance. Norms especially help maintain focus for team members who are dispersed, since there may be less opportunity for day-to-day interactions with the team leader and other team members.

☐ **5. Develop an operating contract within the team.** Let the team members develop their own roles and responsibilities. Once this happens, the team can decide how to apply its human resources to its goals. This process leads members to some heartfelt discussion around who may be best- (and worst-) suited for specific tasks and how all the individual roles and assignments come together to achieve a successful outcome. Don't equate team with sameness in roles. Effective teams deploy resources based on human strengths and weaknesses rather than trying to fit people into a cookie-cutter mold. Clear clarification of roles and responsibilities helps increase goal commitment among virtual team members. A team directory that includes each member's training, experience, and assignments should be posted on the team Web page or virtual space. It should also identify the go-to person for particular issues to guide team members when they need help.

☐ **6. Distribute the work and challenges evenly among members.** Teams won't be successful over the long run if only a few of the members are doing nearly all of the work. If members perceive they are carrying equal loads, they are more likely to band together to achieve their goals. Also, try to evenly divide the challenging parts of the work among the team members. An even better goal is to match each challenge with the needs of each team member. Some are motivated by some aspects of the work and some by different tasks. It is natural in teams for the most challenging work to go to some combination of the most senior or the most talented—those who are most likely to do it well. Avoid this. Strive for balance and alignment. Involve the team in this division of labor. The members probably know best.

☐ **7. Reward and compensate team members.** People will be more committed to team goals when they are rewarded and promoted based on the metrics that support those goals. Research suggests that a combination of team and individual incentives is the most effective in driving team performance. Use both tangible and intangible rewards to reward against benchmarks that are based on individual and team performance. Ask team members what rewards are essential to them to create a sense of ownership. Leaders of virtual teams need to pay special attention to what motivates these team members to keep them engaged and provide opportunities for them to excel. Whatever method is selected, rewards and compensation should be given in a timely manner.

☐ **8. Address missed commitments by individual members of the team.** Find out what happened to cause the problem. One bad apple or less motivated team member can spoil it for the rest. If one team member is not as committed as the others, he/she will impact and frustrate the rest of the team, especially if the person is still reaping the same benefits and rewards as the rest of the team. The team leader and team members need to confront this behavior. Ask a few questions:

- Was this person committed before?
- If so, what has changed?
- Can the situation be reversed?
- How can the team and the leader address the problem?
- If this can't be reversed, is there a more suitable role for this person elsewhere, perhaps outside the team?

☐ **9. Involve the customers.** Bring customers into your organization if the team's activities have direct consequences for customers. Link communications, schedules, technology, and any other support systems you can think of to make sure both organizations reap the maximum benefit from their partnership. Getting customers and team members to work closely together builds commitment on both sides and leads to a win-win link. Getting customer feedback helps the team know how it is performing in the eyes of a key constituency. When possible, teams should interact directly with the external customers who make buying decisions about services and products. It is especially true for problem-solving or consulting teams. Although the beneficiaries of problem-solving teams will most likely be their coworkers in the organization (because their mandate is usually to improve internal operations), the teams should still use external customers to gather information on what actually constitutes an improvement in the product or service.

☐ **10. Build a team brand.** Limited face-to-face interaction often results in loss of team identity for virtual team members. Limited opportunities for bonding in virtual teams make it more difficult to establish trust and commitment, to build commitment to goals, and to create shared values and perspectives. To address this, create a theme that captures the essence of the team's purpose and objectives. Catchphrases, team names, and even logos help a team to build an identity to rally around. And, as the team reaches out beyond its boundaries to external stakeholders, it can begin to build a team brand, one that illustrates its mission and performance focus. If a team theme or symbol doesn't arise naturally, have the team brainstorm to identify a theme embedded in the team's mission or nature of its work that can be used as a rallying point.

Suggested Readings

Beyerlein, M. M., Freedman, S., McGee, C., & Moran, L. (2003). *Beyond teams: Building the collaborative organization.* San Francisco: Jossey-Bass/Pfeiffer.

Cascio, W. F. (2000). Managing a virtual workplace. *Academy of Management Executive, 14*(3), 81-90.

Hackman, J. R. (2002). *Leading teams: Setting the stage for great performances.* Boston: Harvard Business School Press.

Herrenkohl, R. C. (2004). *Becoming a team, achieving a goal.* Mason, OH: South-Western.

Hoefling, T. (2003). *Working virtually: Managing people for successful virtual teams and organizations.* Sterling, VA: Stylus.

Katzenbach, J. R., & Smith, D. K. (1993). *The wisdom of teams.* New York: HarperCollins.

Katzenbach, J. R., & Smith, D. K. (2005). The discipline of teams. *Harvard Business Review, 83*(7/8), 162-171.

Lawler, E. E., III. (2000). *From the ground up: Six principles for building the new logic corporation.* San Francisco: Jossey-Bass.

Malhotra, A., Majchrzak, A., & Rosen, B. (2007). Leading virtual teams. *Academy of Management Perspectives, 21*(1), 60-70.

Massey, T. (2005). *Ten commitments for building high performance teams.* Bandon, OR: Robert D. Reed.

Surplus, S. H. (2004). Motivating the troops: Moving from the power of "me" to the power of "we." *Supervision, 65*(4), 9-12.

3

Translation to the Leadership Architect® Competency Library

In order for a team or individuals on a team to perform well in this area, these are the competencies that would most likely be in play. Aside from a team improvement plan where everybody works on the same thing, some individual team members may need to work on some of these competencies. A critical number (but not necessarily all) of team members would have to be good at:

Mission Critical:	**Important:**	**Nice to Have:**
35. Managing and Measuring Work	36. Motivating Others	15. Customer Focus
53. *Drive for* Results	42. Peer Relationships	22. Ethics and Values
60. *Building Effective* Teams	50. Priority Setting	43. Perseverance
	65. *Managing* Vision and Purpose	

In addition to the 10 tips listed for this dimension, there are some tips that may apply from *FYI For Your Improvement*™. Below are the four items from the Team Architect® that make up this dimension. The item number appears to the left of each item. Immediately below the text of each item are competency and tip numbers from *FYI*. The competency is listed first (from 1 to 67), followed by the tip number (1 to 10). For example, 33-4 refers to competency 33 (Listening), tip number 4. The tips are generally written for individual development, so some adaptation might be needed in the team context.

3. There is an observable sense of commitment in the team.
   35-1,2,3,7; 36-3; 53-7; 60-1,3,7; 110-4

21. Team members are committed to their collective work goals and products—what can only be achieved by all pulling together.
   36-3; 53-1,3; 60-1,3,5,6,7; 65-2; 110-4

39. All team members feel responsible for customer commitments.
   15-1,2,3,4,8,9; 35-2,7; 50-3; 53-3

57. Team members are expected to share the values of the team and the organization.
   22-1,2,3,4; 51-8; 60-1,5,6,7,8

3

Dimension 4
Trust in Truthful Communication

Definition:
Communication inside the team is open, honest, and complete.

Addresses the question:
Does the team's communication have the appropriate level of directness, transparency, and honesty to benefit the team and the organization?

A Dimension in the TRUST Factor
Trusting others to do what's right for the team and for each other.

> *The genius of communication is the ability to be both totally honest and totally kind at the same time.*
> John Powell – British film music composer

Items
4. Team members speak up and say what's on their minds.
22. Team members take the time to understand one another's differences and expertise.
40. Team members are open with one another about their viewpoints.
58. Team members are receptive to candidly observing and improving their own team process.

Unskilled
- ☐ Team members aren't willing to stand alone and voice critical thoughts, ideas, and feelings
- ☐ Team avoids internal conflict
- ☐ Issues are not out in the open; undiscussables exist and may be brewing beneath the surface
- ☐ Team doesn't take the time to identify, understand, or leverage individual differences, including both strengths and weaknesses
- ☐ Team members are not forthcoming or honest with one another
- ☐ Team members are stuck in their ways of doing things
- ☐ Issues are only discussed off-line, not in public or out in the open
- ☐ There are cliques in the team that keep information from others

☐ Team is arrogant and not willing to examine itself critically

☐ Some team members are not truthful communicators

Skilled

☐ Significant issues are always surfaced in public and solved collectively

☐ Team members help each other to surface issues sensitively

☐ Team members give each other time to vent

☐ Team goes into problem-solving mode when issues are surfaced rather than finding blame or dismissing

☐ Team members have both professional and personal conversations with each other

☐ Team members allow each other to express their feelings and thoughts without judging

☐ The team willingly, openly, and directly deals with issues, challenges, and conflict

☐ Team members respect each other's opinions

☐ The team supports and encourages open and honest communication

☐ Information is shared democratically in the team; relevant information is made available to all members

Overused

☐ Team spends too much time collecting input from members

☐ Members are overly critical of one another and themselves

☐ There is too much raw negative information being surfaced

☐ Team spends too much time focusing on the negative

☐ Team members get too personal in discussions and meetings

☐ Team spends too much time reengineering their processes

Note on overused strengths: Overused skills and disproportionately used strengths tend to have the negative effects listed above. To decrease those negative consequences, you have two alternatives. You can scale down or use the strength less, or you can compensate for it with another skill or behavior. In practice, it is very difficult to get an individual or a team to use a strength less. In most cases, the best path is to develop compensators. Team Architect® Dimensions that can compensate for overusing this dimension and compensating skills from the Leadership Architect® Library's 67 Competencies are listed below.

(Note: Team Dimension numbers are listed in parentheses. Competencies are listed in numerical order by competency number.)

30

Compensating Team Dimensions:
- ☐ Resource Management (9)
- ☐ Decision Making (11)
- ☐ Conflict Resolution (12)
- ☐ Focusing (15)
- ☐ Delivering the Goods (18)

Compensating Competencies:
- ☐ 10. Compassion
- ☐ 12. Conflict Management
- ☐ 23. Fairness to Direct Reports
- ☐ 36. Motivating Others
- ☐ 51. Problem Solving
- ☐ 60. *Building Effective* Teams

Some Causes of Poor Performance
- ☐ Members are averse to conflict
- ☐ Team is afraid to take risks
- ☐ Organizational culture is too accommodating, too nice; cultural boundaries stifle open communication
- ☐ Members lack courage
- ☐ Team dismisses differences and diversity
- ☐ Members don't trust one another; trust has been betrayed
- ☐ Members are too sensitive; direct communication hurts feelings or causes misunderstandings
- ☐ Members avoid speaking up for fear of rejection or failure
- ☐ Members are slow learners
- ☐ There is little interest in making this a team
- ☐ There are cliques that keep to themselves
- ☐ Team is new and has not yet fully formed
- ☐ There is one bad apple that spoils it for the rest

The Map
One of the hallmarks of high-performing teams is a climate that promotes truthful communication. Absent that climate, any team will be challenged to keep dysfunction in check. Establishing a climate of truthful communication is one of the most commonly faced obstacles for teams. With virtual teams, lack of face-to-face interaction coupled with diversity in cultural norms can make it more difficult to create a climate where truthful communication is the

norm. False information, hidden agendas, lack of openness, late information, and interpersonal noise all chill team performance. Successful teams have an open, timely, and truthful communication process. Members on successful teams understand one another. They spend as much time listening and understanding as they do speaking. Members on high-performing teams take risks, speak up, trust others, and resolve conflict. This requires teams to practice frank and open communication. This can be a challenge if the organization's culture avoids honesty out of a misguided attempt to be politically correct or polite. To be successful, the team has to make it safe to openly communicate with a lot of give-and-take.

Some Remedies

☐ 1. **Honesty is the policy.** Trust is often slow to develop and easy to lose. The first step in gaining trust is to ensure that it is deserved. To build trust, admit mistakes. Keep confidences. Don't excessively soften messages to avoid conflict or discomfort. Promptly reveal critical information. Take a risk by placing trust in others. These behaviors should be demonstrated, promoted, and reinforced in all team members. New teams start with low levels of trust. For many virtual teams, trust tends to decrease rather than increase over time due to the geographic limitations that prevent frequent in-person contact. It is especially important that virtual team members are honest and prompt in their communication to sustain trust. *More help? See* FYI For Your Improvement™, *Chapter 29 – Integrity and Trust.*

☐ 2. **Make it safe.** Team members should not play games with each another. If they don't know, they should just say so. If they aren't sure, they should ask for input. Directness builds an expectation that people will be constructive with each other. Withholding information, ideas, or feelings can be destructive in teams. Some members, of course, don't have the courage or the tools to be forthright and candid when they communicate. Therefore, transparency in communication needs to be the norm in the team. With transparency as a communication linchpin, straight talk can prevail. Team members will feel safe to air concerns without fear of reprisal. People will be asked for input regularly. They'll be listened to. Respected. They'll feel safe. Encourage team members to be succinct and factual, to listen carefully before speaking, to avoid inflammatory language and, perhaps most dangerous of all, to not make sweeping generalizations and judgments. *More help? See* FYI For Your Improvement™, *Chapter 34 – Managerial Courage.*

☐ 3. **Respect opinions of others.** The best teams are made up of people with the biggest diversity of perceptions. People who learn to understand and value the opinions of others. Virtual team members from different cultural and geographical backgrounds will likely have widely varying values and points of view. That can be a great advantage for the team, but when there are different opinions and disagreements, it is crucial to talk through things and respect each other's opinions. The importance of gaining and sustaining respect within the team cannot be overstated. Respect generally comes before trust. And it's hard to have one without the other. Basically, if you don't or can't respect someone, especially on your team, you likely will never trust them. Many people don't openly give respect to others; rather, they are stingy with it and think it needs to be earned. If you are stingy with respect, here are some things you can do:

- Acknowledge that it is at least partially your problem. Everyone deserves a basic level of respect.
- Focus on the task, not the person.
- Avoid gossip—it kills respect. Form your opinions about your teammates from your working with them, not from the secondhand gossip you may hear from others.
- Be aware and respect teammates' cultures.
- Allow the time for people to tell what they think and feel.

☐ 4. **Leverage differences.** Use a coach to administer a diagnostic tool (FIRO-B®, Myers-Briggs Type Indicator® [MBTI], DiSC®, etc.) on personality style, type, or team roles. Have a coach use some common exercises with such tools to help members understand each other's preferences, how they can best contribute to the team, and what their liabilities might look like. Typical exercises include what is comfortable and difficult for each type (style) to do, what each style can gain from the other, and simulated problem-solving situations where each type can see what valuable perspectives another brings to the problem. Identify ways to incorporate this newly discovered information into team roles, assignments, and responsibilities. Find ways to leverage strengths and create developmental opportunities for individuals, while at the same time minimizing situations where people may not be temperamentally suited for tasks or assignments. Use this process to balance the team. Remember, groupthink—a lack of independent thinking—often occurs when a team has been together as a unit for more than three years, according to some research. So use all the naturally occurring diversity of views you can. It prevents staleness. One caution: don't confuse personality with effectiveness, which is a common misuse of the above-mentioned tools. *More help? See* FYI For Your Improvement™, *Chapter 14 – Creativity, or read* YOU: Being More Effective in Your MBTI® Type.

4

33

☐ **5. Value diversity.** Research indicates that more diverse teams outperform narrow teams in problem-solving tasks, especially when the task has some uniqueness to it. Virtual teams actually may have an advantage here since dispersed team members, particularly when located globally, bring experiences and cultural knowledge that expand the overall team's perspective. People do not need to be alike or think the same to work well together and be a successful team. Rather, successful teams utilize individual differences to achieve the team's common purpose. Following are tips to help teams value diversity:

  – Remember that reasonable people can and do differ with each other.
  – Try to learn as much as you can from others.
  – Evaluate a new idea based on its merits (not on who submitted it).
  – Avoid comments and remarks that draw negative attention to a person's unique characteristics.
  – Don't ignore differences among team members; instead, leverage the differences.
  – Take advantage of global perspectives in virtual teams—this may open windows of thought never considered before.

If you or someone on the team needs to work on a diversity-related issue, see *FYI For Your Improvement*™, Chapter 21 – *Managing* Diversity.

☐ **6. Exchange information.** Create a regular process or meeting time for the team that is focused on information sharing. Use some guidelines or agenda norms that set expectations for each member to come prepared to discuss their status on assignments, things they've learned from internal and external customers, organizational issues that may impact the team's performance, etc. Encourage all members to ask questions and to challenge one another on issues. Pay attention to the quantity and quality of information sharing. Exchange information in a timely manner. Create knowledge-management systems like shared databases that include work-relevant information. Virtual teams can use chat rooms, instant messaging, blogs, a team Web site, or other virtual space to share information. Electronic postings or distribution lists make it easy to exchange information promptly. People from different cultures may vary in terms of their communication and information-sharing norms, so team members need to be sensitive to these differences. Information sharing can help team members develop a greater appreciation of one another based on their communication, technical abilities, and performance rather than personalities or style preferences. Information should be exchanged with all team members to build trust so that team members know what is going on and what is relevant. The team leader sets the stage for open communication. The leader's behavior is crucial in building trust and opening communication. The leader must encourage discussion of problems and key issues and then model a response that is non-judgmental, without invading team members' privacy.

☐ **7. Increase interdependence.** Open communication and trust can be best facilitated when people work interdependently and have an opportunity to get to know and observe each other on a regular basis. When people depend on the actions, information, and resources of each other to complete work, it leads to higher communication and information sharing. Common space and high levels of personal interaction are also critical for most project teams because their members come from different backgrounds and are usually only together for a short period of time. As a result, members need activities that cause them to talk to each other. One expert says that self-managing work teams seem to require both interaction time and common physical space. Members may be spread out over a large facility, but they definitely need dedicated meeting and gathering spaces to allow them to operate as a team. When practical, physically locating the team close together is best. If this isn't feasible, create virtual common spaces by using team chat rooms, instant messaging, or other electronic means to build a common team "space."

☐ **8. Debrief successes and failures.** A regular debriefing process can help to facilitate both open communication and learning. The process also can elicit both positive and negative feedback about the team, their work processes, and individual contributions. This type of group debrief might help to create an environment that makes it more comfortable for team members to give and take feedback. A coach or facilitator should ask and flipchart answers to the following questions after a key accomplishment or setback:

  – What went well?
  – What should we have done differently?
  – What did we learn?
  – How can we apply that learning?

Before jumping into this exercise, establish ground rules to be used during the discussion (e.g., all comments will be presented as constructively as possible, or members will share all thoughts and not withhold feelings). Also, make sure each member contributes at least one response to each of the questions. Use these learnings for future challenges or situations that might be similar so as to not make the same mistakes again. For geographically dispersed team members, conduct regular virtual meetings through audio- or videoconferences so virtual team members can spend time discussing issues, problems, and work progress.

4

☐ **9. Assign an issue manager.** When controversies arise that are personal and subjective rather than issue-based and factual, assign a neutral, relatively uninvolved member of the team to manage the situation. That person should control the agenda, speaking times, and problem-solving tactics used to settle the issue. As the issue referee, that person should avoid taking sides. His/her task is to manage it through to completion. The issue manager's role is to treat the problem as a team problem, even if it is personal. What are the causes, the viewpoints, the theories people are operating under? As in any conflict situation, the manager must get people to be specific and talk about feelings. Formally present both pros and cons of the issues. Post the issues on the Web site for team members to read. *More help? See* FYI For Your Improvement™, *Chapter 12 – Conflict Management.*

☐ **10. Establish electronic communication norms.** It is critical for all teams to establish communication norms regarding how information will be communicated, both in person and, especially, electronically. With electronic communication, keep in mind that expressing feelings and thought in written form, like e-mails and instant messaging, can be more difficult than talking to someone in person or over the phone due to the loss of the non-verbal cues that aid the communication process. Audio- or videoconferencing technologies may replace face-to-face meetings for teams that are geographically dispersed. Virtual team members may not trust each other if they lack a common set of norms or ways of communicating via communication technology. These norms should include:

  – How often to check the team's knowledge repository.
  – When, how, and where to use any communication technologies.
  – When, what, how, and where to post on the virtual space.
  – How to inform others about the upcoming meetings or news.
  – When to have face-to-face meetings.
  – Who has access to the information.

These communication norms need to be revisited and revised over time. Research shows that clear and visible communication strategies are vital to team success.

Suggested Readings

Fisher, K., Rayner, S., Belgard, W., & the Belgard-Fisher-Rayner Team. (1995). *Tips for teams: A ready reference for solving common team problems* (2nd ed.). New York: McGraw-Hill.

Gibson, C. B., & Manuel, J. A. (2003). Building trust: Effective multicultural communication processes in virtual teams. In C. B. Gibson & S. G. Cohen (Eds.), *Virtual teams that work: Creating conditions for virtual team effectiveness* (pp. 59-86). San Francisco: Jossey-Bass.

Hackman, J. R. (2002). *Leading teams: Setting the stage for great performances.* Boston: Harvard Business School Press.

Hoefling, T. (2003). *Working virtually: Managing people for successful virtual teams and organizations.* Sterling, VA: Stylus.

Jarvenpaa, S. L., & Leidner, D. E. (1999). Communication and trust in global virtual teams. *Organization Science, 10*(6), 791-815.

Katzenbach, J. R., & Smith, D. K. (1993). *The wisdom of teams.* New York: HarperCollins.

Lawler, E. E., III. (2000). *From the ground up: Six principles for building the new logic corporation.* San Francisco: Jossey-Bass.

Malhotra, A., Majchrzak, A., & Rosen, B. (2007). Leading virtual teams. *Academy of Management Perspectives, 21*(1), 60-70.

Marquardt, M. J., & Horvath, L. (2001). *Global teams: How top multinationals span boundaries and cultures with high-speed teamwork.* Mountain View, CA: Davies-Black.

McKenna, P. J., & Maister, D. H. (2002). Team trust. *Executive Excellence, 19*(5), 13-14.

Robbins, H., & Finley, M. (2000). *The new why teams don't work: What goes wrong and how to make it right.* San Francisco: Berrett-Koehler Publishers.

Thompson, L. F., & Coovert, M. D. (2006). Overcoming barriers to information sharing in virtual teams. In C. Bowers, E. Salas, & F. Jentsch (Eds.), *Creating high-tech teams: Practical guidance on work performance and technology* (pp. 213-241). Washington, DC: American Psychological Association.

Vukotich, G. (2008). *Breaking the chains of culture: Building trust in individuals, teams, and organizations.* Charleston, SC: Booksurge.

4

Translation to the Leadership Architect® Competency Library

In order for a team or individuals on a team to perform well in this area, these are the competencies that would most likely be in play. Aside from a team improvement plan where everybody works on the same thing, some individual team members may need to work on some of these competencies. A critical number (but not necessarily all) of team members would have to be good at:

Mission Critical:	**Important:**	**Nice to Have:**
12. Conflict Management	29. Integrity and Trust	21. *Managing* Diversity
33. Listening	42. Peer Relationships	22. Ethics and Values
34. Managerial Courage	60. *Building Effective*	45. Personal Learning
44. Personal Disclosure	Teams	56. Sizing Up People
57. Standing Alone		

In addition to the 10 tips listed for this dimension, there are some tips that may apply from *FYI For Your Improvement*™. Below are the four items from the Team Architect® that make up this dimension. The item number appears to the left of each item. Immediately below the text of each item are competency and tip numbers from *FYI*. The competency is listed first (from 1 to 67), followed by the tip number (1 to 10). For example, 33-4 refers to competency 33 (Listening), tip number 4. The tips are generally written for individual development, so some adaptation might be needed in the team context.

4. Team members speak up and say what's on their minds.
   12-2,5,7; 34-1,2,3,7; 57-2,8,9

22. Team members take the time to understand one another's differences and expertise.
   21-4,5,6,9; 33-2,3; 42-6; 56-1,3; 60-5

40. Team members are open with one another about their viewpoints.
   29-1,2,4,7; 33-2,3; 34-2,3; 44-7,8

58. Team members are receptive to candidly observing and improving their own team process.
   12-1,2,5,7; 27-2; 34-2,3,4; 35-2,7

Dimension 5
Trust in Actions

Definition:
Team decisions are supported and team members "walk their talk"; stated values equal actual behavior.

Addresses the question:
Do the individual team members do what they say they are going to do?

A Dimension in the TRUST Factor
Trusting others to do what's right for the team and for each other.

> *When we are debating an issue, loyalty means giving me your honest opinion,*
> *whether you think I'll like it or not. Disagreement, at this stage, stimulates me.*
> *But once a decision has been made, the debate ends. From that point on,*
> *loyalty means executing the decision as if it were your own.*
> Colin Powell – Former Chairman of the U. S. Joint Chiefs of Staff
> and U. S. Secretary of State

Items
5. Team members back each other up.
23. Team members may disagree with a decision, but they will still support it.
41. Team members "walk their talk"; stated values equal actual behavior.
59. Team members work well with other teams and are seen as cooperative.

Unskilled
☐ Members abandon each other during difficulty and don't give support
☐ A few members politic off-line for decisions they prefer
☐ Members act two-faced and bad-mouth decisions made by others on the team
☐ Members contradict team values; say one thing, do another
☐ Team operates in a vacuum and doesn't relate well or interact with other teams
☐ Team openly criticizes the work of other teams without trying to help
☐ Some team members agree with a decision in the meeting, then question it after the meeting

☐ Some team members are working their own agendas without regard for the team as a whole

☐ Cliques in the team are accepted

Skilled

☐ Team surfaces and resolves its issues and problems openly as a team

☐ Team members on the losing side of a decision act in line with the rest of the team

☐ Team members keep conflicts within the team private to other teams; dirty laundry is not aired outside the team

☐ All team members operate within the rules of engagement agreed to by the whole team; they act and behave within team norms and values

☐ Team members keep their promises, even if circumstances have changed

☐ Team members don't speak negatively about their team or team members

☐ Once the decision is made, team members fully support it

☐ Team members live up to their commitments; there is consistency between words and actions

Overused

☐ Team members with opposing views give up too soon just to keep the peace

☐ Team may only select those candidates for membership who already walk and talk like the team prefers, thereby passing up some needed diversity

☐ Team members are so cooperative and supportive with each other that they don't get their individual work done

☐ Team is so driven by values and norms that individual members give up their urge for doing something different

Note on overused strengths: Overused skills and disproportionately used strengths tend to have the negative effects listed above. To decrease those negative consequences, you have two alternatives. You can scale down or use the strength less, or you can compensate for it with another skill or behavior. In practice, it is very difficult to get an individual or a team to use a strength less. In most cases, the best path is to develop compensators. Team Architect® Dimensions that can compensate for overusing this dimension and compensating skills from the Leadership Architect® Library's 67 Competencies are listed below.

(Note: Team Dimension numbers are listed in parentheses. Competencies are listed in numerical order by competency number.)

5

40

Compensating Team Dimensions:

☐ Thrust Management (1)
☐ Talent Acquisition and Enhancement (7)
☐ Conflict Resolution (12)

Compensating Competencies:

☐ 12. Conflict Management
☐ 21. *Managing* Diversity
☐ 31. Interpersonal Savvy
☐ 53. *Drive for* Results

Some Causes of Poor Performance

☐ Some individual members aren't trustworthy
☐ Some team members have a private agenda contrary to the team's agenda
☐ Some team members have poor interpersonal/social skills
☐ Team doesn't finish making decisions in team meetings, and team leaves things hanging
☐ Team and/or organization has not defined its values
☐ Team members are too competitive with one another
☐ Team members sabotage one another
☐ Team doesn't handle conflict about decisions well
☐ Team members do not respect each other
☐ Organizational culture is excessively political

The Map

Building and sustaining trust has been identified in the research as a key success factor in high-performing teams. Trust in action exists when team members not only mean what they say but follow through on commitments. When they operate in good faith toward each other regardless of how interpersonally tense a situation might be. When individual members are comfortable taking tough and decisive actions under tension and conflict, knowing that the rest of the team is there to back them up. Team members need to know that if they go out on a limb on behalf of the team, that there isn't someone cutting the branch behind them. Positive team players will argue their points with intensity during team meetings and decision-making processes, but win or lose, they will support the outcome publicly as if it were their own preference. In the absence of trust, it's common for negative team members to bad-mouth the work of the team, to revisit decisions that are already made, and withhold support from their teammates. They may deal under the table and use deceptive ploys in attempts to sway key members of the team. This destructive behavior can't be tolerated. Team players must speak with pride and enthusiasm about their team and the decisions that have been made, regardless of their own personal position. Just as individuals need to support all internal team goals, they likewise need to support the team in all interactions outside the team. This includes working with other teams and functions in the organization.

Some Remedies

☐ **1. Set an example for others.** The improvement process begins with "the best are modeled by the rest." Walking the talk of the team is for every team member and requires a strong set of personal convictions, open communication with others, and a lot of self-awareness. Each member of the team should ask:

- Do people know what I stand for? If not, find ways to communicate what performance means to you. Be clear about what your values are and the team will align their expectations accordingly.

- How do others perceive me? If you don't know, find out. Get 360° feedback. How others perceive your actions may determine how likely they will be to support you.

- Do I look for ways to demonstrate my convictions? If not, find ways to make supportive comments to the team and about the team.

- What do I say or do that may lead others to think I'm not in line with the team?

- What is the difference between what I do or say and what the most respected member of the team does?

☐ **2. No off-line processing.** Nothing frustrates a team more than to spend time investigating and deliberating an issue and reaching a decision, only to have it reopened by a few members off-line. Off-line processing betrays trust in the team. One of the key rules to high-performing teams is that members can't pull rank. Facts and solutions rule and they have no rank. If a team is truly all for one and one for all, decisions need to be made "in-house" and adhered to by everyone. Team norms should include consequences for off-line processing. When virtual team members are located far apart, it is crucial to make their work and discussions visible to each other. Share and exchange information using collaboration technology, such as team Web sites and blogs, which allows virtual team members to more easily participate in team debates. Post the discussions and issues on the team Web site for all team members to read. Without these communication-sharing tools, team members may be less likely to roll up

42

their sleeves to put a lot of effort into the problem-solving and decision-making process since they won't feel involved. Off-line processing and politicking by its very nature shows disregard for others. Those that rely on off-line influence to have their way are usually the weakest team members from a teamwork standpoint. *More help? See* FYI For Your Improvement™, *Chapter 29 – Integrity and Trust.*

☐ **3. Let dissenters be heard.** When someone does not appear to be supportive of the team effort, the team has to examine why. What is it that a team member isn't supporting? Has the team considered that maybe the person has a point? Rather than just condoning a team member who is neither backing teammates nor supporting decisions that were made by the team, it is important to find out the reason they are not being supportive. Did the team member challenge the decision while it was being made? Was the challenge heard? Did the challenge have merit? Did the team listen? If not, why? Was it a style issue? Was it because the team didn't want to truly examine what the team member was saying because it would have meant major changes in implementation? Many times a discordant team member acts out because he/she has trouble getting heard. Before the team decides the person isn't a team player, the team needs to give the person a fair forum. If, after fully heard and then collectively rejected, the person still is not supportive, then the team has a deeper issue. *More help? See* FYI For Your Improvement™, *Chapter 33 – Listening.*

☐ **4. Reestablish team norms.** If there are people causing trouble by not supporting team members or team decisions, consider revisiting team norms. The team leader (or team coach) should facilitate a discussion of team member expectations at team meetings. Develop a list of norms or acceptable behaviors. These should be things like attendance at team meetings, decision making, dealing with conflict, and supporting the team to outsiders. Team norms have two functions: (1) they provide a guide for self-monitoring by team members, and (2) they provide a basis for the team leader or member to give feedback to a member who has violated the norm. Use the discussion on developing a set of team norms to assess how well the team is functioning in its current state. The team must be open to change if something is not working. Assuming everyone is acting in good faith and wants the team to succeed, most problems center around a lack of communication and the absence of a forum for complete discussion of tough issues.

☐ **5. Give timely private feedback.** If the team has already established values, norms, and the rules of engagement, giving quality feedback should be easy and expected. The reality is that giving critical feedback isn't always easy. Instead of looking at it as confronting the person, consider that you are confronting the ineffective behavior which is causing the entire team to suffer. Feedback that provides insight about how the project evolves and what can be improved is crucial. Giving timely, relevant feedback can be a challenge for leaders of virtual teams since the leader has limited opportunity to personally observe performance. Using two-way communication media, such as teleconferences, is highly recommended. When delivering feedback, do it in private and, if at all possible, in person. Be specific about how the person's behavior is impacting the team. Give the person an opportunity to respond. Be sure to then agree to next steps to resolve the damage that has already been done or to ensure that it doesn't happen again.

☐ **6. Give the naysayer the boot.** If you've tried everything mentioned up to this point without success, you may need to consider removing the troublemaking team member from the group. Some people may steadfastly refuse to modify their behavior, even after they've been given feedback and a chance to present their side. And sometimes you can't fix the damage that has been done. If that is the case, this individual may need to be transferred or let go. While it's dangerous to generalize, many teams have had trouble with those members who personalize decisions (how it affects them only), those on a mission who think their approach is the best one, those out for personal advancement, gossipers, and chronic conflict avoiders who simply can't overcome an obstacle. Any of these must change or go.

☐ **7. Build bridges.** Teams also need to pay attention to the relationships outside the boundaries of their team. Here are some tips to help:

– Identify the key stakeholders. List all the people and groups the team needs in order to be successful. What do you need from these stakeholders? Make another list of the people and groups who have something to gain and lose from the work of your team.

– Look for commonalities. Look beyond what you need from the stakeholders on your list to see what you can do for them. List the ways they need your ideas, your help. This list should be a set of common objectives—outcomes you both share. Use this list to remind the team of the allegiances that can be formed.

– Communicate. Find ways to tell others about your team. Make presentations to stakeholders.

– Assign boundary managers. Carefully select team members who will handle the key interfaces with stakeholders. Ask what needs to be done and who is the best person to do it. Don't assume it is the team leader.

    — Be credible. The above-mentioned strategies only work if your team is credible. Do other people trust your team? Can they count on your team to deliver the goods? To enhance your team's relationships with key stakeholders, don't ask for more than you need, don't promise more than you plan to deliver, don't set a due date you can't meet, and don't exaggerate project benefits or results.

☐ **8. Identify barriers to working with other groups.** Inter-team collaboration is done poorly in many organizations. In particular, cross-functional teams frequently do not manage their boundaries well, do not get the support they need, do not get the resources they require, and fail as a result. There are several reasons teams have difficulty working well with other teams, including:

    — Stereotyping. Preconceived ideas about how certain groups behave.

    — Competition. Teams compete for things like budget dollars, opportunities to work on high-visibility projects, etc. Some competition among teams is healthy. But if a team tries to achieve a goal at another's expense, i.e., by not sharing resources or information, it creates a situation that can stand in the way of healthy collaboration.

    — Differentiation. As groups become more differentiated in their practices, the challenge of integrating them increases. Although this differentiation helps units pull together to get the work done, it can be a barrier when they have to work collaboratively with a cross-functional team. Tension builds because the need to maintain differentiation is at odds with the need to integrate efforts.

If you think your team has barriers to working with other groups in the organization, ask the following questions:

    — Are there any past problems that need to be resolved or overcome?

    — Are you in competition with this group?

    — Does this group stand to lose as a result of your team's project?

    — Does this group support the concept of cross-functional teamwork?

    — Do you respect this group?

Once the team has identified the actual barriers, it can prepare a plan for overcoming them and achieving successful relationships with stakeholders.

☐ **9. Prevent issues from festering.** A major problem for teams occurs when they let things fester, which almost always makes things worse. The reason for this is that most people try to avoid face-to-face conflict. Most teams have inadequate conflict-resolution skills and routines. In general, the sooner you address a problem in the team, the easier it is to solve. Each team has to design and execute a method for the quick surfacing of issues.

45

FACTOR II: TRUST

Post issues or problems on a shared team Web site so all team members can access. Hold regular teleconferences or other meetings to discuss issues and problems. Be sensitive to cultural differences and language barriers. Generally, it's the responsibility of the leader to put issues on the agenda, to model conflict resolution practices, and to support individual team members seeking resolution of trust issues.

☐ **10. Follow through on commitment.** Probably nothing chills trust more than a person saying one thing and doing something else. In a team setting, individual contributions matter, but it's the collective output that distinguishes a high-performing team from the rest. So, team members rely on each other to follow through on commitments. Trust in action is developed when team members live up to their commitments, meet deadlines (or have a good reason for not meeting them), and contribute their fair share to team performance. There needs to be consistency between words and actions for trust to flourish. Focus on keeping commitments on team deliverables. Make the commitments visible to team members via e-mails or other means. Have a method in place to ensure follow through. Inform and explain to team members early if the task cannot be completed on time or if assistance is needed. *More help? See* FYI For Your Improvement™, *Chapter 29 – Integrity and Trust.*

Suggested Readings

Duarte, D. L., & Snyder, N. T. (2006). *Mastering virtual teams: Strategies, tools, and techniques that succeed* (3rd ed.). San Francisco: Jossey-Bass.

Fisher, K., Rayner, S., Belgard, W., & the Belgard-Fisher-Rayner Team. (1995). *Tips for teams: A ready reference for solving common team problems* (2nd ed.). New York: McGraw-Hill.

Hackman, J. R. (2002). *Leading teams: Setting the stage for great performances.* Boston: Harvard Business School Press.

Herzog, V. L. (2001). Trust building on corporate collaborative project teams. *Project Management Journal, 32*(1), 28-37.

Katzenbach, J. R., & Smith, D. K. (1993). *The wisdom of teams.* New York: HarperCollins.

Kirkman, B. L., Rosen, B., Gibson, C. B., Tesluk, P. E., & McPherson, S. O. (2002). Five challenges to virtual team success: Lessons from Sabre, Inc. *Academy of Management Executive, 16*(3), 67-79.

Lencioni, P. (2005). *Overcoming the five dysfunctions of a team: A field guide for leaders, managers, and facilitators.* San Francisco: Jossey-Bass.

Parker, G. M. (2002). *Cross-functional teams: Working with allies, enemies, and other strangers.* San Francisco: Jossey-Bass.

Ross, J. A. (2006). Trust makes the team go 'round. *Harvard Management Update, 11*(6), 3-6.

Vukotich, G. (2008). *Breaking the chains of culture: Building trust in individuals, teams, and organizations.* Charleston, SC: Booksurge.

Translation to the Leadership Architect® Competency Library

In order for a team or individuals on a team to perform well in this area, these are the competencies that would most likely be in play. Aside from a team improvement plan where everybody works on the same thing, some individual team members may need to work on some of these competencies. A critical number (but not necessarily all) of team members would have to be good at:

Mission Critical:	Important:	Nice to Have:
12. Conflict Management	18. Delegation	29. Integrity and Trust
22. Ethics and Values	27. Informing	31. Interpersonal Savvy
33. Listening	57. Standing Alone	36. Motivating Others
42. Peer Relationships		37. Negotiating
44. Personal Disclosure		40. *Dealing with* Paradox
60. *Building Effective* Teams		53. *Drive for* Results

In addition to the 10 tips listed for this dimension, there are some tips that may apply from *FYI For Your Improvement™*. Below are the four items from the Team Architect® that make up this dimension. The item number appears to the left of each item. Immediately below the text of each item are competency and tip numbers from *FYI*. The competency is listed first (from 1 to 67), followed by the tip number (1 to 10). For example, 33-4 refers to competency 33 (Listening), tip number 4. The tips are generally written for individual development, so some adaptation might be needed in the team context.

5. Team members back each other up.
   42-1,2,5,6,7,9; 57-2,6; 60-1,7

23. Team members may disagree with a decision, but they will still support it.
   12-1,2,3,4; 40-2,4; 53-1; 60-6; 65-4,7

41. Team members "walk their talk"; stated values equal actual behavior.
   22-1,2,3,4,5; 27-1,2,9; 40-4; 44-8

59. Team members work well with other teams and are seen as cooperative.
   12-1; 27-5; 31-2,3; 36-4; 37-7; 38-4,8; 42-5,6

Dimension 6
Trust Inside the Team

Definition:
Little to no internal competition in the team; team members motivate one another, engage in regular open feedback, and readily assist fellow team members when needed.

Addresses the question:
Do members of the team trust each other?

A Dimension in the TRUST Factor
Trusting others to do what's right for the team and for each other.

I am a member of a team, and I rely on the team, I defer to it and sacrifice for it, because the team, not the individual, is the ultimate champion.
Mia Hamm – American Olympic Gold Medalist and World Cup soccer player

Items
6. Team members sacrifice their own needs for the good of the team.
24. Little or no internal competition undermines team efforts.
42. Team members put effort into building team cohesion.
60. When one person struggles, other team members are there to help.

Unskilled
☐ Team members perform more like a collection of individual contributors than a team
☐ Team members compete with each other
☐ Members do and say things to get ahead at the expense of other team members
☐ Team does not spend adequate time together to gel
☐ Individuals are focused on getting their own results and don't look out for or help others
☐ Team lets some individual members fail or slip behind
☐ There is little interest in improving as a team
☐ Team members are following their own agendas without much regard for the team agenda
☐ Members dislike or distrust each other

Skilled

- [ ] The team acts as one
- [ ] Team members motivate one another
- [ ] Team members back each other up when needed
- [ ] The team spends scheduled time improving itself
- [ ] Helpful feedback regularly occurs
- [ ] Team members spend scheduled time focused on building and maintaining rapport
- [ ] Team members willingly share resources with each other
- [ ] Team members focus on team performance, not individual performance
- [ ] The team equally shares both accountability and recognition for results
- [ ] The team celebrates successes

Overused

- [ ] Team spends too much time focused on internal morale at the expense of performance
- [ ] Too much collaboration makes the team lose momentum
- [ ] Members may help each other out but neglect their individual priorities
- [ ] Individual strengths may get lost due to the emphasis on the team
- [ ] Individuals may hesitate to go against the learnings of the team for fear of causing internal conflict
- [ ] Team may support laggard members too long and is hesitant to address performance problems in a timely way

Note on overused strengths: Overused skills and disproportionately used strengths tend to have the negative effects listed above. To decrease those negative consequences, you have two alternatives. You can scale down or use the strength less, or you can compensate for it with another skill or behavior. In practice, it is very difficult to get an individual or a team to use a strength less. In most cases, the best path is to develop compensators. Team Architect® Dimensions that can compensate for overusing this dimension and compensating skills from the Leadership Architect® Library's 67 Competencies are listed below.

(Note: Team Dimension numbers are listed in parentheses. Competencies are listed in numerical order by competency number.)

6

Compensating Team Dimensions:

☐ Talent Acquisition and Enhancement (7)
☐ Talent Allocation and Deployment (8)
☐ Resource Management (9)
☐ Conflict Resolution (12)
☐ Focusing (15)
☐ Delivering the Goods (18)

Compensating Competencies:

☐ 13. Confronting Direct Reports
☐ 35. Managing and Measuring Work
☐ 50. Priority Setting
☐ 53. *Drive for* Results

Some Causes of Poor Performance

☐ Some team members act selfishly
☐ Some team members take competitiveness too far
☐ Members have poor peer relationship skills
☐ Team is too focused on technical or business issues at the expense of people issues
☐ Team fails to spend enough time together to build trust
☐ Some team members fit poorly with the rest of the team; weak team member links
☐ Reward systems encourage individual performance over teamwork
☐ Team has a history of trust issues that is hard to fix
☐ Team has poor conflict-resolution skills

The Map

You might think it reasonable to expect team members to get along and work smoothly together. However, the reality is that in many organizations, teamwork and team productivity take a backseat to individual performance. Most people, regardless of level or role in an organization, possess skills that are most closely linked to the strengths of individual contributors. In fact, most people never develop much beyond that profile. Individual responsibility and self-preservation remain the rule; shared responsibility based on trusting others is the exception. The majority of reward and incentive systems are targeted at individual performance. Teaming skills are rare and outstanding team leaders are in short supply. One key characteristic of high-performing teams is that members collaborate to overcome obstacles that get in the way of team success. Facing adversity together reinforces the team's intention to pursue their common purpose above and beyond individual or functional agendas. Team members who trust each other willingly share and exchange information, help each other when needed, have less internal competition, and stand squarely behind the team's mission. The payoff is that high-performing teams outperform the collective results of a collection of individual performers.

Some Remedies

☐ **1. Prioritize team building.** Bring in a team-building coach to help the team with its forming process. Don't do just the feel-good, warm and fuzzy light stuff. Face the most difficult development challenges and take some risks as a team. Learn to understand each other in an environment outside of work. Create a situation where everyone's skills get discovered and where no one has an advantage because of rank, tenure, or technical expertise. Arrange for team members to leave their comfort zones and depend on one another. Use exercises where individual performance means nothing if the team's performance doesn't prevail. (Many exercises are impossible to complete unless everyone contributes.) Make sure the exercises focus on team outcomes, not individual success. Also, make sure the outcomes can be translated into meaning back on the team. Building a virtual team often means recruiting individuals from different regions and locations. Research suggests that virtual team members often feel like they do not belong to a team as they do not have much direct interaction with their colleagues. Virtual teams need to go beyond just connecting team members electronically. If the budget allows, virtual teams should meet face-to-face periodically. If the budget does not allow this, members can still have team building electronically via team-building games, quizzes, and puzzles. They can increase their bonding opportunities using communication technologies such as instant messaging, group chat rooms, tele- and videoconferencing, and electronic bulletin boards.

☐ **2. Align reward systems.** What is the incentive for team members to make individual sacrifices? Will they be recognized or rewarded for doing so? Has the performance management and compensation system been aligned to measure and reward team performance? If not, why? If people are put on a team, but evaluated by their supervisor and compensated for individual work, it is unlikely that the team will reach optimal performance. This is especially so if raises are distributed from a competitive or rank order rating system. Follow the cash because money talks. There has to be a consequence for not being a good team member. Similarly, there should be a reward for the group doing it well. Work with your compensation department to align a performance management process where team members can evaluate each other's performance and be compensated for the team's results. The degree of virtuality needs to be taken into account when deciding how virtual teams are rewarded. For most teams, what seems to work best is a combination of individual and team rewards and incentives. The balance depends upon the extent to which working as a team produces superior results. The more performance depends on effective teamwork, the higher the proportion of rewards needs to be for team effort.

☐ **3. Develop the performance capability of others.** What happens if a member on the team is struggling with performance? Does it frustrate other team members? How do they respond? Do they complain about that person to the other team members? Do they go to the boss? Do they shun the person? If other team members recognize the performance gap and see the path to recovery, why aren't they helping that person discover it? Do they want the other member to fail? Team members should take the lead in bringing the person along. Developing others takes time more than anything. And since developing others is consistently the lowest-rated competency, use this as an opportunity to improve someone's performance. Grow a skill that most don't have. Trust grows when team members have confidence in each other's skills, knowledge, and abilities. Collocated teams have ample opportunities to observe teammates' performance. Virtual teams might not have the same advantage. For virtual teams, create a personalized Web directory that includes pictures and a brief summary of everyone's expertise and background and make it available to everyone on a team Web site. To sustain a high-performing team, keep the focus on continuously building on existing skills and acquiring new ones. *More help? See* FYI For Your Improvement™, *Chapter 19 – Developing Direct Reports and Others, and Chapter 54 – Self-Development.*

☐ **4. Spread the credit around.** One way to build trust is to generously acknowledge the accomplishments of others. Some of the most valuable team members, those with the best ideas, are also the same members who can single-handedly destroy trust on the team. Do some members insist on taking all the credit or attention for work? If so, learning to shine the spotlight on others in the team can help. If members are genuine with their recognition of teammate accomplishments, trust will grow. Are individuals on the team sincere? Do they share? Most of us are pretty selfish, so giving credit does not come naturally. Work on a system of proportional credit to spotlight the contributions of all contributors. Most of the time, many members contribute to an outcome even though one person might be the main contributor. Work with the dominant contributors on the team and help them thank others who helped. Who copied the report at the last

53

minute before the meeting? Remember that stealing someone's thunder is one of the worst things a teammate can do to betray trust on the team. Read *The New Why Teams Don't Work: What Goes Wrong and How to Make It Right* by Harvey Robbins and Michael Finley. They have an entire chapter dedicated to team trust.

☐ **5. Look for lack of trust danger signals.** Know what the signs are of trust breaking down in the team. Are people talking about one another behind their backs? Are members withholding information and resources? Are they undermining one another to benefit themselves? Are they stifling their feelings? Are they blaming or criticizing one another? Do members feel like they need to cover their tracks? Is there off-line processing going on? Are there cliques? Any of these behaviors can crash the trust in a team. Directly confront the warning signs and talk about the issues right away. Bring in a coach or facilitator if things get too heated. Revisit the team's values to look for violations of the rules of engagement and identify the positive behaviors that can get the team back on track. Trust takes a long time to build and a short time to break down. And remember that the majority of trust issues are due to incomplete and inadequate communication. Human nature being what it is, we may begin to wonder if the work is distributed fairly, if others are really committed, if teammates are doing their fair share. *More help? See* FYI For Your Improvement™, *Chapter 29 – Integrity and Trust.*

☐ **6. Help a sinking team member.** Most teams don't get to select their teammates directly. Sometimes we don't know what we've got on the team until it is too late. Everybody has problems, but some have bigger problems than others. Working in a team will allow team members to develop a lot of insight regarding on- and off-work situations. Members might discover that a teammate's performance problems are linked to some other outside issue. Is the team member late all the time? Tired? Disoriented? Stressed out? Some of these symptoms may be linked to physical or emotional problems. If a problem is suspected, don't speculate or gossip. After all, if you had the problem, would you want to be judged or helped? Get the team leader involved and let the leader work with professionals to help the member. It might be as simple as giving the person feedback. Most companies have policies in place to deal with drug or alcohol abuse. And most companies have EAP programs to help with other non-work issues. The important thing is to seek to understand first, and then provide the help or support the team member needs to get back on track.

☐ **7. Minimize cross-functional noise.** Not all functions, departments, units, and businesses work well with each other. So when we group people together that represent different functions on a cross-functional team, there may be some conflict and holding back. Conflicting priorities of different business groups can impede trust-building on a cross-functional team. Many employees in large organizations tend to operate almost exclusively in silos. They view their membership and loyalty as belonging to a certain subunit in the organization. Consequently, they behave in a manner that benefits their subunit but is potentially detrimental to the team as a whole. Such a focus can lead to an "us versus them" mentality that impedes the coordination and collaboration required for a high-performing team. Make team cohesion a priority. Each member of the team must make team mission and objectives a priority to build trust. Design reward systems to give equal weighting to team and "home unit" goals. Members need to take ownership for the information they exchange between the team and their function (and vice versa) and do it in a manner that is resourceful for both sides. Lack of face-to-face interactions with cross-functional team members makes it harder for virtual team members to build and retain a sense of team identity. Developing trust is vital in the early life of virtual teams. Frequent communication helps to increase early trust and team cohesion. Since trust takes time, there should be a couple of meetings where the team simply gets to know one another and sets its charter and rules of engagement before tackling the task.

☐ **8. Help new team members get on board.** New team members and leaders are added all the time to existing teams. In order for a new team entrant to get a fair start in adapting to the new environment, the team needs to roll up their sleeves and spend some time integrating new members. Create an orientation process for new members. Some ideas of things to help ensure the success of the new member include:

– Team charter and goals. Check for clarity to make sure the new team member understands the purpose of the group. Given his/her fresh perspective, does the member have any value-adding suggestions?

– Role clarity for the new member. Map out his/her role and explain the roles of other members.

– A candid assessment of how the team is doing. What's working, what isn't, what's needed.

– Team supplier, customer, and competitor data.

– Team values and rules of engagement. It is a good idea to revisit and perhaps amend the values to include the new team member's input. You can't just expect him/her to have the same values initially. Virtual team leaders should initiate the development of team communication norms and ensure that new members are brought up to speed on the team communication process.

- Organizational boundaries and guidelines the team follows. Political or cultural issues.
- Miscellaneous group processes (e.g., regular meeting times, presentations, and workflow).
- Skills or competencies needed for success on the team.
- Training to learn needed technical or functional skills.

Finally, assign the new team member a buddy who will be responsible for ensuring that the orientation is executed. Make this person accountable for the new team member's onboarding process. Rather than holding back until the rest of the team is sure the person is the right fit, assume fit until events prove otherwise. Trust first.

☐ **9. Vision team success.** Have the team imagine working together much better than they are now. Have someone flipchart answers to questions such as: If we worked together more effectively, we would be able to do what? What outcomes would be possible? What do we have to do individually and collectively to bring that off? What rewards would there be at the end of the team rainbow? Nothing breeds a success-driven culture like winning. Great generals and coaches have always known this and make extensive use of symbols of success and small wins, such as:

- Team dress, team parties, team celebrations, and secret team language all are signs of a tight-knit unit that believes in itself.
- Great coaches often overprepare for the lesser teams. Great generals often take the easy cities first. They do this to build a culture of success, near invincibility, and to discourage opponents. What are five quick, small wins your team can have that are visible, tied to your goals, and have the smell of success? Success, not rah-rah, builds confidence.

☐ **10. Capitalize on team diversity.** Virtual teams often consist of individuals from different cultures, locations, business units, or organizations. One of the key benefits of pulling together a group of individuals to form a high-performing team is the gathering of various perspectives. A wide array of thinking likely will yield broader, more inventive results. Diversity in a team should be embraced but not at the expense of team unity. It's important to remember that when people identify themselves as a team, they are more willing to engage in cooperative behavior and share resources. Here are some ways to build a sense of team unity while honoring the unique contributions of each member:

- Focus on the team's common mind-set, or thrust, such as goals, vision, purpose.
- Treat all team members equitably.
- Create a team image or brand.

– Make team assignments interdependent.
– Enhance group interest rather than self-interest; focus on the team's welfare rather than personal welfare.

Suggested Readings

Brandon, D. P., & Pratt, M. G. (1999). Managing the formation of virtual team categories and prototypes by managing information: A SIT/SCT perspective. *Academy of Management Proceedings*, D1-D6.

Duarte, D. L., & Snyder, N. T. (2006). *Mastering virtual teams: Strategies, tools, and techniques that succeed* (3rd ed.). San Francisco: Jossey-Bass.

Fisher, K., Rayner, S., Belgard, W., & the Belgard-Fisher-Rayner Team. (1995). *Tips for teams: A ready reference for solving common team problems* (2nd ed.). New York: McGraw-Hill.

Harvey, M., Novicevic, M. M., & Garrison, G. (2004). Challenges to staffing global virtual teams. *Human Resource Management, 14*, 275-294.

Jarvenpaa, S. L., & Leidner, D. E. (1999). Communication and trust in global virtual teams. *Organization Science, 10*(6), 791-815.

Katzenbach, J. R., & Smith, D. K. (1993). *The wisdom of teams*. New York: HarperCollins.

Kirkman, B. L., Rosen, B., Gibson, C. B., Tesluk, P. E., & McPherson, S. O. (2002). Five challenges to virtual team success: Lessons from Sabre, Inc. *Academy of Management Executive, 16*(3), 67-79.

Lawler, E. E., III. (2003). Pay systems for virtual teams. In C. B. Gibson & S. G. Cohen (Eds.), *Virtual teams that work: Creating conditions for virtual team effectiveness* (pp. 121-144). San Francisco: Jossey-Bass.

Lencioni, P. (2005). *Overcoming the five dysfunctions of a team: A field guide for leaders, managers, and facilitators*. San Francisco: Jossey-Bass.

Robbins, H., & Finley, M. (2000). *The new why teams don't work: What goes wrong and how to make it right*. San Francisco: Berrett-Koehler Publishers.

Spector, M. D., & Jones, G. E. (2004). Trust in the workplace: Factors affecting trust formation between team members. *Journal of Social Psychology, 144*(3), 311-321.

Vukotich, G. (2008). *Breaking the chains of culture: Building trust in individuals, teams, and organizations*. Charleston, SC: Booksurge.

6

Translation to the Leadership Architect® Competency Library

In order for a team or individuals on a team to perform well in this area, these are the competencies that would most likely be in play. Aside from a team improvement plan where everybody works on the same thing, some individual team members may need to work on some of these competencies. A critical number (but not necessarily all) of team members would have to be good at:

Mission Critical:	Important:	Nice to Have:
42. Peer Relationships	12. Conflict Management	7. Caring About Direct
51. Problem Solving	27. Informing	Reports
53. *Drive for* Results	45. Personal Learning	15. Customer Focus
60. *Building Effective*	50. Priority Setting	36. Motivating Others
Teams	62. Time Management	57. Standing Alone

In addition to the 10 tips listed for this dimension, there are some tips that may apply from *FYI For Your Improvement*™. Below are the four items from the Team Architect® that make up this dimension. The item number appears to the left of each item. Immediately below the text of each item are competency and tip numbers from *FYI*. The competency is listed first (from 1 to 67), followed by the tip number (1 to 10). For example, 33-4 refers to competency 33 (Listening), tip number 4. The tips are generally written for individual development, so some adaptation might be needed in the team context.

6. Team members sacrifice their own needs for the good of the team.
   40-1; 42-6; 50-3; 53-1; 60-1,5,6,9; 62-3,7

24. Little or no internal competition undermines team efforts.
   12-1,3; 27-2; 42-5; 51-1,3; 60-1,5,7; 63-1

42. Team members put effort into building team cohesion.
   36-1,3,5; 42-1,7,8; 60-1,6,7; 110-4

60. When one person struggles, other team members are there to help.
   3-6; 10-6; 42-1,5; 53-2; 56-2,3; 60-3,8; 110-4

Dimension 7
Talent Acquisition and Enhancement

Definition:
Team ensures it has the range of talents necessary to achieve its goals and uses a systematic process to improve team member skills.

Addresses the question:
Is there sufficient talent on the team to do what needs to be done?

A Dimension in the TALENT Factor
The necessary collective skills to get the job done.

> *All of us do not have equal talents, but all of us should have*
> *an equal opportunity to develop our talents.*
> John Fitzgerald Kennedy – 35th President of the United States

Items
7. The team has systems in place to help its members gain the skills and information they need.
25. Team members give each other positive and negative feedback to improve performance and team functioning.
43. The team follows a recruiting and staffing process to ensure it has the range of talents necessary to achieve its goals.
61. If the team has a knowledge or skill limitation, it faces it promptly and looks for help to fill the gap.

Unskilled
- ☐ The team does not possess the necessary skills and talent to accomplish its mission
- ☐ The team is made up of people who fit the culture or fit the style preferences of the team, but not the skill requirements
- ☐ Team members do not upgrade their skills or retool their capabilities
- ☐ Team members do not provide much improvement feedback to each other
- ☐ Team hires new members they know or with whom they are comfortable, rather than follow best practices for selection

☐ The team does not have processes and metrics in place to align skills and talent with its charter

☐ Team tries to get by with existing skills; ignores its limitations

☐ The team has a strong "not invented here" viewpoint and will not ask for nor seek help outside the team to achieve its goals

☐ The team is slow to recognize the need to change

Skilled

☐ When the team has an opening to fill, it tries to get the best talent it can, even if the new member is better than existing members at some skills and talents

☐ The team has measures in place to help it align talent against its mission

☐ The team debriefs both successes and failures looking for opportunities for improvement

☐ The team is not hesitant to go outside to get the skills and talents it needs on a short-term basis

☐ Team members trust that critical feedback from other team members is given solely with the collective interest of improving

☐ Continuous team development is an integral part of team norms

☐ The team has an objective hiring process in place to select the best talent to achieve team objectives

☐ The team has a skill road map which shows necessary skills, knowledge, and abilities for team tasks and assignments

☐ Once a performance gap is identified, team members make serious efforts to improve in that area

Overused

☐ Team spends too much time cross-training or learning new skills that are not mission critical

☐ Members exchange so much direct critical feedback that personal relationships have been damaged beyond repair

☐ Team is so rigid in following alignment staffing processes that they are slow adding people in time

☐ Team hires too many narrow experts to fill short-term technical needs at the expense of hiring members with more general or future skills

☐ Team spends too much time analyzing skill gaps and not acting on integrating skill resources

☐ Team goes outside so much for what it needs that internal development is stalled

Note on overused strengths: Overused skills and disproportionately used strengths tend to have the negative effects listed above. To decrease those negative consequences, you have two alternatives. You can scale down or use the strength less, or you can compensate for it with another skill or behavior. In practice, it is very difficult to get an individual or a team to use a strength less. In most cases, the best path is to develop compensators. Team Architect® Dimensions that can compensate for overusing this dimension and compensating skills from the Leadership Architect® Library's 67 Competencies are listed below.

(Note: Team Dimension numbers are listed in parentheses. Competencies are listed in numerical order by competency number.)

Compensating Team Dimensions:
☐ Talent Allocation and Deployment (8)
☐ Team Atmosphere (13)
☐ Focusing (15)
☐ Assignment Flexibility (16)

Compensating Competencies:
☐ 19. Developing Direct Reports and Others
☐ 31. Interpersonal Savvy
☐ 36. Motivating Others
☐ 53. *Drive for* Results
☐ 60. *Building Effective* Teams

Some Causes of Poor Performance
☐ Arrogance; team members think they know it all
☐ Unconscious incompetence; members don't know what they don't know
☐ Team members are blocked learners
☐ Organization has poor training resources
☐ Organization has poor staffing resources
☐ Organization isn't focused on development
☐ Organization is not open with information and communication
☐ Organizational culture is too polite; doesn't give critical feedback
☐ Members avoid conflict
☐ Team members are defensive when receiving feedback
☐ Good-old-boy network rules staffing decisions
☐ Team has had too many changes in team membership
☐ Change has been so rapid that the team can't keep up

7

The Map

A team can't be high performing if it does not collectively possess the skills that match the requirements of the objectives. It doesn't matter if the team has set its sights on being first. It doesn't matter if it has laid out an elaborate plan to get there. It doesn't even matter if it has an enlightened leader. If the team lacks the skills or a process to get needed skills, it cannot perform. The top priority when assembling a team is to get the skills on board needed to achieve the mission. It's important to not stack the deck too much in favor of some skills at the expense of others. Technical skills are vital; teaming and interpersonal skills are important as well. A high-performing team is well-rounded, comprised of talented individuals who bring complementary skills and abilities to the table. Individual member knowledge, skills, and abilities, taken in aggregate, create a formidable arsenal for achieving the team's mission. Another important priority is having a systematic process in place to keep the skills fresh as challenges shift. Consistent upgrading of skill keeps the team sharp. Embedding a feedback protocol into team norms helps surface skill gaps and areas for improvement. Using tasks and assignments targeted at developing capabilities in the team allows the team to grow and produce at the same time.

Some Remedies

☐ 1. **Align task requirements and skills.** Every permanent or temporary team has a set of work challenges, issues, goals, and objectives—stated or implied. Successfully performing against those requirements takes a certain mix of skills, styles, and talents. As part of the chartering exercise, the team should list the challenges, issues, goals, and objectives on one side of a chart, and then list the specific technical, functional, teaming, and personal skills necessary to effectively work against those tasks on the other side. That list of skills and talents can then be used for assessing skill gaps in the team, selecting new team members, assigning members to tasks, training members in new skills, and acquiring outside resources where significant gaps exist.

☐ 2. **Identify teaming skill requirements.** Identify the competencies needed to be a successful team member on this team at this time. Research has identified the following team-player skills: planning and goal setting, meeting management, listening, resolving conflict, consensus building, presentation skills, risk taking, problem solving, role clarification, mentorship, ethics, assertiveness, and giving/receiving feedback, among other things. Each team will have unique requirements based upon its stage of development and what tasks need to be accomplished. Communicate the skill requirements so people understand where they fit and where they don't. This approach will help with the skills inventory that needs to occur.

☐ **3. Conduct a continuous skills inventory.** Once the teaming requirements have been identified, it is important to continually inventory the talent on the team. Figure out what you have and what gaps might slow the team down. The boss, other team members, and self should assess each team member. Use the results of this team skills inventory to prioritize training needs for specific individuals or the entire team, and to determine the need for outside resources. In high-performing teams, the skills need to be in the team collectively, that is, not all team members need to be good at everything. (This will be addressed later in Dimension 8, Talent Allocation and Deployment.)

☐ **4. Use a disciplined recruiting process.** There are research-based and experience-tested best practices for selecting the people that best fit the needs of a position and a team. Those practices include structured interviewing on team competencies, multiple interviewers, and a disciplined decision-making process. Select members based on skills and potential, not personalities. With virtual teams, the interview protocol should uncover potential team candidates' skills and comfort level working either remotely or interacting with remotely located teammates. A key issue for teams is striking the right balance between members who already possess the needed skill levels versus developing the skills after they join the team. Far too many leaders overemphasize selection of all skills up front. With the exception of some advanced technical or functional skills, many people can develop needed skills after selection. If the organization is willing to help team members grow, selecting for potential may be the best bet. Hiring someone with all the skills will be difficult; hiring someone with many of the skills and an orientation for learning may be more productive.

☐ **5. Systemize team development.** While initial selection is important to team performance, it is important to foster the conditions that allow members to continuously develop after selection and earn their membership in the team. Development is happening all the time. Remember that most development doesn't happen away from work. The process of learning and being more productive in the team is not mutually exclusive. Create a system in your team that integrates development into team members' work. Put people who are willing to learn into first-time, new, and tougher situations. Research suggests that the people who develop the most have had numerous small versions of first-time tasks that prepared them for more significant challenges later. Have these team members take on tasks

63

that are challenging, or even ones they might dislike doing. Pair them with someone on the team who is an expert who can provide guidance. Avoid the out-of-sight, out-of-mind trap when it comes to virtual team members' development. Assign them to a high-impact task, one that doesn't require a lot of physical interaction with other team members in order to be successful. Create action learning assignments to simultaneously solve team problems and develop team member capabilities. The key is to integrate development into the team's work. Use formal workshops on technical or teaming topics as a complement to on-the-job development. For formal training, make accommodations for remote team members. Ensure that all who participate in training get equal benefit from the content.

☐ **6. Develop a feedback preference matrix.** If the team established values early in the process, giving feedback was probably one of them. Have the team leader or coach facilitate a preferred feedback exercise. Encourage team members to ask for feedback. Have each team member identify how they prefer to give and receive feedback. Have them explain why it is their preference. Everyone isn't the same. Some people get their feelings hurt more than others. Some will get embarrassed. Some will get mad and turn red. Some really want to learn from the feedback. Create a matrix of the feedback preference results that members feel strongly about. Post the matrix and make sure everyone has a copy and follows the preferences if possible.

Feedback Preference Matrix

	Face-to-face	One-on-one	With the team	Immediately	After a cool-down period	Via e-mail	Other
Joe	Always					Never	
Mary	Sometimes			Always		Sometimes	
Tim	Always		Never				

☐ **7. Follow feedback-giving guidelines.** Have the team review the following tips on how to provide useful feedback:

- Be sensitive. Give the feedback privately unless it calls for a group intervention, or unless you are in a group debriefing or processing session.
- Be balanced. Don't sandwich or sugarcoat the feedback, but do mention some good things the person does that leaves him/her feeling resourceful rather than beaten up.
- Be specific. Try to avoid words like "usually" or "sometimes." Give specific examples with behaviors that were observed.
- Have courage. Say what needs to be said. Don't hold back. Avoid a long preamble where the person hears nothing while waiting for the bad news. "Here's where you can make a 3% improvement on your performance" is often all that needs to be said as an opener. This statement clearly implies that the person is competent, can improve, and that this is not an 80%-improvement-needed situation.
- Own the feedback. Avoid saying things like "I heard" or "the team thinks." If you are giving the feedback, say what you think, how you feel, and what you saw or heard.
- Hear the person out. Give him/her a chance to absorb your feedback and hear the other side of the story.
- Give direction. Help the person process the situation. Ask how the situation could have been handled differently. Don't give all the answers. Let the person figure it out as much as possible.
- Keep it private. If your intention is to help the person, keep the situation confidential.

☐ **8. Receive feedback graciously.** Have the team work on receiving feedback. Receiving feedback is sometimes more difficult than giving it. Remember that it takes a lot of courage for a teammate to sit down and share some negative information with you. If you are a team member receiving feedback, consider the following tips:

- Listen. Have an open mind. Hear the person out. Don't let any biases you have toward the person giving feedback get in the way of hearing the message.
- Be patient. If you cut the person off, he/she will be less apt to help you in the future.
- Manage your non-verbal reaction. The signals you send off can speak louder than words. Make eye contact; don't roll your eyes; don't fold your arms, etc.

7

- Stay composed. It is normal to have feelings, but try to productively manage them. Don't shoot the messenger.
- Don't get defensive. Try not to explain yourself out of the situation or defend your actions if the messenger has a point.
- Accept all feedback, even if it's wrong. Now is not the time to point out that this view is incorrect. If on reflection and further counsel it is factually wrong, the question becomes why are you seen that way? Why would someone see you that way? Your goal will then be to devise a plan to present yourself as you are and not engage in misleading behaviors.
- Rephrase for clarity. Repeat the message back that you are hearing to make sure you have it straight.
- Apologize if necessary. If remorse is warranted, show it. Don't let your arrogance or pride block it.
- Identify a strategy for improvement. Process what you could have done differently. Ask the messenger for input and agreement.
- Ask for more feedback. If you are willing to improve, ask the messenger to continue to observe you and give regular feedback on your progress (or lack thereof).
- Thank the feedback giver. This is true, even if you are having trouble accepting the feedback.

☐ **9. Solicit outside expertise.** If the team has a knowledge or skill limitation, it needs to identify ways to fill the gap. When possible, build the skills in the team. Research shows that providing developmental opportunities not only helps overcome skill gaps, but can be a powerful tool for retention as well. Some skill gaps are harder to close with existing team resources. If the needed skills are in highly technical or functional areas, it may be necessary to look outside the team, at least in the short-term. When seeking help from outside expertise is necessary, use a disciplined recruiting process. Find individuals who not only possess the needed skills, but will also mesh well with the existing team. If full-time membership is not warranted in these areas, consider ad-hoc members or part-time members or consultants. Invite these valuable contributors in when it makes sense.

☐ **10. Adjust to changes in team membership.** High-performing teams are sometimes fragile. The loss of a valued team member can be painful and the loss of the team leader can completely derail a team. Virtual team membership can be more fluid than traditional team membership. Virtual teams are characterized by frequent changes in membership, whether caused by new members joining the team or completion of a team assignment, at which point some members may drop off the team.

FACTOR III: TALENT

If forming has occurred and the team is mature and used to working with each other, members may not realize how much they really depend on one another until someone leaves. If the loss is due to an accepted or planned event (i.e., retirement), it is difficult but the team can generally cope. However, if the loss is due to health problems, unexpected resignation, organizational politics, sabotage, or defection, the effects can be serious. Change in team membership is not always a bad thing. It can provide opportunities to learn new skills and knowledge acquired by new members. Here are a few suggestions:

- Look for signs of unexpected defections. Most departures have warning signals. If the team is forewarned, it can cope better.
- Try a radical organ transplant. Immediately replace the member. Realize that organ transplants many times don't work, though, and the new member may be rejected.
- Provide lots of support for the team. Have a facilitator help the team acknowledge the impact of the loss and target some strategies to get the group back on track.
- Let team members own restaffing issues. If a team is truly high performing, it has spent a lot of time forming, storming, and norming, and it doesn't want to start all over again because of a change in team membership. High-performing teams may require some bending of the rules in existing corporate staffing policies. Although recruiting for a new member means some deviation from work, most high-performing teams would rather do it themselves.

7

Suggested Readings

Blackburn, R., Furst, S., & Rosen, B. (2003). Building a winning virtual team: KSAs, selection, training, and evaluation. In C. B. Gibson & S. G. Cohen (Eds.), *Virtual teams that work: Creating conditions for virtual team effectiveness* (pp. 95-120). San Francisco: Jossey-Bass.

Ellis, L. (2003). *Leading talents, leading teams: Aligning people, passions, and positions for maximum performance.* Chicago: Northfield.

Hackman, J. R. (2002). *Leading teams: Setting the stage for great performances.* Boston: Harvard Business School Press.

Katzenbach, J. R., & Smith, D. K. (1993). *The wisdom of teams.* New York: HarperCollins.

Kirkman, B. L., Rosen, B., Gibson, C. B., Tesluk, P. E., & McPherson, S. O. (2002). Five challenges to virtual team success: Lessons from Sabre, Inc. *Academy of Management Executive, 16*(3), 67-79.

Lipman-Blumen, J., & Leavitt, H. J. (1999). *Hot groups: Seeding them, feeding them, and using them to ignite your organization.* New York: Oxford University Press.

Marks, A., & Lockyer, C. (2004). Producing knowledge: The use of the project team as a vehicle for knowledge and skill acquisition for software employees. *Economic & Industrial Democracy, 25*(2), 219-245.

Massey, T. (2005). *Ten commitments for building high performance teams.* Bandon, OR: Robert D. Reed.

Parker, G. M. (2008). *Team players and teamwork: New strategies for developing successful collaboration* (2nd ed.). San Francisco: Jossey-Bass.

Rosen, B., Furst, S., & Blackburn, R. (2006). Training for virtual teams: An investigation of current practices and future needs. *Human Resource Management, 45*(2), 229-247.

Ruyle, K. R., Eichinger, R. W., & De Meuse, K. P. (2009). *FYI for Talent Engagement™: Drivers of best practice.* Minneapolis, MN: Lominger International: A Korn/Ferry Company.

Translation to the Leadership Architect® Competency Library

In order for a team or individuals on a team to perform well in this area, these are the competencies that would most likely be in play. Aside from a team improvement plan where everybody works on the same thing, some individual team members may need to work on some of these competencies. A critical number (but not necessarily all) of team members would have to be good at:

Mission Critical:	Important:	Nice to Have:
25. Hiring and Staffing	19. Developing Direct	1. Action Oriented
27. Informing	Reports and Others	12. Conflict Management
50. Priority Setting	39. Organizing	17. Decision Quality
51. Problem Solving	62. Time Management	18. Delegation
53. *Drive for* Results		29. Integrity and Trust
56. Sizing Up People		34. Managerial Courage

In addition to the 10 tips listed for this dimension, there are some tips that may apply from *FYI For Your Improvement*™. Below are the four items from the Team Architect® that make up this dimension. The item number appears to the left of each item. Immediately below the text of each item are competency and tip numbers from *FYI*. The competency is listed first (from 1 to 67), followed by the tip number (1 to 10). For example, 33-4 refers to competency 33 (Listening), tip number 4. The tips are generally written for individual development, so some adaptation might be needed in the team context.

7. The team has systems in place to help its members gain the skills and information they need.
   27-1,2,3,4,5,10; 39-5; 50-2; 52-3; 62-2

25. Team members give each other positive and negative feedback to improve performance and team functioning.
   12-7; 29-1,7,8; 34-1,2,3,7,8; 35-7

43. The team follows a recruiting and staffing process to ensure it has the range of talents necessary to achieve its goals.
   25-1,3,6,7,8; 53-1; 56-1,3,4,7

61. If the team has a knowledge or skill limitation, it faces it promptly and looks for help to fill the gap.
   1-1; 18-5,9; 25-1,6; 53-1; 56-4,5; 110-4,8

FACTOR III: TALENT

7

Dimension 8
Talent Allocation and Deployment

Definition:
Team talent is complementary and balanced; talent is viewed collectively and team members readily defer to one another when one is more skilled or knowledgeable in an area.

Addresses the question:
Are the right people assigned to the right tasks?

A Dimension in the TALENT Factor
The necessary collective skills to get the job done.

> *Get the right people on the bus, get the wrong people off the bus,*
> *and put the right people in the right place in the bus.*
> Jim Collins – American business consultant and author

Items
8. Team members readily defer to one another where the other is more skilled or knowledgeable in an area.
26. Talent is viewed collectively; there is little or no individual competition.
44. Each team member's strengths and weaknesses are known to all.
62. Talent is reasonably balanced across the whole team; one or a few people do not dominate it.

Unskilled
- ☐ Team does not leverage all of the strengths of individual members
- ☐ Team allows individual shortcomings to stall team performance
- ☐ Individual team members compete for space and credit
- ☐ Team members are not aware of one another's strengths
- ☐ Team is carried by one or a few star performers
- ☐ Team has one or more poor performers
- ☐ Talent within the team is neither complementary nor balanced
- ☐ Roles are not clear; team members aren't sure who is responsible for what
- ☐ New members of the team are given the less desirable jobs
- ☐ Team members show little interest in understanding each other's strengths and weaknesses

Skilled

☐ Team has clarity on roles and responsibilities

☐ Team is not worried about who does what; they are just interested in achieving the mission of the team

☐ Team members have no trouble delegating part of their jobs or roles to others on the team

☐ Team members are willing to seek help when they need help

☐ The team focuses on team results, not individual results

☐ Team members have an understanding of each other's skills and abilities

☐ The team assigns tasks to individuals based on their expertise, skills, knowledge, and abilities

☐ Team fosters a collaborative rather than a competitive culture

☐ Team celebrates wins and victories, even when all have not been involved

Overused

☐ Team members are so good at leveraging each other's individual strengths that few new skills are developed

☐ Team members are labeled due to strengths or weaknesses and can't overcome stereotypes associated with the labels

☐ Team becomes hesitant to let anyone try anything for the first time

☐ The team is so well-oiled that it's hard for a new team member to fit in and get up to speed

☐ Team is so well-balanced that no one stands out for promotion to the next level

☐ Team may have trouble competing outside the team since it tries so hard not to be competitive inside

Note on overused strengths: Overused skills and disproportionately used strengths tend to have the negative effects listed above. To decrease those negative consequences, you have two alternatives. You can scale down or use the strength less, or you can compensate for it with another skill or behavior. In practice, it is very difficult to get an individual or a team to use a strength less. In most cases, the best path is to develop compensators. Team Architect® Dimensions that can compensate for overusing this dimension and compensating skills from the Leadership Architect® Library's 67 Competencies are listed below.

(Note: Team Dimension numbers are listed in parentheses. Competencies are listed in numerical order by competency number.)

Compensating Team Dimensions:

- ☐ Talent Acquisition and Enhancement (7)
- ☐ Team Learning (10)
- ☐ Assignment Flexibility (16)
- ☐ Delivering the Goods (18)

Compensating Competencies:

- ☐ 7. Caring About Direct Reports
- ☐ 19. Developing Direct Reports and Others
- ☐ 23. Fairness to Direct Reports
- ☐ 31. Interpersonal Savvy
- ☐ 36. Motivating Others

Some Causes of Poor Performance

- ☐ Team may be very new and therefore does not know each other well enough
- ☐ The team's tasks and specialties may not benefit from cooperation
- ☐ The team's manager does not allow the team to work together much
- ☐ Members may be too stubborn or arrogant to defer work to others who have more expertise or capability
- ☐ Members may be overly ambitious
- ☐ Team has not conducted self- or team skill assessments
- ☐ Members are not self-aware of their own strengths and weaknesses
- ☐ Members avoid conflict, so they don't discuss skill limitations or gaps
- ☐ Team leader may not be good at sizing up others and allocating work
- ☐ Team staffs poorly; team clones skills they already have
- ☐ Team has not identified clear roles and responsibilities

The Map

Having talented team members is not enough. A unique characteristic of a high-performing team is its ability and willingness to apply the strengths of individuals against key tasks, regardless of whose specific job it is. The best presenter makes mission-critical presentations. The best analyst analyzes in situations where it has to be right. The best at assessing talent manages the selection of new team members. Not all team members of a high-performing team need to be skilled in everything. In a well-functioning team, the real key is that the team has all skill requirements covered collectively. High-performing teams bring together complementary skills and experiences that far exceed any individual on the team or the output of all the team members acting alone.

8

FACTOR III: TALENT

It doesn't do any good to build a team with the right capabilities if the team doesn't deploy them collectively and effectively. Talent deployment requires, first, an understanding of capabilities (and liabilities) within the team, and then willingness and flexibility in using these individual skills collectively to achieve successful outcomes. That means team members have to share, step aside from time to time, or step into the breach if needed. Balance the knowledge, skills, and expertise of team members to reach shared goals.

Some Remedies

☐ **1. Determine the skill requirements for the team.** The first step in team success is to determine what skill requirements are crucial for the team to accomplish its objectives. Have the team spend time carefully looking at the issues and challenges that will be facing the team during the next business cycle—usually a year. The team already has its charter from previous steps. Now, the question is what the team will face in trying to reach its goals in terms of:

- Economics
- Markets
- Availability of talent
- Regulatory issues
- Competitor activity
- Environmental requirements
- Resources
- Political considerations
- Constituencies in the way
- Constituencies that can help
- Customer requirements
- Time frames
- Alliances needed
- Technology

Once the issues and challenges are identified, derive the skills that will be needed to solve the challenge or face the issue. So if the challenge is getting several reluctant constituents on board, the key skills might be influencing and motivating others. If the issue is tight time frames, then some key skills might be timely decision making or priority setting.

☐ **2. Clearly assign roles and responsibilities.** Teams need to have a clear and systematic process for assigning roles. One of the best ways to get members to defer to one another is to carefully identify roles and responsibilities. Lack of role clarity can derail a team's success. When

74

team members do not work at the same time or in the same physical location and rely heavily on communication technology, role conflict or ambiguity can cause considerable stress, resulting in lost productivity and dissatisfaction. One way to achieve role clarity is to develop a job description for each member. The concept of role goes beyond listing tasks for each team member. Effective teamwork involves task interdependence, so agreement on team roles and responsibilities is very important. Align the roles and tasks with the team goals. Research suggests the following tips to building clear roles:

– Break down the work to be done into tasks.
– Define shared responsibilities. Which tasks cannot be performed by individuals alone?
– Define individual responsibilities. Have members exchange input on each role. Team effectiveness is optimized when members know what others expect of them and understand the source of conflict in expectations.
– Identify the importance of each role. Many team conflicts are often related to roles or procedures.
– Revisit role clarification often. Especially when (1) there is role conflict or ambiguity, (2) a new team is forming, or (3) a new member joins the team.

After the roles and responsibilities are identified, they are assigned to each team member based on his/her strengths, expertise, skills, knowledge, and ability. Each work assignment should be communicated widely in the team to avoid mistrust and misunderstanding. Every team member should be well informed of others' roles so they know whom to call on for help when needed.

☐ **3. Uncover strengths and weaknesses within the team.** There are many options for skill assessment. Self-assessment is an OK starting place, but input from others is the best source for real assessment data. You can conduct a formal 360° assessment process of the mission-critical skills identified in Remedy 1 above. A formal 360° assessment identifies strengths and weaknesses by comparing the mission-critical skills with the current skills. Each individual should get his/her individual report. Each individual should have a development plan. The individual reports then can be rolled up into a group report. Have the team examine the group report to locate common strengths and weaknesses. Then have the team create a group development plan—a plan everyone will work on. Alternately, the coach can facilitate a live feedback process for each member. This approach will increase the awareness of various capabilities within the team, help each member direct his/her own development, and decrease defensive reactions to feedback in the future. This process will work best after the team has been in place for several months so that members have had experience in observing behaviors within the team.

☐ **4. Allow all individuals to contribute.** High-performing teams always find ways for each individual to contribute. If the team purpose or goal calls for output for which certain individual members are best-suited, let them perform. This requires that some members on the team step back from time to time to let their peer(s) shine. High-performing teams understand that certain situations may call for expertise and speed to get the needed performance results. Remember to keep remote team members top of mind for exposure opportunities as they may not have the same amount of informal and spontaneous opportunities to shine as team members who physically work together or are situated in more high-profile locations.

☐ **5. Ensure talent mix and balance.** The most effective teams have a balance of skills and abilities. Effective teams realize that having balance does not mean equal use of all skills at all times. Balance means having the capability to use the various skills when required. A team's need for particular skills is situational, driven by team objectives and business demands. Beware of stacking the deck too much in favor of certain skills. If a team is full of idea generators but no one can execute, it's highly unlikely team objectives will be met. On the other hand, if the team is full of technically smart people who aren't the best listeners, you'll likely have team conflict. Successful teams use workarounds to compensate for skill deficiencies. For example, if someone possesses a skill that another doesn't, he/she can then serve as a workaround for that person. A team member may be stellar at presenting to large groups but hopeless at running the audiovisual. Enter the teammate who is both proficient and passionate about that type of technology. A well-put-together team will have a breadth of skills at their disposal. A high-performing team will know when and where to use those skills most efficiently.

☐ **6. Address talent imbalances.** There are several types of talent imbalances on teams:
- One or more members are star performers.
- One or more members are poor performers.
- One or more members may be dominating or bullying the team.
- Member styles are too similar.
- A needed style may be lacking.

Once the imbalance is identified, possible solutions include:
- Aggressively coaching laggard performers.
- Confronting dominating or bullying team members.
- Revisiting team values and discussing the implications on other members.
- Removing poor performers from the team.
- Adding members who fill talent or style gaps.

It is important to understand potential pitfalls of not addressing talent imbalances:
- Workload may become more and more unbalanced as a result of talent differences.
- Star performers likely will resent poor performers for their lack of contribution.
- Poor performers may resent star performers for getting all the recognition.
- Star performers may leave.
- Poor performers may eventually give up and coast or let others carry the load.

☐ **7. Distribute the workload equitably.** One potential pitfall of deferring to skill or expertise within the team is the possibility that one or more members may continually inherit the least desirable jobs or get overburdened with tasks. Teams will always have some undesirable assignments. On the mundane end, they could be tasks like team paperwork, monthly reporting, or housekeeping. When distributing team tasks, be careful not to overburden the go-to people on the team—the ones that can always be counted on and, as a result, get more than their fair share of the workload. Avoid a potential situation where these team members may start to feel that good performance is actually more punitive than rewarding. Here are a few tips on distributing workload:
- Attempt to get rid of bad jobs. Asking the same people to always do the bad jobs creates tension and inequality in the team. If you cannot eliminate these jobs, consider contracting them out.
- Rotate them. If bad jobs can't be taken out of a team, consider rotating them. Create a visual on a poster that lists a schedule of team members assigned to the bad jobs. Everyone on the team must pull his/her fair share of unappetizing work if the team is to succeed.
- Speak up. If you are the team member who is frustrated because you feel like you always get the bad jobs or do the heavy lifting on the team, say something about it.

☐ **8. Address turf wars.** Just like there are bad jobs, there are also jobs that members perceive to be glory jobs. Problems often occur when one person on a team consistently has responsibility for a single (usually appealing) task. This happens often on cross-functional or senior management teams. When two parties perceive a task as their turf, they can be prepared to violate the spirit of collaboration to ensure the turf remains theirs. Conflict and team noise occur when members perceive the turf issue to represent power for them (or lack thereof). Turf wars can mean trouble for a team. Here are some tips to overcome turf wars:

– Negotiate specific desirable (and undesirable) tasks.

– Agree on procedures to update team members on progress of collaborative efforts.

– Collaborate with team members who have a vested interest.

– Assign clear accountabilities for results (to avoid later blame).

☐ **9. Celebrate wins as a team.** No matter who does what, celebrate as a team. If everyone on the team is dedicated to collective success and is willing to either take or defer tasks for the benefit of the team, then it follows that all successes and wins belong to everyone. For example, have parties, raffles that everyone can participate in regardless of location, or team dress on special occasions, or roast each other after work. Get virtual team members involved by using Web-based technology to advertise and celebrate team successes. Have fun with it.

☐ **10. Publish skills online.** With virtual teams, organizations can recruit talent quickly from different locations and regions. The goal is to increase competitive advantage by leveraging intellectual capital as fast as possible. Oftentimes, virtual team members never have a chance to meet face-to-face. Collaboration between virtual team members starts once they know more about each other's backgrounds, expertise, and skills. Publish an online directory that includes each team member's photo, expertise and experience, and current role and responsibilities. It will also help to find out whom to contact when they need help and when they assign the tasks.

Suggested Readings

Blackburn, R., Furst, S., & Rosen, B. (2003). Building a winning virtual team: KSAs, selection, training, and evaluation. In C. B. Gibson & S. G. Cohen (Eds.), *Virtual teams that work: Creating conditions for virtual team effectiveness* (pp. 95-120). San Francisco: Jossey-Bass.

Duarte, D. L., & Snyder, N. T. (2006). *Mastering virtual teams: Strategies, tools, and techniques that succeed* (3rd ed.). San Francisco: Jossey-Bass.

Ellis, L. (2003). *Leading talents, leading teams: Aligning people, passions, and positions for maximum performance.* Chicago: Northfield.

Fisher, K., Rayner, S., Belgard, W., & the Belgard-Fisher-Rayner Team. (1995). *Tips for teams: A ready reference for solving common team problems* (2nd ed.). New York: McGraw-Hill.

Hackman, J. R. (2002). *Leading teams: Setting the stage for great performances.* Boston: Harvard Business School Press.

Katzenbach, J. R., & Smith, D. K. (1993). *The wisdom of teams.* New York: HarperCollins.

Malhotra, A., Majchrzak, A., & Rosen, B. (2007). Leading virtual teams. *Academy of Management Perspectives, 21*(1), 60-70.

Massey, T. (2005). *Ten commitments for building high performance teams.* Bandon, OR: Robert D. Reed.

Parker, G. M. (2008). *Team players and teamwork: New strategies for developing successful collaboration* (2nd ed.). San Francisco: Jossey-Bass.

Robbins, H., & Finley, M. (2000). *The new why teams don't work: What goes wrong and how to make it right.* San Francisco: Berrett-Koehler Publishers.

Tavcar, J., Zavbi, R., Verlinden, J., & Duhovnik, J. (2005). Skills for effective communication and work in global product development teams. *Journal of Engineering Design, 16*(6), 557-576.

∞

Translation to the Leadership Architect® Competency Library

In order for a team or individuals on a team to perform well in this area, these are the competencies that would most likely be in play. Aside from a team improvement plan where everybody works on the same thing, some individual team members may need to work on some of these competencies. A critical number (but not necessarily all) of team members would have to be good at:

Mission Critical:	**Important:**	**Nice to Have:**
44. Personal Disclosure	12. Conflict Management	25. Hiring and Staffing
55. Self-Knowledge	18. Delegation	39. Organizing
56. Sizing Up People	53. *Drive for* Results	40. *Dealing with* Paradox
60. *Building Effective* Teams		42. Peer Relationships

In addition to the 10 tips listed for this dimension, there are some tips that may apply from *FYI For Your Improvement*™. Below are the four items from the Team Architect® that make up this dimension. The item number appears to the left of each item. Immediately below the text of each item are competency and tip numbers from *FYI*. The competency is listed first (from 1 to 67), followed by the tip number (1 to 10). For example, 33-4 refers to competency 33 (Listening), tip number 4. The tips are generally written for individual development, so some adaptation might be needed in the team context.

8. Team members readily defer to one another where the other is more skilled or knowledgeable in an area.
   18-5,9; 55-1,3,5; 56-2,3,4; 60-8,10

26. Talent is viewed collectively; there is little or no individual competition.
   12-1; 23-5; 27-3; 42-5; 60-1,6,8; 110-2,4,6

44. Each team member's strengths and weaknesses are known to all.
   31-5; 44-1,6,7; 55-1,3; 56-2,3,5; 60-8

62. Talent is reasonably balanced across the whole team; one or a few people do not dominate it.
   25-1,3,6,7,8; 56-1,3,4,7; 60-8

Dimension 9
Resource Management

Definition:
Team plans and uses its resources effectively, utilizes its members' experiences, and seeks outside help if needed.

Addresses the question:
Does the team effectively use all the resources at its disposal and acquire resources when needed?

A Dimension in the TEAMING SKILLS Factor
Operating the team's business efficiently and effectively.

> *A particular shot or way of moving the ball can be a player's personal signature, but efficiency of performance is what wins the game for the team.*
> Pat Riley – American National Basketball Association head coach

Items
9. Team members use their experiences to strengthen how the team operates.
27. The team uses time well (in meetings, on assignments); there is little wasted motion.
45. The team is not afraid to ask for and use outside help.
63. The team organizes and uses its resources efficiently.

Unskilled
- ☐ Team spends too much time on unimportant things
- ☐ Team is not productive when working together
- ☐ Team members complain about spinning wheels but don't do anything to get traction
- ☐ Team is very internally focused; afflicted by not-invented-here syndrome
- ☐ Team doesn't look for or ask for external resources
- ☐ Team is disorganized with approach, assignments, and resources
- ☐ Members do not leverage previous experiences as learnings that improve future team performance
- ☐ The team has to do a lot of rework on things that weren't done right the first time

9

Skilled

☐ This team gets more done with less compared to other teams

☐ Most events come off on time and on schedule

☐ It's easy to find the resources you need when you need them, even when they are controlled and managed by another team member

☐ The team successfully obtains additional resources when it needs them

☐ The team is realistic and objective when it comes to planning and estimating

☐ The team doesn't hesitate to go outside for resources when warranted

☐ The team has a schedule or deadline for all projects or tasks

☐ There is a process to make and update resource assignment decisions

Overused

☐ Team members are too focused on the tried-and-true; limit creativity and experimentation

☐ Team is so structured with time that it becomes inflexible and lacks spontaneity

☐ Team outsources too much, stifling internal opportunities for development

☐ Everything is run so tight that there is hardly any room or time to relax and enjoy the work

☐ Everything is so structured that there is little time for reflection, looking for unscheduled opportunities for adding value

☐ Team is held in such esteem that there is little time for rapport-building and social conversation when the team gets together

Note on overused strengths: Overused skills and disproportionately used strengths tend to have the negative effects listed above. To decrease those negative consequences, you have two alternatives. You can scale down or use the strength less, or you can compensate for it with another skill or behavior. In practice, it is very difficult to get an individual or a team to use a strength less. In most cases, the best path is to develop compensators. Team Architect® Dimensions that can compensate for overusing this dimension and compensating skills from the Leadership Architect® Library's 67 Competencies are listed below.

(Note: Team Dimension numbers are listed in parentheses. Competencies are listed in numerical order by competency number.)

Compensating Team Dimensions:

☐ Team Learning (10)
☐ Team Atmosphere (13)
☐ Managing Process (14)

Compensating Competencies:

☐ 14. Creativity
☐ 19. Developing Direct Reports and Others
☐ 28. Innovation Management
☐ 32. Learning on the Fly
☐ 60. *Building Effective* Teams

Some Causes of Poor Performance

☐ Some team members are blocked learners
☐ Team members are disorganized
☐ Team members are arrogant
☐ Team members are not good time managers
☐ Team members have narrow experiences
☐ Team members are not focused on results
☐ Some members are rigid
☐ Team members are not resourceful
☐ Team members do not follow through on commitments
☐ Team members prefer to avoid conflict
☐ Team is impulsive and reactive

The Map

High-performing teams effectively manage their resources to achieve goals. Resources include people, skills, time, money, and influence. Lack of resources has been identified as a core source of dissatisfaction and frustration for teams. It's tough to perform if a team is unable to secure the means necessary to do so. When armed with a set of clear, solid objectives, a team can be more effective in scoping the work effort and getting the needed resources up front. Once secured, managing resources is critical. It requires the ability to juggle multiple tasks, organize things into sensible solutions and, most of all, disciplined execution by team members. A key is doing more with less or getting more value per pound of resource than other teams. Teams with a solid grasp of each member's skills have a head start in resource planning. These teams know how and where to deploy resources to achieve team goals. And, when there's a lack of resources within the team, the team is not afraid to look outside itself for help.

9

Some Remedies

☐ **1. Use team goals as a foundation for resource planning.** Setting specific and realistic goals that support the team's mission helps guide team decisions on budgeting, resource allocation, and time management. Make sure the goals are agreed upon and that each team member feels a sense of ownership for the outcomes. When planning for resources, focus on what is really needed to achieve the goals. Plan for contingencies. Once resource planning is complete, establish metrics to keep track of the progress against the goals and use of resources. Progress metrics help keep the team focused on the goals and provide status on how efficiently the team is utilizing its resources. For virtual teams, set up audio- or videoconference calls frequently to track progress and prioritize tasks. *More help? See* FYI For Your Improvement™, *Chapter 35 – Managing and Measuring Work.*

☐ **2. Get organized.** Plan the work, then work the plan. What needs to be accomplished? What is the time line? What resources will be needed? Does the team have a resource allocation plan? What are the priorities? Who on the team is best at organizing people and things? Put that person in charge of managing the team's budget, meeting agendas and things that require discipline, priority setting and follow-up. Not everyone has an eye for detail or can juggle multiple things at once. Make resource management a priority for the team so that efficiency and organization are at the forefront of all activities. *More help? See* FYI For Your Improvement™, *Chapter 39 – Organizing, and Chapter 47 – Planning.*

☐ **3. Involve the whole team.** Involve the whole team when making decisions about how to use the resources effectively. Individuals are more willing to accept decisions when they have a say in how the resources should be used. Open discussions and negotiation on resource assignments are crucial to help build consensus and promote ownership. When team members are dispersed across different regions, prioritizing the use of resources can be done using both formal and informal communication technologies. Some ground rules need to be set to manage discussion and constructive team conflict. When planning and allocating resources, team members should focus on what works best for the team, not for individuals.

☐ **4. Catalog team member skills and experience.** Solid resource planning starts with a clear understanding of how each member can contribute to achieving team objectives. Conduct a skill and experience audit for each team member. Review the types of experiences each team member has had throughout his/her career (both on- and off-work experiences) to identify which skills and competencies he/she should have developed along the way. Compare those competencies to the team member profile and identify

9

matches and gaps for each team member. Team members may have had some experiences via development in current job assignments, off-work, or full-time jobs that have fostered the growth of certain competencies critical for success in the team environment. Utilize your HR partner or team coach to help each member identify how he/she can apply the lessons of experience from the past to current challenges facing the team. Publish each team member's expertise and experiences so that team members know whom to go to for help.

☐ **5. Ask for resources.** Learn to speak up to lobby for team needs. Ask for help obtaining the amount of human and monetary resources needed by the team to achieve its goals. You may not get it, but at least you tried. Who is best at constructing the case? Who on the team is best at stating the case? What type of argument works best to those with resource authority? Results? Outcomes? Innovation? Customer satisfaction? Create a compelling case to inspire the resource providers. Paint a vivid picture of what results these resources will bring. High-performing teams are, in a sense, self-renewing because great results are usually followed by a larger share of the resources next cycle.

☐ **6. Beware of dwindling resources.** When teams have sizable goals, they can become a major consumer of resources. Long projects typically cost big money and require different types of organizational support. Generally, when an organization charters a team for a significant cause, it will also budget money. However, when a project team's funding rolls into future budget years, or when cross-functional teams lose a key sponsor, things can change. Oddly enough, resource support can also change as a result of a team achieving lots of success. While it's just as true that resources go to the successful, success of the team can cause resentment in other parts of the organization. Competition and jealousy can spark sabotage against a high-performing team. Resource reduction can become a quick and easy target. When a team's resources dwindle under the guise that the team doesn't need the degree of support other teams do, the team may begin to falter and become discouraged. Most high-performing teams will persevere; however, a cut in resources could sink an average team. In sum, keep an eye on resources, especially if they are at risk. Make sure the team is aligned with the right sponsors and support arms to maintain its resources. Have your case ready to go and be prepared to repeat it.

9

☐ **7. Tame the meeting beast.** Research has shown that teams can waste much time and resources on meetings. Basically, meetings break down if there is no agenda, participants arrive late, airtime is not managed, and topics are not closed. Here are some ground rules that help to make meetings more effective:

- Before the meeting, send a written agenda with topics to be covered in advance so that team members know what they are going to do in the meeting. It is especially critical for virtual teams who rely on more formal updates and communication to stay on top of team activities.

- Be on time. When one person arrives late to a meeting, multiply that delay by the number of people kept waiting. It can add up to a significant waste of resources. Additionally, tardiness signals a lack of respect for other team members.

- During the meeting, be sure to engage all team members. Encourage those team members who usually do not speak up to do so. Many times they have a perspective that would move the process ahead. Virtual team leaders can check in frequently with their team members by asking for their opinions. There should be someone to keep track of the time and make sure all items on the agenda are covered. This person can be the team leader or a team member.

- After the meeting, send out a meeting recap or meeting minutes. Post it on the team repository. Assign different people to take minutes for every meeting. Action items like task assignments and deadlines should be distributed to all team members and posted on the team Web page.

☐ **8. Improve team processes.** Use process improvement techniques such as Six Sigma to reduce cycle times, improve quality, and remove friction from business processes. Look for ways to take steps out of processes. Have a detailed plan that scopes out length and tasks. Clarify the steps of all processes. Develop schedules for work assignments. Do things in a shorter period of time. Use fewer resources per process step. Identify future problems and opportunities. Provide training and other developmental opportunities. Measure and monitor team progress. *More help? See* FYI for Teams™, *Chapter 14 – Managing Process, or* FYI For Your Improvement™, *Chapter 52 – Process Management, and Chapter 63 – Total Work Systems.*

☐ **9. Share leadership.** Working virtually requires team members to be masters in self-management. Due to lack of face-to-face interactions and long distances, it is difficult for virtual team leaders to closely monitor and coach their team members. Virtual team members need to share some leadership with their team leader. They may not be able to depend totally on the team leader at all times due to proximity constraints. Virtual team

9

86

leaders can explicitly inform their team members about what decisions they are empowered to make. All team members should be encouraged to set personal agendas and motivate themselves to take necessary action. Leadership doesn't have to be assumed by the person with the position power. In successful teams, task and process leadership roles are shared. It often shifts among team members, depending on the needs of the group and the skills of members. There are two types of shared leadership responsibilities:

– Task Responsibilities. Actions that help the team reach its goals, accomplish its tasks, make a decision, or solve a problem (e.g., time management, meeting planning, goal setting).

– Process Responsibilities. How the team goes about accomplishing its tasks. In many cases, the process is interpersonal.

Identify opportunities to share both types of leadership and to reinforce positive examples of supporting leadership behaviors within the team.

☐ **10. Ensure the team really needs to be a team.** When the team meets, are the major relationships of the team members with each other or primarily with customers and technology? If the answer is the latter, the team may not really be a team. Is there opportunity to set and enforce productivity or quality norms that the entire group is responsible for? Or, is the work self-contained and repetitive? If the answer is the latter, the team may not really be a team.

Bottom line: teams only pay off when there are critical interdependencies that a team can manage. If working together doesn't add value, team meetings may not add much. If the team really isn't a team, call it something else and quit pretending.

9

87

Suggested Readings

Cramton, C. D., & Orvis, K. L. (2003). Overcoming barriers to information sharing in virtual teams. In C. B. Gibson & S. G. Cohen (Eds.), *Virtual teams that work: Creating conditions for virtual team effectiveness* (pp. 214-229). San Francisco: Jossey-Bass.

Duarte, D. L., & Snyder, N. T. (2006). *Mastering virtual teams: Strategies, tools, and techniques that succeed* (3rd ed.). San Francisco: Jossey-Bass.

Eichinger, R. W., Ruyle, K. E., & Lombardo, M. M. (2007). *FYI for Performance Management™: Universal dimensions for success.* Minneapolis, MN: Lominger International: A Korn/Ferry Company.

Fisher, K., Rayner, S., Belgard, W., & the Belgard-Fisher-Rayner Team. (1995). *Tips for teams: A ready reference for solving common team problems* (2nd ed.). New York: McGraw-Hill.

Katzenbach, J. R., & Smith, D. K. (1993). *The wisdom of teams.* New York: HarperCollins.

LaFasto, F., & Larson, C. (2001). *When teams work best.* Thousand Oaks, CA: Sage.

Malhotra, A., Majchrzak, A., & Rosen, B. (2007). Leading virtual teams. *Academy of Management Perspectives, 21*(1), 60-70.

Parker, G. M. (2008). *Team players and teamwork: New strategies for developing successful collaboration* (2nd ed.). San Francisco: Jossey-Bass.

Robbins, H., & Finley, M. (2000). *The new why teams don't work: What goes wrong and how to make it right.* San Francisco: Berrett-Koehler Publishers.

Rosen, B., Furst, S., & Blackburn, R. (2007). Overcoming barriers to knowledge sharing in virtual teams. *Organizational Dynamics, 36*(3), 259-273.

9

Translation to the Leadership Architect® Competency Library

In order for a team or individuals on a team to perform well in this area, these are the competencies that would most likely be in play. Aside from a team improvement plan where everybody works on the same thing, some individual team members may need to work on some of these competencies. A critical number (but not necessarily all) of team members would have to be good at:

Mission Critical:	**Important:**	**Nice to Have:**
39. Organizing	47. Planning	37. Negotiating
50. Priority Setting	53. *Drive for* Results	38. Organizational Agility
51. Problem Solving	62. Time Management	63. Total Work Systems
52. Process Management		

In addition to the ten tips listed for this dimension, there are additional tips that may apply from *FYI For Your Improvement*™. Below are the four items from the Team Architect® that make up this dimension. The item number appears to the left of each item. Immediately below the text of each item are competency and tip numbers from *FYI*. The competency is listed first (from 1 to 67), followed by the tip number (1 to 10). For example, 33-4 refers to competency 33 (Listening), tip number 4. The tips are generally written for individual development, so some adaptation might be needed in the team context.

9. Team members use their experiences to strengthen how the team operates.
   24-10; 32-1,2,3; 51-3,8; 52-2,3; 63-2,6

27. The team uses time well (in meetings, on assignments); there is little wasted motion.
   50-1,3,7,9; 52-3,7,8; 62-1,3,10

45. The team is not afraid to ask for and use outside help.
   37-1,4; 38-3,4,8; 39-2; 42-1,5; 51-5; 53-6

63. The team organizes and uses its resources efficiently.
   39-1,2,6; 47-6,7; 50-2,3; 52-3,5; 53-3

9

FACTOR IV: TEAMING SKILLS

9

Dimension 10
Team Learning

Definition:
Team members use failures, mistakes, and successes as models; continue to improve by learning new skills and technology.

Addresses the question:
Does the team improve by learning from its successes and failures as well as the successes and failures of others?

A Dimension in the TEAMING SKILLS Factor
Operating the team's business efficiently and effectively.

> *The greatest danger a team faces isn't that it won't become successful,*
> *but that it will, and then cease to improve.*
> Mark Sanborn – American author and consultant

Items
10. The team debriefs its successes in order to find "repeatables" and perform better.
28. The team debriefs its failures and mistakes in order to perform better.
46. The team practices continuous improvement; team members are more skilled than they were a year ago.
64. Team members are receptive to innovative approaches and new technology to improve team effectiveness.

Unskilled
- ☐ The team makes the same mistakes over and over again; no learning occurs
- ☐ The team tries to apply the same strengths to every situation
- ☐ Individual team members are not enhancing their skills or growing from their experience on the team
- ☐ The team does not make time for development and learning
- ☐ Some team members are stuck in their ways of doing things
- ☐ The team does not leverage new technology to improve its processes
- ☐ The team is often surprised by turmoil and unanticipated roadblocks
- ☐ The team attributes successes to itself and failures to others

Skilled

☐ The team has put in place a set of practices that keep it up-to-date

☐ The team makes learning new skills a priority

☐ The team constantly projects ahead to anticipate opportunities and potholes

☐ The team is open to learning from others inside the organization and adopting best practices that were not created in the team

☐ The team parts with tried-and-true methods to make room for new and better ones

☐ Team members are encouraged to learn from each other and provide feedback to each other

☐ The team views mistakes as learning opportunities

☐ The team experiments with new technology and innovative approaches to stay ahead

Overused

☐ Team spends so much time reviewing their successes that they develop a false sense of security

☐ Team debriefs failures to such an extent that it demotivates individuals

☐ Team is always trying to reinvent processes at the expense of keeping an eye on results

☐ Team tries so many new approaches that it leaves others in the organization behind

☐ Team casts out the old and the past too readily

☐ Team's advanced technology may not be compatible with the rest of the organization

☐ Team gets easily bored when things don't change fast enough

☐ Team spends too much time on developing skills for the future at the expense of current needs

Note on overused strengths: Overused skills and disproportionately used strengths tend to have the negative effects listed above. To decrease those negative consequences, you have two alternatives. You can scale down or use the strength less, or you can compensate for it with another skill or behavior. In practice, it is very difficult to get an individual or a team to use a strength less. In most cases, the best path is to develop compensators. Team Architect® Dimensions that can compensate for overusing this dimension and compensating skills from the Leadership Architect® Library's 67 Competencies are listed below.

(Note: Team Dimension numbers are listed in parentheses. Competencies are listed in numerical order by competency number.)

10

Compensating Team Dimensions:

☐ Thrust Management (1)
☐ Managing Process (14)
☐ Focusing (15)
☐ Measurement (17)
☐ Delivering the Goods (18)

Compensating Competencies:

☐   7. Caring About Direct Reports
☐ 23. Fairness to Direct Reports
☐ 36. Motivating Others
☐ 38. Organizational Agility
☐ 41. Patience
☐ 48. Political Savvy
☐ 50. Priority Setting

Some Causes of Poor Performance

☐ Team members are arrogant
☐ Team members lack the self-confidence to explore and experiment with the new
☐ Some members are blocked learners
☐ Team members are uncomfortable with change; can't deal with uncertainty and ambiguity
☐ Team does not manage time well
☐ Team is overextended
☐ Organization surrounding the team does not value learning or development
☐ Team leader does not model or recognize continuous learning

The Map

A culture of learning is crucial for high-performing teams. The world is changing rapidly. Staying the same year after year is the equivalent of losing ground when it comes to performance. Few teams will be successful next year if they do exactly what they did last year this year. Markets are changing. Technology is changing. Competition is changing. Customer requirements are shifting. At one time, two-week photo processing was the norm. Then overnight. Then one hour. Now instant digital. Organizations, teams, and individuals have to keep up. Teams need to expand their knowledge and skills in order to stay ahead of the competition. They have to set aside valuable time to get prepared for

10

93

FACTOR IV: TEAMING SKILLS

what's to come. High-performing teams are ones that seek out opportunities to develop new skills and knowledge. They view learning and development as an inherent team value. They are willing to take on challenging assignments and tasks. Create mechanisms and foster a team culture that supports skill enhancement, process improvement, and best practices or be prepared to watch team performance inevitably degrade.

Some Remedies

☐ **1. Strengthen team learning capacity.** There are countless ways to improve your learning acumen as a team. Study two competitors. Look at similar situations where teams succeeded and failed and figure out some guiding principles. Storyboard (represent with pictures) a complex process so it is easier to visualize. Have team members study a new trend or technology and present it to the team. Set up a competition with another group, or find a team that faces similar problems to yours and use each other as consultants. If speed is your problem, practice quick experiments. Start small, try lots of things, make decisions quickly. Many problem-solving studies show that it's the second or third time through before we really understand the dynamics of the problem we're working on. The more times you cycle through a problem, the more feedback, and the more opportunity to learn. *More help? See* FYI For Your Improvement™, *Chapter 28 – Innovation Management, and Chapter 32 – Learning on the Fly.*

☐ **2. Strengthen individual learning capacities.** Teams won't do well if their members are not motivated to learn. Following are some tips on increasing individual learning:

– Throw out past solutions to a problem, even though they may have worked for you. Come up with something completely different by freewheeling and allowing no evaluation of the ideas initially.

– Look for parallels in other organizations and other industries. Don't be too local—ask the broader question. If your problem is poor order processing, ask: Who is the absolute best in this area? The likely answers may not be in your direct business.

– Accept challenging and difficult assignments or tasks that require stretching to build skills and knowledge.

– Turn a problem upside down—ask what is the least likely cause of it, what the problem is not, or what the mirror image of the problem is.

– Ask more questions. Studies of problem-solving groups show that only about 7% of comments are questions.

10

94

– Look for patterns in your successes and failures. What is common in each success? What is never present in a failure? What is always present in a failure but never present in a success?

More help? See FYI For Your Improvement™, *Chapter 14 – Creativity.*

☐ **3. Prioritize team development.** When there is no support from the top, it's tough for a team to focus on continuous learning. Teams view support for training and development as symbols of the organization's commitment to investing in them. Make learning a part of your team culture. Build an expectation of learning and developing skills into team role descriptions. Have a clear message about the value of continuous learning. A shared understanding helps build commitment and energy for learning. Celebrate learning milestones with the same vigor as other performance results. Allocate resources such as funding, time, and equipment to providing learning opportunities.

☐ **4. Debrief team successes and failures.** A simple debriefing process can help to facilitate both open communication and learning. The process can also elicit both good and bad feedback about the team, its work processes, and individual contributions. Use audio- or videoconference technology to involve all team members. Create a safe environment to give and receive feedback. The team leader, a coach, or a facilitator should flipchart answers to the following questions after a key accomplishment or setback:

– What went well?
– What would we have done differently?
– What did we learn?
– How can we apply that learning?

Before jumping into the exercise, establish ground rules to be used during the discussion (e.g., all comments will be presented as constructively as possible, or members will share all thoughts and not withhold feelings). Also, make sure each member contributes at least one response to each of the questions. Use the learning for future challenges or situations that might be similar so as to not make the same mistakes again. In the case of debriefing successes, it's important for the team to honestly distinguish between things it did that directly contributed to success rather than by luck or happenstance. Successful teams own up to the parts of success that were due to others and to circumstances not related directly to what they did.

☐ **5. Encourage experimentation.** It is common knowledge that high risk has the potential to yield high rewards. This is especially true when applied to team member development. Real development involves real work the person largely hasn't done before. Real development is rewarding but

10

scary. Research indicates that individuals gain developmental experiences in a supportive environment with role models, constructive support, and mentors who provide counsel. If the team is experimenting and looking for better, bigger, faster ways to do things, they will most likely make some mistakes along the way. That's OK, as long as it is in search of performance and getting results. Start having a high tolerance for failure. There is no surer way to suffocate experimentation than by adopting a punitive stance when it doesn't succeed. Since some of the richest learning comes from adversity, a failed task or assignment that the team collectively learns from and then applies in the future is a success from a developmental standpoint. Consider a few rules of thumb when it comes to making mistakes:

- Was there a decent chance for success? Did the team carefully analyze the idea or approach? You can minimize the impact associated with a mistake by considering the worst thing that could happen if the team fails. Dig deep when problem solving to find out if the team's idea has ever been tried before. If so, what was the result? Is your team's idea or approach better? Can you measure it to know if the team has achieved success?

- Make different mistakes. If the team continues to make the same mistake, there is a problem. The whole point of promoting experimentation and tolerating mistakes is the assumption that learning occurs as a result. So figure out what went wrong and why. Was it an organizational issue, a team issue, or an individual issue? Or was it just a bad idea, broken process, or just bad timing? Get input from others inside and outside the team when analyzing a mistake.

☐ **6. Develop those who learn best.** If you are the team leader and you discover that you really do have one or more high-potential members on the team, learn how to manage them more effectively. They may not only contribute to the team and raise the performance bar for the other team members, but they may also be future executives in the making. To develop a new skill, the person must:

- Take on challenging, uncomfortable tasks/assignments. Research suggests that this accounts for about 70% of reported skill development in all organizations. Essentially, development is performing the skill or failing at something important to you. All lousy listeners have had countless opportunities to learn. They don't because under stress they fall back on their strengths. Tasks that develop listening or anything else are those in which not doing it is not a viable option— coaching children's sports, running a task force of computer experts when you barely know how to turn one on, negotiating with someone who doesn't want to negotiate with you and doesn't really have to.

– Get continuing feedback on the skill compared to a target of success. This can take the form of a developmental partner, keeping a written summary of what's working and not working and then having that reviewed periodically, or preferably as a formal assessment. There are three types that work well: (1) having the person take a standard questionnaire three to six months into his/her change project; (2) having an agreed-upon list of people answer what they would like to have this person keep doing, start doing, or stop doing in the developmental area three to six months into his/her change project; (3) a 360° performance appraisal. Research indicates that without this further feedback, even the best developmental plan usually fails miserably.

– Have some new/different things to do—typically these come from coursework/reading and account for about 10% of development. The lion's share is self-learning from tough tasks and the learning from other people that comes from feedback. Many people can benefit from studying models of the behavior. This is a more direct way to learn than reading and easier for most people to assimilate.

– In studies of development, those who are best at it are high learners: they tend to get out of their comfort zone, try many different ways to improve, and actively search for ways to make sense out of their experiences.

More help? See FYI For Your Improvement™, *Chapter 19 – Developing Others.*

☐ **7. Get unstuck.** Is the team stuck in its way of doing things or stale in its approach? If so, inject new information and approaches. Teams develop and learn when they get new and fresh facts or different perspectives on things that inside team members may not be able to provide. Look for ways to be resourceful and to gain new insight. Benchmark a competitor. Identify best practices outside the team. Bring in an outsider. Attend a conference. Interview your customers. Learn the principles of total process reengineering, six sigma, or other total work systems. Read about the teams that win the Malcolm Baldrige Award or other best-in-class business team competitions. Study workflows around you. Then make sure you find ways to apply the new information in the team. *More help? See* FYI For Your Improvement™, *Chapter 63 – Total Work Systems.*

☐ **8. Define problems more thoroughly.** Most of us do a poor job of defining problems. We assume that we know what it is, spend a minute or two on it at most, then leap in with numerous solutions. Argument and discussion then follow until something is selected, often the solution with the most vocal support. These instant and early conclusions often lead to safe,

10

historical solutions which attack the wrong problem. High-performing teams don't do this—they devote much time, sometimes as much as 50% of the discussion, to defining the nature of the problem. To do this:

- Ask what the problem is and what it isn't.
- See how many causes you can come up with.
- Organize the causes into themes or patterns.

Don't suggest any solutions, just keep asking why this would happen or why this would not happen. Viewing a problem or an opportunity from many angles can provide some exciting payoffs and learning for an organization, a department, and a team. Actively search for ways to see possible changes on the horizon that may cause problems or provide opportunities for new products, systems, or services.

☐ **9. Use change agents in the team.** Do some team members rock the boat so much that they make the rest of the crew seasick? Are these members free spirits who lack patience, discipline, or due process courtesies in the process of their breakthrough discoveries? The challenge for the team leader and members is to find ways to integrate those differences within the team. Here are a few ways to keep the creative, always-forward-moving types engaged, while at the same time keeping some level of peace and balance within the team:

- Keep the creators challenged. You can do this by empowering them to come up with their own assignments and workload. They don't like to be bored.
- Recognize their contributions and give feedback when they aren't taking the needs of others into consideration. They want to know how they are perceived.
- Create a method of having them share their creative ideas with the rest of the team, especially those who think differently than they do.
- Don't overdirect creators or tell them how to get results, solve problems, or make decisions. They like to figure it out on their own, and many times they come up with improved team processes along the way.

☐ **10. Leverage GroupWare technology.** New communication and information technology has increased e-learning or distance-learning opportunities. Cheap, fast, and easy communication makes it possible for all teams to learn online as a team, even when members are physically distant from one another. Participation in virtual classrooms can give team members the impression that they are in the same place, learning collaboratively. Make online discussion rooms available for team members to engage in communication, decision-making processes, and information sharing. Set

98

up communities of practice within the team and between the team and outside stakeholders that share common concerns. Find ways to centralize information so that it can be easily accessed in the team. Be aware that any learning materials need to be presented in a way that all team members, regardless of location or cultural differences, are comfortable using. Have an operational learning plan that includes goals and purpose, agendas and schedules, and process and progress evaluation.

Suggested Readings

Bardwick, J. (1993). *Danger in the comfort zone.* New York: AMACOM.

Blackburn, R., Furst, S., & Rosen, B. (2003). Building a winning virtual team: KSAs, selection, training, and evaluation. In C. B. Gibson & S. G. Cohen (Eds.), *Virtual teams that work: Creating conditions for virtual team effectiveness* (pp. 95-120). San Francisco: Jossey-Bass.

Clark, D. N., & Gibb, J. L. (2006). Virtual team learning: An introductory study team exercise. *Journal of Management Education, 30*(6), 765-787.

Hackman, J. R. (2002). *Leading teams: Setting the stage for great performances.* Boston: Harvard Business School Press.

Hall, B. (2008). Building exceptional virtual learning teams: Five ways to enhance virtual learning and work environments. *Chief Learning Officer, 7*(5), 20.

Harvey, M., Novicevic, M. M., & Garrison, G. (2004). Challenges to staffing global virtual teams. *Human Resource Management, 14,* 275-294.

Katzenbach, J. R., & Smith, D. K. (1993). *The wisdom of teams.* New York: HarperCollins.

Lombardo, M. M., & Eichinger, R. W. (2004). *The leadership machine: Architecture to develop leaders for any future.* Minneapolis, MN: Lominger International: A Korn/Ferry Company.

Massey, T. (2005). *Ten commitments for building high performance teams.* Bandon, OR: Robert D. Reed.

Parker, G. M. (2008). *Team players and teamwork: New strategies for developing successful collaboration* (2nd ed.). San Francisco: Jossey-Bass.

Rosen, B., Furst, S., & Blackburn, R. (2006). Training for virtual teams: An investigation of current practices and future needs. *Human Resource Management, 45*(2), 229-247.

Rugelj, J. (2000). Collaborative virtual environments for problem based learning. In G. Orange & D. Hobbs (Eds.), *International perspectives on tele-education and virtual learning environments* (pp. 140-155). Aldershot, UK: Ashgate.

Stinson, L., Pearson, D., & Lucas, B. (2006). Developing a learning culture: Twelve tips for individuals, teams, and organizations. *Medical Teacher, 28*(4), 309-312.

10

Translation to the Leadership Architect® Competency Library

In order for a team or individuals on a team to perform well in this area, these are the competencies that would most likely be in play. Aside from a team improvement plan where everybody works on the same thing, some individual team members may need to work on some of these competencies. A critical number (but not necessarily all) of team members would have to be good at:

Mission Critical:	Important:	Nice to Have:
32. Learning on the Fly	2. *Dealing with*	28. Innovation
33. Listening	*Ambiguity*	Management
51. Problem Solving	35. Managing and	54. Self-Development
	Measuring Work	61. Technical Learning
	45. Personal Learning	
	50. Priority Setting	
	62. Time Management	

In addition to the 10 tips listed for this dimension, there are some tips that may apply from *FYI For Your Improvement*™. Below are the four items from the Team Architect® that make up this dimension. The item number appears to the left of each item. Immediately below the text of each item are competency and tip numbers from *FYI*. The competency is listed first (from 1 to 67), followed by the tip number (1 to 10). For example, 33-4 refers to competency 33 (Listening), tip number 4. The tips are generally written for individual development, so some adaptation might be needed in the team context.

10. The team debriefs its successes in order to find "repeatables" and perform better.
    15-10; 32-1,2,3; 33-4,5; 50-3; 51-1,3,8

28. The team debriefs its failures and mistakes in order to perform better.
    2-1,7; 29-5; 32-3; 33-7; 34-3,4; 35-2,7; 44-6

46. The team practices continuous improvement; team members are more skilled than they were a year ago.
    32-1,2,3; 35-2; 51-1,2; 53-1,3; 54-10; 63-6

64. Team members are receptive to innovative approaches and new technology to improve team effectiveness.
    14-2,8; 28-1,4,5,7; 32-2,3; 46-1; 61-7

Dimension 11
Decision Making

Definition:
Team makes timely decisions, collects enough information to make objective decisions, and has open decision-making processes.

Addresses the question:
Does the team have trouble making effective decisions in a timely manner?

A Dimension in the TEAMING SKILLS Factor
Operating the team's business efficiently and effectively.

> *The man who insists upon seeing with perfect clearness before he decides, never decides. Accept life, and you must accept regret.*
> Henri-Frédéric Amiel – Swiss philosopher, poet, and critic

Items
11. The team makes timely decisions; everything is not open for endless debate and fact finding.
29. All decisions do not have to be made as a team; one or a few may make decisions at times based on expertise.
47. Team members resist jumping to conclusions.
65. Team members discuss problems objectively; they do not form coalitions to pressure others into agreement.

Unskilled
☐ Team spends too much time collecting information and problem solving at the expense of making timely decisions
☐ Team spends too much time getting everyone's input, approval, or consensus before making decisions
☐ Team members are too quick to decide; overuse their gut; or don't seek out enough information
☐ Team has internal cliques or alliances that dominate decision making
☐ Decisions are made off-line, outside of open decision-making processes
☐ Some team members use subjective approaches to decision making
☐ Team members cover their true feelings about decisions to keep peace
☐ Team endlessly deliberates decisions without coming to resolution
☐ One or a few members dominate team discussions

Skilled

- ☐ Team selects most appropriate decision-making technique based on the situation
- ☐ Team has a process to follow when it needs to make complex decisions
- ☐ The team is comfortable making significant decisions before all the data are in
- ☐ Team is quick to correct a previous decision when additional information is known
- ☐ Team members rotate and step up to role of decision manager
- ☐ The team takes on tough issues, has discussions around them, and then reaches a consensus
- ☐ The team sets a decision time frame
- ☐ The team takes external and internal customers' perspectives into consideration when making decisions
- ☐ The team balances the need for information with the need for speed when making decisions

Overused

- ☐ Team is too patient with the decision-making process; the team tolerates unlimited debate
- ☐ Team may force a decision prematurely in order to meet a self-imposed deadline
- ☐ The team leaves others behind as it rockets through decisions
- ☐ The team has trouble backing up and reprocessing a decision when additional information comes in
- ☐ Team is so speedy that others with legitimate input are not given a chance
- ☐ Decision making procedures receive higher priority in the team than discussion on what needs to be decided; procedure becomes an end unto itself

Note on overused strengths: Overused skills and disproportionately used strengths tend to have the negative effects listed above. To decrease those negative consequences, you have two alternatives. You can scale down or use the strength less, or you can compensate for it with another skill or behavior. In practice, it is very difficult to get an individual or a team to use a strength less. In most cases, the best path is to develop compensators. Team Architect® Dimensions that can compensate for overusing this dimension and compensating skills from the Leadership Architect® Library's 67 Competencies are listed below.

102

(Note: Team Dimension numbers are listed in parentheses. Competencies are listed in numerical order by competency number.)

Compensating Team Dimensions:
☐ Team Learning (10)
☐ Conflict Resolution (12)
☐ Managing Process (14)
☐ Team Leader Fit (20)

Compensating Competencies:
☐ 12. Conflict Management
☐ 17. Decision Quality
☐ 40. *Dealing with* Paradox
☐ 41. Patience
☐ 51. Problem Solving

Some Causes of Poor Performance
☐ Team does not handle uncertainty or ambiguity comfortably
☐ Team avoids the conflict involved in debating sides of a decision
☐ Some members need too much information to make a decision
☐ Team is afraid to make a bad decision
☐ Failures related to poor decision making in the past have made the team timid
☐ Team has little perspective, a narrow outlook on issues
☐ Some team members are impatient
☐ Team makes timely decisions but fails to follow up and plan for implementation
☐ A single key team member tends to hold things up
☐ A single key team member is extremely conservative
☐ A single key team member is not a clear-headed problem-solver

The Map
Making good decisions can be challenging. Throw in the need for speed and the challenge becomes nearly impossible. Timely decision making often means deciding before we're ready. Before we have all the data. Before everyone on the team is on board. Before everyone feels they've had a fair shot at giving input. Uncomfortably short time frames. Limited information. The difficulty is compounded in a team setting. How do you move quickly when there is the need for debate and collaboration? When busy schedules of multiple team members compound logistics issues? When a key member is unavailable?

When political considerations are heightened? To do it requires a high tolerance for ambiguity and skill in dealing with uncertainty. It means not fearing mistakes. While timeliness is important, it shouldn't trump decision quality. There needs to be a balance between speed and quality in decision making. Good decisions are based upon a mixture of data, analysis, intuition, and wisdom. Team members need to have patience enough to collect the available information and be humble enough to ask for other teammates' opinions and thoughts. Teams must be able to identify the problems and opportunities they face, evaluate the options they have for moving forward, and then make the decision about how to proceed. Correct isn't enough. Correct enough in time to create competitive advantage is the key.

Some Remedies

☐ 1. Define the issue. When teams are studied making decisions, a consistent finding is that most do not take enough time up front to define the issue. They start with a solution or conclusion. They fall back on what they have done in the past instead of exploring new ideas. So the first thing the team should do is spend scheduled time defining the issue. No one is allowed to offer a solution. All that is allowed is to define aspects of the issue. The next step is to define the goal of the decision. What goal will be accomplished? What is being determined? How will it be measured? Next, have the team create multiple solutions. Research shows that generally the first solution people generate is not the best one. Somewhere between the second and third solution is the highest-quality solution. After honing in on a solution, have the team spend a little time test-driving the decision. Unintended consequences are an all-too-common problem when implementing a decision. The decision may cause unanticipated noise with other groups. Once the solution is selected and the decision is made, monitor what was intended against what actually happens and make course corrections as you go.

☐ 2. Make timely decisions. Most individuals and, therefore, most teams have more trouble making timely decisions than accurate ones. This is usually due to the fear of mistakes and failures and the low tolerance for ambiguity and uncertainty. It also comes from the unrealistic expectation of perfection. Always making the right decision is the unfortunate standard. The important measure for individuals and teams is net accuracy over time. There are no perfect decisions in real life. Have the team discuss its expectations for accuracy of decisions. Compare that to other teams who are high performing. Timeliness is making a decision before you really are ready or want to. For most, making quick decisions is hard because it opens them up to potential criticism. Have the team set out a timetable for making timely decisions. Set an end date. Work backwards from there to lay out the decision-making process. Along the way, periodically check with the team and poll them on what they would decide if the decision were due in the next five minutes. Track that data over time to check to see when the team settled in to what turns out to be the final decision.

☐ **3. Balance decision-making styles in the team.** A complicating element when teams have to make timely decisions is the diversity of decision-making styles and preferences in the team. A few individuals are comfortable making seat-of-the-pants decisions. More are comfortable taking what they consider to be ample time and thinking things through. This can lead to noise and conflict in teams as the slow paced resist the speed merchants. Try this approach: do a team assessment, either self-ratings or, better yet, have the team members rate each other on comfort with making timely decisions. Line up the members of the team—from those that make decisions with a minimum of information, sometimes called satisficers, to the ones who prefer to analyze at a slower pace, known as maximizers. When faced with a significant decision, assign those that prefer to analyze a lot of information (the maximizers) to work on it first, defining the elements and analyzing the issues. The maximizers can then present their analysis to those more comfortable deciding with a minimum of information (the satisficers). That way, everyone on the team will start from about the same place. The satisficers will be seeing the issue for the first time and the maximizers will have had time to analyze the issue in detail. *More help? See Chapter 10 – Team Learning, in this book.*

☐ **4. Pick the right people to make decisions.** It's hard enough for an individual to make a decision. It's even harder for a team. Ideally, everyone has a piece of the puzzle. Everyone is without bias and contributes evenly. The discussions are balanced and the time managed efficiently. When the decision is made, the whole team supports and feels ownership because they've been involved in the process. In real life, contributions to a solution or a decision are often unbalanced. Some team members have significant contributions to make and others have little to offer or may even have a chilling effect on arriving at the best decision. Teams need to be careful to not confuse the need for inclusion, collaboration, consensus, and participation with making quality decisions. High-performing teams allow unbalanced inputs and distribute authority to those who have the most to offer, decision by decision. There is less need in a high-performing team for collaboration simply for the sake of collaboration. Collaboration is used when more than one person has the pieces and parts needed to put together a good decision. Get familiar with team members' expertise and backgrounds. Put directories that include each team member's skills and experience on the team Web site or repository. Have the team determine for each decision that needs to be made who is the best person or combination of people to make the decision. Figure out who has the needed information. Monitor the size of the decision team. When quick decisions are needed, a team may need to delegate them to certain team members (who are the experts) so decisions can be expedited.

☐ **5. Assign a devil's advocate.** When team members see issues surrounding a decision in a similar way, it makes the decision-making process faster. However, it does not mean that the decision made will be the best one. Typically, it's better to have some open discussion and debate in the decision-making process. Welcome dissenting voices in the team. Dissenters enhance decision quality by forcing team members to think within a broader set of information and perspectives. Encourage team members to express disagreement in a way that will foster new understanding without damaging team morale and cohesion. One way of ensuring debate is to assign a person to play devil's advocate when making decisions. A devil's advocate helps reduce group conformity or groupthink. The devil's advocate can encourage team members to think outside their normal paradigms.

☐ **6. Use different decision methods.** Decision making isn't one size fits all. Teams need to be flexible in determining what type of decision-making method is called for based on the business challenge at hand. Variety works best in teams. Too much decision-making regulation can bog a team down. Make sure the team understands the different ways a decision can be made and when to use various approaches. It is important that the team decide in advance what decision-making method will be used for the pending issue. No surprises in the decision-making process midway. Here are some of the most common methods and when to use them:

- Autocratic. Made by one person (the team leader or sponsor) or a small group of individuals with expertise and power. This method is useful for simple, routine, administrative decisions or when team members lack the skills or information to make the decision. Also, an autocratic approach is needed when timeliness is vital.
- Expert. One person has expertise on this topic. This method is useful when the expertise of one person is far superior to all other team members. Little is gained from team discussion.
- Democratic. Everybody contributes, gets a vote, and the majority wins. This method should be used when there isn't time for consensus or when the decision is not so important that consensus is necessary. Be careful not to alienate those who didn't vote for the decision.

- Consensus. Input and ideas from all team members is gathered and discussed to arrive at a final acceptable decision to all. This method is helpful in situations where you can take the time to hammer out a decision. It is not practical in emergency situations or when there are extreme time pressures.
- Unanimous. Everyone agrees that the best decision has been made. This method is useful when 100% member commitment is critical for implementing the decision, like in a jury trial.

☐ **7. Use decision managers.** Studies have shown that the decision-making process has a lot of downtime where nothing is being done. Issues get stalled as much as 85% of the time while information sits in someone's in-box, on the bottom of the pile of things to do, or in the briefcase in the car. If each decision has a manager, that person can walk the decision through the various inputs and approval steps needed to move the decision along. The decision manager also manages the discussions and debates over the decision. The decision manager makes sure everyone with input has a place to provide it. That all sides of the issues are examined. That expert advice is sought from outside the team. It's best if the decision manager is not involved passionately in the decision. This technique serves a dual purpose. Not only does it speed decisions, it offers development for decision managers on how to manage decision-making processes.

☐ **8. Don't ask for input on a decision if you don't intend to use it.** This tip is especially useful for team leaders and decision managers. In some circumstances, it may be more appropriate for everyone to provide input and reach consensus. However, in some circumstances, everyone's input in decision making may not be appropriate. The degree of participation depends on the characteristics of a decision, such as complexity, importance of team acceptance, capability of the team members and team leader, and impact of a wrong decision. Don't ask if you aren't going to consider the input or if you have already made up your mind. If a decision requires you to use your authority without discussion, just say so. One of the best ways to kill trust in your team is to lead team members to think their opinions really affect the decision. Team members know when you are jerking them around. It is also important to explain to others whether the decision will be made autocratically or whether team members' input will be considered to avoid misunderstanding.

☐ **9. Learn how to make better decisions.** Team members need to be able to problem solve, make timely decisions, make quality decisions, and relate well to others in a team setting. These skills can make or break a team's ability to make fair and reasonable decisions, be open in their communications, confront one another, work through conflict, and develop an effective approach to decision making. If too many members are lacking in these key skills, a team is likely to be inefficient. Consequently, teams will have unproductive meetings trying to get decisions made and work done. To improve team decision-making ability, have individuals focus on their personal development and training around any gaps that may get in the way of them being a productive contributor on the team. Collectively participate in some team-building exercises to learn how to integrate the skills of individual members and develop decision-making methods that make sense for the team and the business challenges. Team members should be trained together so they can determine how the team will make decisions in certain situations and how they will deal with one another. Assess the past decision-making processes. What went right? What went wrong? What could be done to make the decision making better? Learn from mistakes and feedback. *More help? See* FYI For Your Improvement™, *Chapter 16 – Timely Decision Making, and Chapter 17 – Decision Quality.*

☐ **10. Use collaborative technology.** As globalization increases, more organizations are using virtual teams as a means to recruit experts from different disciplines and regions to work on projects. When it comes to decision making, virtual teams may make the process more complicated. Some of the complication is logistical (e.g., different time zones). Some is due to lack of face-to-face collaboration on decisions. For virtual teams that consist of members from different cultures, language can be a barrier. To help streamline the decision-making process in virtual teams, use collaborative technologies to encourage team members to dialog about pending decisions. Team chat rooms or Web site postings provide a forum for debate and commentary. Asynchronous communication like this allows team members time to analyze issues before responding. Collaborative technologies allow data, analysis, and other relevant information on the decision to be archived and stored until such time that the team has a need to retrieve it in the future. Lack of face-to-face interactions can increase the likelihood that team members are swayed by information, reasons, and ideas.

Suggested Readings

Brousseau, K. R., Driver, M. J., Hourihan, G., & Larsson, R. (2006). The seasoned executive's decision-making style. *Harvard Business Review, 84*(2), 110-122.

Fisher, K., Rayner, S., Belgard, W., & the Belgard-Fisher-Rayner Team. (1995). *Tips for teams: A ready reference for solving common team problems* (2nd ed.). New York: McGraw-Hill.

Hackman, J. R. (2002). *Leading teams: Setting the stage for great performances.* Boston: Harvard Business School Press.

Katzenbach, J. R., & Smith, D. K. (1993). *The wisdom of teams.* New York: HarperCollins.

Kellermanns, F. W., Floyd, S. W., Pearson, A. W., & Spencer, B. (2008). The contingent effect of constructive confrontation on the relationship between shared mental models and decision quality. *Journal of Organizational Behavior, 29,* 119-137.

Kemp, J. M. (2008). *Moving out of the box: Tools for team decision making.* Westport, CT: Praeger.

McNamara, K., Dennis, A. R., & Carte, T. A. (2008). It's the thought that counts: The mediating effects of information processing in virtual team decision making. *Information Systems Management, 25*(1), 20-32.

Mulvey, P. W., Veiga, J. F., & Elsass, P. M. (1996). When teammates raise a white flag. *Academy of Management Executive, 10*(1), 40-49.

Nemiro, J., Beyerlein, M. M., Bradley, L., & Beyerlein, S. (Eds.). (2008). *The handbook of high-performance virtual teams: A toolkit for collaborating across boundaries.* San Francisco: Jossey-Bass.

Pokras, S. (2006). *Problem solving for teams: A systematic approach to consensus decision making* (Rev. ed.). Los Altos, CA: Crisp Learning.

Robbins, H., & Finley, M. (2000). *The new why teams don't work: What goes wrong and how to make it right.* San Francisco: Berrett-Koehler Publishers.

Schmidt, J. B., Montoya-Weiss, M. M., & Massey, A. P. (2001). New product development decision-making effectiveness: Comparing individuals, face-to-face teams, and virtual teams. *Decision Sciences, 32*(4), 575-599.

Schulz-Hardt, S., Brodbeck, F. C., Mojzisch, A., Kerschreiter, R., & Frey, D. (2006). Group decision making in hidden profile situations: Dissent as a facilitator for decision quality. *Journal of Personality & Social Psychology, 91*(6), 1080-1093.

Shachaf, P. (2008). Cultural diversity and information and communication technology impacts on global virtual teams: An exploratory study. *Information & Management, 45*(2), 131-142.

Zhang, D., Lowry, P. B., Zhou, L., & Fu, X. (2007). The impact of individualism-collectivism, social presence, and group diversity on group decision making under majority influence. *Journal of Management Information Systems, 23*(4), 53-80.

Translation to the Leadership Architect® Competency Library

In order for a team or individuals on a team to perform well in this area, these are the competencies that would most likely be in play. Aside from a team improvement plan where everybody works on the same thing, some individual team members may need to work on some of these competencies. A critical number (but not necessarily all) of team members would have to be good at:

Mission Critical:	**Important:**	**Nice to Have:**
16. *Timely* Decision Making	12. Conflict Management	1. Action Oriented
17. Decision Quality	33. Listening	2. *Dealing with* Ambiguity
51. Problem Solving	50. Priority Setting	11. Composure
	53. *Drive for* Results	18. Delegation
		42. Peer Relationships

In addition to the 10 tips listed for this dimension, there are some tips that may apply from *FYI For Your Improvement*™. Below are the four items from the Team Architect® that make up this dimension. The item number appears to the left of each item. Immediately below the text of each item are competency and tip numbers from *FYI*. The competency is listed first (from 1 to 67), followed by the tip number (1 to 10). For example, 33-4 refers to competency 33 (Listening), tip number 4. The tips are generally written for individual development, so some adaptation might be needed in the team context.

11. The team makes timely decisions; everything is not open for endless debate and fact finding.
    1-5,7; 16-1,2,3,5,6,7; 50-9; 51-1

29. All decisions do not have to be made as a team; based on expertise, one or a few may make decisions at times.
    18-2,5,9; 53-2; 56-3,5; 60-3,8; 110-4,8

47. Team members resist jumping to conclusions.
    11-2,3,9; 33-3,6,7; 41-4,7; 51-1,2

65. Team members discuss problems objectively; they do not form coalitions to pressure others into agreement.
    12-1,2,4,7; 27-1; 34-8; 51-1,2; 57-2,4

Dimension 12
Conflict Resolution

Definition:
Team members listen empathically and provide opportunities to address the needs of all parties; can calmly have a contentious discussion before a consensus is reached.

Addresses the question:
Is there excessive noise and unresolved conflict that take up time and keep people from working well with one another?

A Dimension in the TEAMING SKILLS Factor
Operating the team's business efficiently and effectively.

> *Conflict is the gadfly of thought. It stirs us to observation and memory.*
> *It instigates to invention. It shocks us out of sheeplike passivity,*
> *and sets us at noting and contriving.*
> John Dewey – American philosopher, psychologist, and educator

Items
12. The team has smooth, freely flowing internal communications.
30. The team takes on the tough issues; the ones many teams would rather not surface.
48. The team can have an exciting, contentious discussion and then reach a consensus.
66. When a serious internal conflict occurs, the team calmly resolves it.

Unskilled
- ☐ Some team members avoid discussing uncomfortable subjects and let things fester
- ☐ Conflict is seen as negative and avoided if at all possible
- ☐ Team members lash out at each other or shut members down in times of conflict; conflict gets personal
- ☐ Team members take too many conflicts to the team leader for resolution
- ☐ Conflict drives the team off course and disrupts normal processes
- ☐ The team's internal communications are ineffective and inconsistent
- ☐ The team has trouble building consensus when conflicts arise

☐ There is a lot of unnecessary noise in the team

☐ It takes too much time for the team to settle down and work together again after a particularly heated conflict

Skilled

☐ Team surfaces conflicts early

☐ All team members don't get distracted by superficial issues during conflict

☐ Those team members on the losing side of an issue don't brood; they become part of the loyal opposition and move on

☐ Surfacing and resolving conflict is seen as a normal part of the team's business

☐ Team members view conflict as constructive, not destructive

☐ Team focuses conflict on objective business issues, not individuals

☐ Team members approach conflict with patience and calm

☐ Respect for fellow team members is top of mind during conflict situations

☐ The team seeks win-win solutions when doing so meets overall team objectives

☐ Team members are not afraid to express their opinions, even if it causes conflict

Overused

☐ Team sometimes is too quick to see conflict; meets trouble more than halfway

☐ Team spends too much time opening and discussing conflicts

☐ Team tries too hard to resolve the unresolvable

☐ Some team members cave in to consensus just to smooth over conflict

☐ Team members may be too accommodating and overanxious to keep peace in the team

☐ The team's internal conflicts may spill out to others around them and be misinterpreted as more negative than they are

☐ It may be really hard for a new member to be comfortable due to the open atmosphere and immediate airing of everything

☐ Team may get buried in communications and e-mails they don't need to know or even want to know

Note on overused strengths: Overused skills and disproportionately used strengths tend to have the negative effects listed above. To decrease those negative consequences, you have two alternatives. You can scale down or use the strength less, or you can compensate for it with another skill or

behavior. In practice, it is very difficult to get an individual or a team to use a strength less. In most cases, the best path is to develop compensators. Team Architect® Dimensions that can compensate for overusing this dimension and compensating skills from the Leadership Architect® Library's 67 Competencies are listed below.

(Note: Team Dimension numbers are listed in parentheses. Competencies are listed in numerical order by competency number.)

Compensating Team Dimensions:
- ☐ Thrust Management (1)
- ☐ Resource Management (9)
- ☐ Decision Making (11)
- ☐ Managing Process (14)
- ☐ Focusing (15)
- ☐ Team Leader Fit (20)

Compensating Competencies:
- ☐ 2. *Dealing with* Ambiguity
- ☐ 41. Patience
- ☐ 48. Political Savvy
- ☐ 51. Problem Solving

Some Causes of Poor Performance
- ☐ Members just want to get along and be liked
- ☐ Some members avoid conflict at all costs
- ☐ Team leader doesn't set a good example on handling conflict
- ☐ Organization is conflict averse; conflict is viewed as politically incorrect and negative
- ☐ Members are shy and reluctant to surface issues
- ☐ Members may take conflict too personally or are too sensitive
- ☐ Team turns little things into conflicts because they enjoy the battle
- ☐ Members are uneven in terms of their tolerance and skill at handling conflict
- ☐ Team views all conflicts in terms of either winning or losing

The Map
There is good news and bad news when it comes to conflict. The good news is that when managed fairly and openly, conflict is a healthy way to address issues and challenges. Conflict can bring out differences of fact and opinion and experience. It can bring things out from under the table into the light of

12

day. It can put passion behind the debate. All members can express their views. In the end, when it is a fair and open process, conflict can lead to better and more lasting solutions because all sides are heard and nothing is held back. On the flip side, the bad news is that conflict can be chilling rather than energizing. Conflict can be uncomfortable and demotivating. If it turns personal, conflict can be destructive. Conflict can decrease personal effectiveness rather than being a means to reach peak performance. When handled poorly and allowed to fester, conflict becomes a permanent storm cloud that breaks down cooperation and threatens team cohesion. Handled well, conflict can be the elixir to better solutions and more effective problem solving.

Some Remedies

☐ 1. **Accept that conflict is normal and necessary.** Conflict is an essential part of becoming a high-performing team. Rarely can you expect a group of people to come together, build a common purpose, set performance goals and measures, assign roles, produce results, and not run into some significant conflict. The key to getting through the conflict is to make conflict constructive—not something that is personal or must be painfully endured by team members. Teams learn through conflict and become stronger, just as individuals learn through personal hardships. The most effective team members intercede when other team members are in conflict to help resolve the disagreement. Bad or weak team members turn their backs on conflict—either ignoring it and hoping it will disappear or letting the other team members battle it out. When conflicts arise, find opportunities to debrief conflict at team meetings to make sure members don't miss the meaning from the experience.

☐ 2. **Identify the causes of conflicts.** Teams need to recognize the causes of their conflicts to effectively work on them and address the causes. Usually the identification of the cause is the first step to resolving a conflict successfully. One or a combination of the following reasons generally causes conflicts:

- Unmet individual needs and wants
- Clashing values
- Different perceptions
- Varying knowledge
- Different assumptions
- Different expectations
- Different backgrounds
- Willingness and ability to deal with conflict
- Communication breakdown or difficulties

114

Review the list of causes with the team and discuss examples for each cause. Identify constructive ways to resolve the examples discussed. Post the list of causes somewhere that is visible to team members. Refer to the list when conflicts arise to facilitate understanding and resolution of disagreements within the team.

☐ **3. Identify the cost of conflict.** Conflict can go beyond being just an irritant for team members. It can be expensive. As a result, teams should view unresolved conflict as affecting the bottom line. If conflict avoidance or ineffective conflict resolution becomes an ongoing problem, consider trying to identify the cost of conflict. Ask each team member privately to identify a team conflict that they have either participated in or observed. Ask the team members to individually identify the costs associated with the conflict, such as:

- Delayed decisions
- Wasted time
- Reduced or poor decision quality
- Turnover or terminations
- Loss of resources
- Restructuring/restaffing to accommodate the conflict
- Sabotage/damaged reputations
- Lowered motivation, reduced performance and productivity
- Absenteeism associated with the conflict
- Stress-related health costs

Ask for a show of hands to gauge the total range of costs associated with the conflict that each team member assessed (i.e., less than $100; $100–$1,000; $1,000–$10,000). Stress that these were cost examples of just one conflict. Imagine what the collective conflicts add up to. Discuss the implications of each category used in the analysis. Identify ways to reduce costs associated with conflict in the future.

☐ **4. Tackle the issues, not the people.** It's likely for teams to have a tendency to avoid negative or uncomfortable subjects. Some team members may even be sensitive to initiating tough discussions because they don't want to be perceived as "rocking the boat." Teams should avoid getting themselves into situations where conflict gets overly personal. When conflict becomes personal, it can harm working relationships. Learn how to focus conflict resolution more on tasks, issues, and process, and less on people. Look past interpersonal styles to stay objective when addressing conflict between team members. When conflict situations focus on objective business issues such as process breakdowns, roadblocks, or misalignment with strategy rather than subjective opinions of people and personalities, it defuses tension and enables better decision making. Collective focus on the process or on the team goals will bring people together to work toward improving performance. It should also lessen common defensive behaviors that can surface in times of conflict. Make statements that focus on the issues, not on individuals. The simplest choices of words can temper discussions, allowing the team to focus on resolution rather than getting sidetracked on personal attacks that will leave hurt feelings and scars that take time to heal (if they ever do). *More help? See* FYI For Your Improvement™, *Chapter 12 – Conflict Management.*

☐ **5. Listen first, talk later.** When teams work closely together, they are bound to have disagreements from time to time. To solve an issue or problem effectively, you have to understand what other people think. Give others opportunities to express their thoughts and perspectives before defending your own position. Pay attention to other team members' underlying concerns, needs, and interests. Listen to verbal cues and don't miss the non-verbal cues as well. Establish eye contact with the speakers. Be patient. Hear people out. You cannot fully understand people's points of view if you are busy judging and arguing mentally about what they are saying. Ask for clarity if you don't understand. In a virtual team setting, we lose the non-verbal cues that can be so telling in a conflict situation. As a workaround, regularly check in with remote team members. Don't assume that silence means agreement. Draw them out and into discussions. Use an independent manager of the issue to help facilitate discussions when needed. The issue manager is the timekeeper, the rule enforcer, and the synthesizer. The issue manager makes sure everyone has a chance to express his/her opinion and decides how long a person can talk. *More help? See* FYI For Your Improvement™, *Chapter 33 – Listening.*

☐ **6. Anticipate organizational or political conflict traps.** High-performing teams learn how to deal with conflict through frank and open communication. However, this is easier said than done. Many people grow up in large companies where they are taught to play by the rules of politics. Conforming to politics usually contributes to career success. Lack of it is almost certain to derail people at some point. Learn how to navigate within the accepted boundaries of the organization. For example, the culture may demand respect for superiors, or supporting the party line, or not pushing crazy or overly creative ideas. There are likely cultural norms around conflict as well. Some cultures may generally restrict conflict, making it difficult or risky to surface conflict. Other cultures may thrive on it and view harmony as a sign of stagnation or lack of innovation. If your organization is extremely political, create new rules within the team to get past it. Make a commitment to keep confidences about things that may be taboo in the rest of the organization. What happens in the team stays in the team. Disagreements are kept inside the team. There is no off-line processing or politicking to get the decision changed. Successful teams find ways to open up to conflict and respond constructively to one another. Such an approach allows individual differences to be surfaced, understood, and ultimately merged into common goals. *More help? See* FYI For Your Improvement™, *Chapter 48 – Political Savvy.*

☐ **7. Build consensus.** Consensus is different from consent. Consent usually means majority rules. Consensus is a decision everyone can live with and typically involves compromise among teammates. All team members must agree, even though their preferred solution may not be the one the team (ultimately) chooses. Consensus means all team members see the agreed-upon solution as acceptable, having a mind-set of "I can live with the decision." The key to consensus is a give-and-take attitude within the team. Offering ideas, respecting differences, and taking in other viewpoints by listening to the opinions of your team members are critical behaviors. It is a lot easier to do this if there are previously established norms that everyone's facts, opinions, and even feelings matter. When facilitating a consensus decision, remember the following tips:

– Focus on the idea or solution, not on the originator or manner of suggestion.

– Look for a meet-me-halfway option that people can live with.

– Analyze the reality of the idea having success in the team, organization, or marketplace.

– Analyze the cost-effectiveness of the option.

A decision made via consensus takes more time and should be viewed as a win-win proposition rather than one that creates winning and losing camps. Not everyone will be delighted with every resolution. Sometimes team members will feel passionately about an issue and feel like they're giving up a lot in order to reach consensus. At these times, it is critical to support them immediately after the decision because they may be feeling alienated since the issue didn't go their way. Generally, all that is needed is some acknowledgment that losing is no fun, that we all lose sometimes, and that they are valued contributors.

☐ **8. Discuss the "undiscussables."** Undiscussables are unpleasant issues recognized by most everyone but addressed by almost no one, at least not in a group setting. Conflict cannot be resolved until it is surfaced and addressed. A team's success is inversely related to the number of issues that remain under the table. The more undiscussables are kept secretive, the more damaging they can be. Compared to traditional teams, virtual teams have more difficulty spotting and addressing conflict in part due

12

12

to their dependence on e-communication for collaboration. Virtual team members may ignore the problem or issue and assume that the problem will go away by itself (especially if it is not something clearly impacting their work). Bring the undiscussables out of the shadows. Use a conflict manager or facilitator or coach to put the undiscussables on the table. Sometimes it is difficult for a team to solve its own conflict problems. The team may be too close to the problem. It might be helpful to bring in a facilitator or conflict coach from time to time for an outside perspective. Give each team member three index cards to write down three separate undiscussable issues. The facilitator should collect them and briefly review to see if there are any trends. A code of conduct or rules of engagement should be established to make the exchange productive. The facilitator should post the first most common undiscussable and ask questions to prompt discussion, such as:

– What does this undiscussable mean?

– What is the cause?

– What is the cost?

– What prompts the issue to reoccur (if applicable)?

If the team agrees that it is something that needs to be addressed and worthy of an action item, the facilitator might ask these types of questions:

– What are the barriers to overcoming this undiscussable?

– What resources do we need to fix it (sponsorship, money, time, etc.)?

– What are the consequences of not fixing it?

– Who will own this?

– How will progress be measured?

☐ **9. Reestablish team conflict rules of engagement.** Team conflict rules of engagement have two functions: (1) they provide a guide to solve team conflict, and (2) they provide a basis for the team leader and members to give feedback to another member who has violated a norm. Team conflict norms are especially crucial for virtual teams that consist of team members who are dispersed across different locations. Conflict can be higher in virtual teams due to time zone differences, reliance on e-communication, lack of face-to-face interactions, and cultural differences. The team leader (or team coach/facilitator) should facilitate a discussion of team member expectations about how conflict is to be handled in the team. Develop a list of norms of acceptable behaviors. They should be things like listening to opposing views, letting each person be heard, staying objective, no interrupting, no shouting, voting if consensus cannot be reached, and so on. Use the discussion on developing a set of conflict norms to lead to

118

an assessment of how well the norms are currently being followed. Make sure norms specifically address potential virtual team conflicts. In conflict discussions with virtual teams, use a round-robin format so all members have an opportunity to share their views and concerns.

☐ **10. Make communication a priority.** Research suggests that virtual teams are more likely to face conflict due to communication delays and difficulties, time zone differences, and diverse perspectives. Cultural differences do not always create conflict but certainly can increase the likelihood of conflict. Geographic dispersion and heavy dependence on communication technologies can increase misunderstanding, misperception, and be a distraction to virtual team functioning. Communication breakdowns that lead to conflict aren't limited to virtual teams. Even teams who sit within the same four walls can miss the signals that lead to conflict. Failure to exchange information. Differences in speed of access to information. Misinterpretation of the meaning of silence. All can create big communication problems which then lead to conflict. Establish communication norms to help enhance communication capabilities. These norms should include:

- Appropriate use of communication media and contact information.
- Meeting and contact schedules.
- Documentation procedures.
- When to make phone or conference calls.
- Verifying that messages are received and understood.

12

Suggested Readings

Fitzgerald, M. (2006). *Corporate circles: Transforming conflict and building trusting teams*. Vancouver, Canada: Quinn.

Garton, C., & Wegryn, K. (2006). *Managing without walls: Maximize success with virtual, global, and cross-cultural teams*. Lewisville, TX: MC Press.

Griffith, T. L., Mannix, E. A., & Neale, M. A. (2003). Conflict and virtual teams. In C. B. Gibson & S. G. Cohen (Eds.), *Virtual teams that work: Creating conditions for virtual team effectiveness* (pp. 335-352). San Francisco: Jossey-Bass.

Hackman, J. R. (2002). *Leading teams: Setting the stage for great performances*. Boston: Harvard Business School Press.

Hoefling, T. (2003). *Working virtually: Managing people for successful virtual teams and organizations*. Sterling, VA: Stylus.

Kankanhalli, A., Tan, B. C. Y., & Wei, K. K. (2007). Conflict and performance in global virtual teams. *Journal of Management Information Systems, 23*(3), 237-274.

Katzenbach, J. R., & Smith, D. K. (1993). *The wisdom of teams*. New York: HarperCollins.

Kimball, F. (1999). *Leading self-directed work teams: A guide to developing new team leadership skills*. New York: McGraw-Hill.

Nemiro, J., Beyerlein, M. M., Bradley, L., & Beyerlein, S. (Eds.). (2008). *The handbook of high-performance virtual teams: A toolkit for collaborating across boundaries*. San Francisco: Jossey-Bass.

Parker, G. M. (Ed.). (1996). *The handbook of best practices for teams*, Volume I. Amherst, MA: HRD Press.

Robbins, H., & Finley, M. (2000). *The new why teams don't work: What goes wrong and how to make it right*. San Francisco: Berrett-Koehler Publishers.

Shin, Y. (2005). Conflict resolution in virtual teams. *Organizational Dynamics, 34*(4), 331-345.

Stevens, M. J., & Campion, M. A. (1994). The knowledge, skill, and ability requirements for teamwork: Implications for human resource management. *Journal of Management, 20*(2), 503-530.

Ulrich, D., Eichinger, R. W., Kulas, J. T., & De Meuse, K. P. (2007). *50 More things you need to know: The science behind best people practices for managers & HR professionals*. Minneapolis, MN: Lominger International: A Korn/Ferry Company.

12

Translation to the Leadership Architect® Competency Library

In order for a team or individuals on a team to perform well in this area, these are the competencies that would most likely be in play. Aside from a team improvement plan where everybody works on the same thing, some individual team members may need to work on some of these competencies. A critical number (but not necessarily all) of team members would have to be good at:

Mission Critical:	**Important:**	**Nice to Have:**
11. Composure	27. Informing	37. Negotiating
12. Conflict Management	33. Listening	50. Priority Setting
34. Managerial Courage	51. Problem Solving	57. Standing Alone
42. Peer Relationships		

In addition to the 10 tips listed for this dimension, there are some tips that may apply from *FYI For Your Improvement*™. Below are the four items from the Team Architect® that make up this dimension. The item number appears to the left of each item. Immediately below the text of each item are competency and tip numbers from *FYI*. The competency is listed first (from 1 to 67), followed by the tip number (1 to 10). For example, 33-4 refers to competency 33 (Listening), tip number 4. The tips are generally written for individual development, so some adaptation might be needed in the team context.

12. The team has smooth, freely flowing internal communications.
    27-2,3,4,10; 33-3,4,5; 42-1,7; 105-1

30. The team takes on the tough issues; the ones many teams would rather not surface.
    12-3,4,5,7; 34-3,9; 43-1,5; 57-1,4

48. The team can have an exciting, contentious discussion and then reach a consensus.
    12-1,3,4,5,7; 17-3; 34-3; 51-1,2,3

66. When a serious internal conflict occurs, the team calmly resolves it.
    11-3,9; 12-2,3,4,5,7; 41-7; 51-1,2

FACTOR IV: TEAMING SKILLS

12

Dimension 13
Team Atmosphere

Definition:
There is a high level of camaraderie in the team; team members celebrate accomplishments collectively; it is apparent to others that the team enjoys working together.

Addresses the question:
Is the atmosphere inside the team conducive to everyone performing at his/her best?

A Dimension in the TEAMING SKILLS Factor
Operating the team's business efficiently and effectively.

> *If you can laugh together, you can work together.*
> Robert Orben – American magician and writer

Items
13. The team has an identity; it is not just a collection of individuals.
31. Team members enjoy working on this team.
49. The team has a positive atmosphere that is commented on by those outside the team.
67. The whole team celebrates its successes.

Unskilled
- ☐ The climate in this team is chilling and negative
- ☐ Individuals look forward to the time they are no longer part of this team
- ☐ Team members show little or no connectivity to one another; they have little in common
- ☐ Team doesn't take the time to celebrate or recognize performance milestones
- ☐ Some team members are all work and no play
- ☐ Individuals on this team don't view one another as friends or agreeable colleagues
- ☐ The team does not spend any off-work time together
- ☐ The team has cliques that tend to do things together but not with others

13

123

☐ Openings on this team are hard to fill; talented people are reluctant to join the team

☐ The team's lack of a positive atmosphere spills over and affects others above and below them

☐ There is little or no team pride, just individual pride or satisfaction

☐ Turnover on the team is a problem

Skilled

☐ High-performing/high-potential employees want to work on this team

☐ Openings on this team are easy to fill

☐ Team members have a true concern for others on the team, even beyond work

☐ Team members truly enjoy one another as people

☐ The team not only works hard together, they also play well together

☐ Others who report to members of this team comment on how well they work together and how positive the tone is

☐ Team members are proud to be part of the team

☐ Team members respect and value each other

☐ Team members are willing to invest time and effort to build up the relationship

☐ The team demonstrates a strong sense of team identity; operates as one

☐ Team members maintain positive attitudes toward each other

☐ Members of the team look out for each other

☐ Team members often do things together outside of the work setting

Overused

☐ Team is too consumed with itself and one another

☐ Team members may have too much fun, spend too much time socializing and bonding

☐ Team is perceived as too tight a clique

☐ Team celebrates so much that others perceive them as arrogant

☐ Team cohesiveness chills diversity of opinion; groupthink prevails

☐ Team spends too much effort trying to outdo other teams

☐ Team is so close that it is hard for outsiders to gain access

☐ Team spends so much time with one another that they do not build effective networks outside the team

☐ Sometimes members are reluctant to give negative feedback for fear of chilling the positive atmosphere

☐ Team goals become more important than organizational goals

13

Note on overused strengths: Overused skills and disproportionately used strengths tend to have the negative effects listed above. To decrease those negative consequences, you have two alternatives. You can scale down or use the strength less, or you can compensate for it with another skill or behavior. In practice, it is very difficult to get an individual or a team to use a strength less. In most cases, the best path is to develop compensators. Team Architect® Dimensions that can compensate for overusing this dimension and compensating skills from the Leadership Architect® Library's 67 Competencies are listed below.

(Note: Team Dimension numbers are listed in parentheses. Competencies are listed in numerical order by competency number.)

Compensating Team Dimensions:
☐ Thrust Management (1)
☐ Resource Management (9)
☐ Conflict Resolution (12)
☐ Focusing (15)
☐ Delivering the Goods (18)
☐ Team Leader Fit (20)

Compensating Competencies:
☐ 3. Approachability
☐ 21. *Managing* Diversity
☐ 42. Peer Relationships
☐ 53. *Drive for* Results
☐ 65. *Managing* Vision and Purpose

Some Causes of Poor Performance
☐ Team members may not have had enough time to bond
☐ Team leader may not create an atmosphere that encourages fun or celebration
☐ Organization is overly formal or stiff and doesn't promote fun at work
☐ Team members can't relax or loosen up
☐ One or more team members are negative and spoil all the fun for the rest
☐ There is a lack of humor in the team
☐ Team is made up of apples and oranges with little in common
☐ Team is under great stress and time pressure and has little time for anything else
☐ The way the team is organized and the work is distributed does not really require cooperation and/or much interaction

13

The Map

A team's ability to play together is a good indication of its ability to work together. A high-functioning, top-performing team is much more than a collection of skilled and well-intentioned individuals. It is a network of relationships between two or more people working closely together to accomplish a common goal. And those relationships need to be nourished. Highly effective teams think team first, individual second. One team member's success is shared by all. People are more productive being part of a team where members trust, respect, and basically like being around each other. They want to work in an environment that's positive and energizing. They want to enjoy and have pride in what they do. These are the teams that emit a palpable, positive energy that others see and want to become a part of. These are teams that openly support their members. These are the teams that know how to have fun. The work on these teams may be hard, but it is not a burden because the team looks forward to the opportunity of spending time together. These teams understand that their camaraderie is a big part of what makes them successful. People like to belong to a team that wins and enjoys the ride along the way.

Some Remedies

☐ **1. Do atmosphere audits.** In the everyday workplace, everyone is busy and there is not much time to stop and reflect. Everybody is hunkered down and doing his/her work. Even so, it's important that the atmosphere of the team be periodically monitored. The monitoring can range from the very simple—asking one-on-one or in team meetings how things are going— to more formal surveys of morale. Team leaders need to ask regularly for constructive feedback from their team members about what they think about the team—what's going well and what's not going well. It's also important to get feedback from people outside the team to learn about their perceptions. The drivers of a positive atmosphere are factors like trust in the leader and coworkers, fairness in assignments and evaluation, energy around doing something worthwhile, and reward for accomplishments. It's also important to surface atmosphere-chilling issues sooner rather than later. A team can quickly lose its positive feel when things go wrong. Here you are looking for noise and barriers. The question is: What's keeping you from performing and having fun doing it?

☐ **2. Plan off-work activities.** Allow time for members of the team to get to know one another outside of work. All work and no play makes for a less effective team environment. Some activities outside of work are especially important in the early stages of team development. Sometimes they happen naturally. A member invites the team to happy hour on Friday afternoon and they all end up spending a little social time together. Other times they are scheduled events. If you are the team leader and your team hasn't had any off-work activities, schedule something. Some events should be team members only. Others can include significant others and families. Invite the team over to your house for a cookout. If your company sponsors community events, get tickets to a sports event or concert to bring the team together. These activities allow team members to see each other in a different light, appreciate differences, and understand each other more clearly. They also help to create a bond of common happenings and pleasant experiences. When possible, find ways to include virtual team members for in-person gatherings. Obviously, for teams that are geographically dispersed, off-work activities will be more challenging. Leaders of virtual teams should encourage team members to make a habit of posting fun and exciting news on the team Web site or using chat rooms to get to know each other professionally and personally.

☐ **3. Celebrate successes.** Effective teams recognize and reward teamwork by celebrating successes. Celebrations keep energy levels high on the team. Find accomplishments and outcomes that warrant a celebration. It can be done formally or informally. Order pizza. Bring in a cake. Give everyone a shirt or something to recognize the team achievement. In a virtual environment, efforts to recognize and reward team successes may be more difficult. When there is lack of face-to-face interaction, it is crucial to reinforce the perception that virtual work is valued. Use Web-based technology, such as a team Web site, audio- or videoconference calls, and electronic bulletin boards, to advertise team successes and performance. Virtual team leaders can promote team successes in speeches, presentations, and discussions with other team leaders and with management. Ask a senior executive to make a personal call to stellar team members. Actively search for ways to lift morale through celebration.

☐ **4. Help new team members get on board.** One of the most challenging tasks a team can face is the introduction of a new member. It can be especially challenging in teams that are highly effective with their current members. Yet, even the most successful teams can get stagnant, succumb to groupthink, or potentially lose their edge without regular infusions of fresh perspectives. It's both common and healthy for members to move in and out of the team. When this happens, the team will require a certain amount of re-forming. Re-forming helps give a new team member a good start and can help lessen any struggles he/she might have adapting into the new environment. Create an onboarding process for the new member.

13

127

Here are some ideas of things to include:
- Team charter and goals. Check for clarity to make sure the new team member understands the purpose of the group. Ask for any value-adding suggestions from the new member.
- Role clarity. Map out his/her role and explain the roles of other members.
- Team norms and rules of engagement. Introduce the new member to team norms and check for buy-in. It is a good idea to revisit and amend to include new ideas from the new team member.
- Team supplier, customer, and competitor data.
- Miscellaneous group processes. Regular meeting times, presentations, workflow, etc.).
- Skills or competencies needed for success on the team.
- Training to learn needed technical or functional skills.
- Socialization. Use lunch times, chat rooms, or other Web-based technology for socialization to get to know the new member personally.
- Necessities. Phone, computer, e-mail, desk, security access, etc.
- Assignments. Give the new member a significant assignment from the start that will expose him/her to key constituencies throughout the team and organization.

Finally, while everyone on the team should have a part in the onboarding of the new member, it may help to assign the new team member to an onboarding coach who will be responsible for ensuring that the orientation is actually completed. Hold this person accountable for the new team member's onboarding process.

☐ **5. Encourage the use of humor.** Working toward team objectives can be stressful and intense. Tight deadlines, high-profile deliverables, high-stake outcomes can mean that team members spend a lot of time with each other. Humor can help in tense situations like this. Think about a person you know who is fairly humorless. Imagine working almost constantly with that person for a prolonged time period. Now, compare that to a person with a great sense of humor (who is also productive). Whom would you rather team with on an important, high-impact deliverable? Who would lighten the load, at least figuratively? Team members need to learn how to laugh at themselves and laugh with (not at) their teammates. Use humor to relieve tension and smooth over awkward moments. Use online chat rooms or the team Web site to post work-appropriate cartoons and articles, make fun of yourself, or point out the lighter side of events. *More help? See* FYI For Your Improvement™, *Chapter 26 – Humor.*

☐ **6. Treat mistakes and failures as team learning opportunities.** Mistakes happen. The key is to learn from them and to create an atmosphere that is free of fear around mistakes. If there is a punitive atmosphere around mistakes, risk taking will become stifled, mistakes will be hidden, and blaming will dominate. And, eventually, trust will erode. Teams can use mistakes as learning opportunities. A respectful, positive, and caring learning environment is pivotal. Here are some suggestions to make it happen:

- The team leader and team members should talk about mistakes openly without embarrassment around the team.
- Team members should respond constructively and maintain composure with a teammate who has made a mistake.
- Keep feedback focused on the process or problem rather than on personalities, unless the team member's behavior was the issue.
- Create strategies to immediately recover with the business, sponsors, or customers when mistakes are made.
- Have a regular team meeting agenda item on learning from experience so that others can learn from things that have happened.
- Present an award to the team member whose resolution of a mistake created the most learning for the team.

☐ **7. Allow work time for banter, rapport building, and small talk.** Team effectiveness can be enhanced when the people on the team really respect each other and get along. It's a good sign when team members are talking and laughing with one another, as long as the environment stays productive. Don't view banter and small talk as a waste of time—it is a sign of healthy rapport among team members. Save time before, during, or after meetings for members to socialize and catch up on things in general that may be company-related or personal. Some teams develop rituals to make this happen on their own. When it comes to virtual teams, small talk takes shape through tools like instant messaging, chat rooms, and electronic bulletin boards.

☐ **8. Encourage and support fellow team members.** Team members are generally willing to work hard if they are respected and valued. Low productivity happens when team members feel discouraged, rejected, daunted, and overall, less confident. Team members are empowered and thrive in an atmosphere that supports them. In a supportive environment, team members compliment and appreciate each other's work. And when one or some team members are struggling, the others happily lend a hand. Rather than shunning a person for failing, the team finds a way to help him/her be successful, recognizing that the success or failure of one affects the team overall.

13

☐ **9. Build energy and enthusiasm in the team.** Effective teams work hard and enthusiastically. They also play hard and enthusiastically. This energy and enthusiasm enables an environment for performance. When energy is high, people are motivated to succeed. You don't have to ask members to put in extra time, they just do it. They hit targets with minimal direction. They find creative ways to knock down barriers. Outsiders and onlookers can sense the energy. They also can feel it when they enter the team's space. The energy attracts others to join the team. The energy cannot be mandated or prescribed by the leader or the organization. It just happens. And it happens primarily from the interactions of the team members. If your team is lacking this energy, use a facilitator or coach to help determine why things seem flat. Or get feedback from people outside the team. The feedback can help pinpoint, or at least surface, some issues that might be dragging down the team.

☐ **10. Build relationships by understanding team members' preferences.** Part of building effective team relationships comes from understanding each other. Some people are more energized by active discussion, while others prefer to reflect on data before weighing in. Different people have different ways of taking in information, making decisions, and organizing the way they go about their work. Friction in the team can develop if members don't have an understanding of and appreciation for these differences. A way to accelerate relationship building and get team members to know each other better is through a personality or style assessment exercise. There are many different tools out there that the team can use—Myers-Briggs®, DiSC®, Golden Personality Type Profiler™, Social Styles—to name a few. Whatever the tool, the goal should be to help team members understand each other better. This is also a great way to build relationships with virtual team members. Without frequent face-to-face interaction, it's impossible to catch non-verbal signals. A baseline understanding of how virtual team members prefer to work and interact minimizes this disadvantage. Everyone takes the assessment and debriefs the results together. Role play or do simulations that show how styles or preferences play out in the team. Enlist the help of a facilitator or coach expert in this area. The end result will be a unified language for the team around personality and work-style preferences and a greater appreciation of how complementary, diverse styles enable the team to be most effective.

Suggested Readings

Duarte, D. L., & Snyder, N. T. (2006). *Mastering virtual teams: Strategies, tools, and techniques that succeed* (3rd ed.). San Francisco: Jossey-Bass.

Fisher, K., Rayner, S., Belgard, W., & the Belgard-Fisher-Rayner Team. (1995). *Tips for teams: A ready reference for solving common team problems* (2nd ed.). New York: McGraw-Hill.

Hertel, G., Geister, S., & Konradt, U. (2005). Managing virtual teams: A review of current empirical research. *Human Resource Management Review, 15*(1), 69-95.

Hinds, P. J., & Weisband, S. P. (2003). Knowledge sharing and shared understanding in virtual teams. In C. B. Gibson & S. G. Cohen (Eds.), *Virtual teams that work: Creating conditions for virtual team effectiveness* (pp. 21-36). San Francisco: Jossey-Bass.

Hoefling, T. (2003). *Working virtually: Managing people for successful virtual teams and organizations.* Sterling, VA: Stylus.

Katzenbach, J. R., & Smith, D. K. (1993). *The wisdom of teams.* New York: HarperCollins.

Kaye, B., & Jordan-Evans, S. (2008). *Love 'em or lose 'em. Getting good people to stay* (4th ed.). San Francisco: Berrett-Koehler Publishers.

Nemiro, J., Beyerlein, M. M., Bradley, L., & Beyerlein, S. (Eds.). (2008). *The handbook of high-performance virtual teams: A toolkit for collaborating across boundaries.* San Francisco: Jossey-Bass.

Parker, G. M. (2008). *Team players and teamwork: New strategies for developing successful collaboration* (2nd ed.). San Francisco: Jossey-Bass.

Robbins, H., & Finley, M. (2000). *The new why teams don't work: What goes wrong and how to make it right.* San Francisco: Berrett-Koehler Publishers.

Surplus, S. H. (2004). Motivating the troops: Moving from the power of "me" to the power of "we." *Supervision, 65*(4), 9-12.

Vukotich, G. (2008). *Breaking the chains of culture: Building trust in individuals, teams, and organizations.* Charleston, SC: Booksurge.

13

Translation to the Leadership Architect® Competency Library

In order for a team or individuals on a team to perform well in this area, these are the competencies that would most likely be in play. Aside from a team improvement plan where everybody works on the same thing, some individual team members may need to work on some of these competencies. A critical number (but not necessarily all) of team members would have to be good at:

Mission Critical:	**Important:**	**Nice to Have:**
36. Motivating Others	26. Humor	29. Integrity and Trust
60. *Building Effective* Teams	27. Informing	65. *Managing* Vision and Purpose
	42. Peer Relationships	
	53. *Drive for* Results	

In addition to the 10 tips listed for this dimension, there are additional tips that may apply from *FYI For Your Improvement*™. Below are the four items from the Team Architect® that make up this dimension. The item number appears to the left of each item. Immediately below the text of each item are competency and tip numbers from *FYI*. The competency is listed first (from 1 to 67), followed by the tip number (1 to 10). For example, 33-4 refers to competency 33 (Listening), tip number 4. The tips are generally written for individual development, so some adaptation might be needed in the team context.

13. The team has an identity; it is not just a collection of individuals.
    36-3,10; 60-1,3,6,7,8; 110-1,2,4

31. Team members enjoy working on this team.
    27-2,3; 36-3,10; 60-1,3,6,7,8; 110-4

49. The team has a positive atmosphere that is commented on by those outside the team.
    36-3,10; 42-2,5,6; 53-6; 60-1,3,4,7

67. The whole team celebrates its successes.
    36-3,10; 60-1,3,7; 110-1,2,8,9

Dimension 14
Managing Process

Definition:
Team is process driven, uses effective work processes to identify and solve problems, and uses best practices to streamline processes for optimal performance.

Addresses the question:
Are the processes the team uses to do its work efficient and effective?

A Dimension in the TEAMING SKILLS Factor
Operating the team's business efficiently and effectively.

> *It is a fact that in the right formation, the lifting power of many wings can achieve twice the distance of any bird flying alone.*
> – Author Unknown

Items
14. The team spots problems early and works to eliminate them.
32. Team meetings are effective and accomplish their agenda.
50. The team is process-driven; it is relentless in streamlining workflows.
68. The team is excellent at designing new processes that work well the first time.

Unskilled
- ☐ Team work processes are haphazard and ineffective
- ☐ Team seldom does things right the first time; is constantly in fix-it mode
- ☐ Team has a not-invented-here mentality and does not seek out best practices
- ☐ Team members do not anticipate problems or roadblocks
- ☐ Team members let process problems fester for too long
- ☐ There is redundancy and waste in the team's processes
- ☐ Team does not accept responsibility for process breakdowns
- ☐ Team does not have an effective problem-resolution process
- ☐ Team has trouble implementing total work systems or continuous process-improvement practices

14

133

Skilled

☐ The team develops best practice processes that are leveraged by others

☐ The team readily scouts for and uses process best practices from others

☐ The team is always tinkering with processes and reengineering for optimal performance

☐ The team places a high value on efficient and effective processes and workflows

☐ The team has measurement systems that provide early warnings on broken processes

☐ The team knows how to organize people and work activities for maximum efficiency

☐ The team regularly examines work processes

☐ The team anticipates problems and makes process adjustments to overcome problems and roadblocks

☐ The team is capable of designing processes and systems that allow distance managing

Overused

☐ The team's emphasis on single best methods chills innovation and creativity

☐ The team reacts immediately to perceived workflow problems without understanding the true impact of the issues

☐ The team spends too much time looking for problems

☐ Team members may be overly critical of one another and leave scars that are difficult to repair

☐ Team spends too much time perfecting processes at the expense of net productivity

☐ Team meetings are so focused on the agenda that they resist needed detours to raise unexpected problems

☐ It is extremely hard for a new team member to fit in because everything is so specified and certain

Note on overused strengths: Overused skills and disproportionately used strengths tend to have the negative effects listed above. To decrease those negative consequences, you have two alternatives. You can scale down or use the strength less, or you can compensate for it with another skill or behavior. In practice, it is very difficult to get an individual or a team to use a strength less. In most cases, the best path is to develop compensators. Team Architect® Dimensions that can compensate for overusing this dimension and compensating skills from the Leadership Architect® Library's 67 Competencies are listed below.

14

(Note: Team Dimension numbers are listed in parentheses. Competencies are listed in numerical order by competency number.)

Compensating Team Dimensions:
- ☐ Thrust Management (1)
- ☐ Thrust Clarity (2)
- ☐ Resource Management (9)
- ☐ Delivering the Goods (18)

Compensating Competencies:
- ☐ 7. Caring About Direct Reports
- ☐ 28. Innovation Management
- ☐ 36. Motivating Others
- ☐ 38. Organizational Agility
- ☐ 50. Priority Setting
- ☐ 51. Problem Solving

Some Causes of Poor Performance
- ☐ Team members avoid the conflict that occurs when existing processes and workflows are challenged
- ☐ Team members are not process oriented; not systems oriented
- ☐ Organization does not value best practices for process improvement
- ☐ Members resist input from outside the team
- ☐ Team has high turnover; takes too long to onboard new members
- ☐ Team demonstrates arrogance
- ☐ Team members are impatient with process design
- ☐ Team members lack process design skills
- ☐ Things don't stay the same long enough for results to be measured

The Map

High-performing teams understand the importance of efficiency. Tight work processes. Little to no wasted motion. Top teams stay ahead of the curve on process innovation. They are among the first to road test the latest in process improvement and methods for maximizing efficiency. And they review their processes. Constantly. They use during- and after-action review to assess their workflows. These teams apply research-based and experience-tested systems to design their workflows and processes. Methods such as process reengineering, human factors engineering, workspace design, quality engineering, statistical process control, and Six Sigma. These are systems-oriented disciplines that generally start with outcomes and the customer in mind and design processes

14

to deliver desired outcomes with the least amount of friction, time, and cost. The methods also include a measurement element so the team can monitor results and a continuous improvement component that constantly looks for opportunities for improvement. In many studies of unexamined workflow, there is 85% downtime when the work is simply suspended between steps or people. You can't have a high-performing work team without effective and efficient processes. That takes discipline and technology.

Some Remedies

☐ **1. Select workflow technologies that fit team objectives.** There are many workflow systems to choose from. Before considering any particular one, the team needs to know what it is looking to achieve in designing or improving processes. Is the goal to eliminate waste? Consider Six Sigma, which sees any variation to the overall process as redundant. (GE is a good example of Six Sigma in action.) Or, does the team want to shed any activity that doesn't add customer value? Then lean manufacturing is worth exploring. Hammer and Champy's process reengineering looks at designing agile processes that can shift easily in a rapidly changing environment. ISO provides a framework for standardization. Whatever the method, the objective is to see which of those various methods will best fit the work of the team. Have each member study a technique and report to the team on his/her findings. Many organizations already use one or more of these techniques. Check with others in the organization to determine if there is already a group that uses any of the technologies. Invite them in to present what they are doing. Remember that workflow or process technologies are a means to an end. Start with the team's objectives, then pick the technology that will help the team meet its process goals.

☐ **2. Do a study of workflow efficiency and effectiveness.** Using one or more of the methods described above, perform a study of the current workflows used by the team. Lay out each process step-by-step to see if each step is really necessary and how much each step costs in terms of resources. Starting from the customer, design each process with as few steps and with the least resources possible. Look for unnecessary signatures. Unnecessary reviews. Decisions that get stuck in the in-box of an out-of-the-office member. Look for where the most errors occur. How can they be prevented? Look for late deliveries or missed milestones. Unnecessary features the customer didn't ask for. Unneeded permissions. Blocked access to resources. Learn how to use workflow software and apply it to the critical processes the team uses to perform.

☐ **3. Hire a process expert or consultant to help.** Sometimes it is best to leave things to the experts. There are many process methods available

14

in the market. If your team is under time pressures, inexperienced with process improvement methods, or if the project has high stakes, consider hiring a process consultant or consulting organization that specializes in your industry. Check references to ensure customer satisfaction. Find out who will be your lead consultant and supporting consultants. Engage the consulting firm to "transfer the technology" to the team. This means not only analyzing the processes, but training the team how to do it on their own in the future.

☐ **4. Recognize common process breakdowns.** Search for trends where high-frequency and high-impact problems occur with the processes. Some common reasons for breakdowns in processes include:

– Duplicate steps or work.
– Unnecessary, non-value-adding steps.
– Excessively time-consuming activities.
– Manual work that might be easily automated.
– Overly complex steps.
– Steps that can be combined.
– Steps or activities in the wrong sequence.
– Lack of compliance with certain steps.
– Steps frequently resulting in waste or rework.
– Steps that result in user or customer complaints.
– Missing steps that are typically added by performers.

Once the team has identified one or more breakdowns, determine adjustments that need to be made in response. Not all processes need to be reengineered; instead, they may simply need tweaking. Others may only require clarification. Maybe some people haven't been informed about how the process works. Or, maybe they have not fully understood communications and training regarding the process.

☐ **5. Create standardized process outcome measures.** Process measures ensure that disconnects and breakdowns do not creep back into the process. The measures should be developed to reflect the extent to which the process produces the desired outputs, the degree to which certain steps have been performed, or both. Outcome measures help teams stay on course and allow for performance benchmarking. Here are some key steps to follow when creating standardized process measures:

– Step 1: Identify subprocesses or activities within the team that are most closely linked to the team's primary products and services. This should be the work most crucial to meeting customer and business results.

14

137

– Step 2: Narrow the work to measure (in Step #1) down to the most critical processes. They should be processes that add the most value to the customer and advance the business.

– Step 3: Carefully quantify the outputs of the processes.

– Step 4: Flowchart the processes and subprocesses to help identify the steps or activities worthy of measurement.

☐ **6. Make work processes and measures open and visible.** Ever notice how athletes keep their eyes on the clock and the scoreboard? They continually monitor their progress against time and the competition in an effort to win. Publish the team processes and measures so that the activities of planning, assigning, monitoring, and measuring of work processes are clear. Post them in the workplace and on the team's virtual space. Use signs or technology to post team goals, processes, data, and progress toward accomplishment. That's the idea behind the United Way Thermometer. The scoreboard that displays number of days without a lost-time injury. Constant reminders such as these place focus on what's important. They involve, motivate, and engage individuals.

☐ **7. Assign team members to search for best practices outside the team.** On a regular basis, have team members scout and scan for best practices outside the team—both inside and outside the organization. What do other top teams do well with their processes? On the flip side, have the team analyze epic team failures where process breakdowns were the cause. Have each member report back what they find and use the data to inform team processes going forward.

☐ **8. Audit team processes regularly.** One way to ensure that team processes are effective is to ensure that they are reviewed, monitored, and continually improved. Make this a standard team meeting agenda item. The process review can be done in person or via audio- or videoconference. Make sure all team members have an opportunity to provide input into the reviews. Solicit feedback from stakeholders inside and outside the team. Determine if processes are really meeting customer and business requirements. After gathering data, figure out how to fix any broken processes and brainstorm how to replicate those processes that are functioning well.

☐ **9. Do roadblock scenario planning.** On a periodic basis, have the team take one process at a time and perform a roadblock analysis. The task is to envision what could go wrong. Play out various scenarios where there are breakdowns in the processes the team uses to produce its products and services. Look for substandard quality. Misplaced orders. Misunderstood specifications from the customer. Delivery errors. Badly handled customer-service inquiries. Typos in instructions. Missing parts. Tool inadequacies. Errant invoices. Payments not logged properly. By thinking about all of the

14

things that could go wrong, the team can design checks and balances so that all of the bad things that could happen won't.

☐ **10. Use technology to monitor team processes.** In today's increasingly virtual workplace, team leaders can get a better handle on team work processes with the assistance of technology. Process monitoring options range from the basic—such as time-tracking software—to complex, rules-driven systems like Electronic Performance Monitoring (EPM), the 21st century equivalent of time and motion studies. Organizations should carefully consider work and organization design when they choose technology to use with their processes for things like manufacturing or service work. Many teams and companies make the mistake of thinking technology first and workflow or process second. Don't separate work design from technology. When technology is chosen in advance or as a stand-alone effort, it can have a limiting effect on workflow options.

Suggested Readings

Beyerlein, M. M., Freedman, S., McGee, C., & Moran, L. (2003). *Beyond teams: Building the collaborative organization.* San Francisco: Jossey-Bass/Pfeiffer.

Carr, D. K., & Johansson, H. J. (1995). *Best practices in reengineering.* New York: McGraw-Hill.

Chinowsky, P. S., & Rojas, E. M. (2003). Virtual teams: Guide to successful implementation. *Journal of Management in Engineering, 19*(3), 98-106.

Davenport, T. H. (2005). The coming commoditization of processes. *Harvard Business Review, 83*(6), 100-108.

Duarte, D. L., & Snyder, N. T. (2006). *Mastering virtual teams: Strategies, tools, and techniques that succeed* (3rd ed.). San Francisco: Jossey-Bass.

Garton, C., & Wegryn, K. (2006). *Managing without walls: Maximize success with virtual, global, and cross-cultural teams.* Lewisville, TX: MC Press.

Gibson, C. B., & Cohen, S. G. (Eds.). (2003). *Virtual teams that work: Creating conditions for virtual team effectiveness.* San Francisco: Jossey-Bass.

Hammer, M., & Champy, J. (2003). *Reengineering the corporation.* New York, NY: HarperCollins Publishers.

Hertel, G., Geister, S., & Konradt, U. (2005). Managing virtual teams: A review of current empirical research. *Human Resource Management Review, 15*(1), 69-95.

Jones, S. D., & Schilling, D. J. (2000). *Measuring team performance: A step-by-step, customizable approach for managers, facilitators, and team leaders.* San Francisco: Jossey-Bass.

Lawler, E. E., III. (2000). *From the ground up: Six principles for building the new logic corporation.* San Francisco: Jossey-Bass.

Malhotra, A., Majchrzak, A., & Rosen, B. (2007). Leading virtual teams. *Academy of Management Perspectives, 21*(1), 60-70.

14

Translation to the Leadership Architect® Competency Library

In order for a team or individuals on a team to perform well in this area, these are the competencies that would most likely be in play. Aside from a team improvement plan where everybody works on the same thing, some individual team members may need to work on some of these competencies. A critical number (but not necessarily all) of team members would have to be good at:

Mission Critical:	Important:	Nice to Have:
51. Problem Solving	53. *Drive for* Results	1. Action Oriented
52. Process Management	63. Total Work Systems	16. *Timely* Decision Making
		32. Learning on the Fly
		47. Planning
		50. Priority Setting

In addition to the ten tips listed for this dimension, there are additional tips that may apply from *FYI For Your Improvement*™. Below are the four items from the Team Architect® that make up this dimension. The item number appears to the left of each item. Immediately below the text of each item are competency and tip numbers from *FYI*. The competency is listed first (from 1 to 67), followed by the tip number (1 to 10). For example, 33-4 refers to competency 33 (Listening), tip number 4. The tips are generally written for individual development, so some adaptation might be needed in the team context.

14. The team spots problems early and works to eliminate them.
    16-2,3; 32-2,3; 51-1,3; 52-3,6,8; 63-1

32. Team meetings are effective and accomplish their agenda.
    16-3; 27-2,4,6; 35-2; 47-1; 50-2,3; 62-3,10

50. The team is process-driven; it is relentless in streamlining workflows.
    51-1,3; 52-3,4,6,8; 63-1,2,3,6

68. The team is excellent at designing new processes that work well the first time.
    51-1,3; 52-3,4,6,8; 62-1,2,3,6

14

Dimension 15
Focusing

Definition:
Team is customer focused, prioritizes critical tasks but shifts easily as things change, and meets goals and targets.

Addresses the question:
Does the team have trouble setting and following priorities?

A Dimension in the TASK SKILLS Factor
The effort necessary to execute successfully.

> *Concentrate all your thoughts upon the work at hand.*
> *The sun's rays do not burn until brought to a focus.*
> Alexander Graham Bell – Scottish-born American scientist,
> inventor, and innovator

Items
15. The team focuses more on its customers than on itself.
33. The team's strategies are insightful and successful.
51. The team's tactics and annual plans are on target.
69. The team focuses on the critical-few priorities; it is not easily diverted.

Unskilled
☐ The team tries to focus on too many things at once
☐ The team doesn't focus enough attention on the customer
☐ The team has too much of an inward focus
☐ Team members are too tactical
☐ Team expends so much energy on urgencies that priorities suffer
☐ The team has a hit-and-miss approach to priority setting
☐ Team members spend too much time on unimportant things
☐ Team members are easily distracted
☐ Team members prefer working on fun, exciting things at the expense of staying focused on what's important
☐ The team struggles when priorities shift

15

☐ The team is surprised by changing trends and shifts in customer requirements

☐ Team members are impatient and impulsive and just react as things happen

Skilled

☐ The team easily shifts focus as things change

☐ The team has measurements in place that track progress against priorities

☐ The team is constantly on the prowl for changes and trends that will affect its priorities

☐ Team members are in personal and constant touch with customers

☐ The team spends the bulk of its time and energy on agreed-upon priorities

☐ Each major action the team takes is first tested against its priorities

☐ The team sheds activities that draw its attention away from critical tasks

☐ The team sets clear, specific, and realistic goals

☐ Team members seek feedback from customers and stakeholders to stay focused on progress

☐ Team members have a clear understanding of priorities

☐ Team members are experts in their customers' businesses

☐ The team constantly reexamines priorities and strategies

Overused

☐ Team is overly responsive to customer needs to the point of ignoring important internal practices and policies

☐ Team members are workaholics

☐ Team responds to unreasonable customer requests and loses focus

☐ Team oversimplifies plans

☐ Team is impatient with day-to-day, tactical details

☐ Team is too rigid with their priorities and not flexible enough to meet changing customer or organizational needs

☐ The team's focus on a few priorities chills innovation and creativity

☐ Team shifts priorities too quickly on false signs of change

☐ Team gets out ahead of its customers before the anticipated need becomes viable in the marketplace

Note on overused strengths: Overused skills and disproportionately used strengths tend to have the negative effects listed above. To decrease those negative consequences, you have two alternatives. You can scale down or use the strength less, or you can compensate for it with another skill or

15

behavior. In practice, it is very difficult to get an individual or a team to use a strength less. In most cases, the best path is to develop compensators. Team Architect® Dimensions that can compensate for overusing this dimension and compensating skills from the Leadership Architect® Library's 67 Competencies are listed below.

(Note: Team Dimension numbers are listed in parentheses. Competencies are listed in numerical order by competency number.)

Compensating Team Dimensions:
- ☐ Thrust Management (1)
- ☐ Thrust Clarity (2)
- ☐ Team Learning (10)
- ☐ Managing Process (14)
- ☐ Delivering the Goods (18)

Compensating Competencies:
- ☐ 2. *Dealing with* Ambiguity
- ☐ 9. Command Skills
- ☐ 12. Conflict Management
- ☐ 28. Innovation Management
- ☐ 41. Patience
- ☐ 53. *Drive for* Results
- ☐ 58. Strategic Agility
- ☐ 65. *Managing* Vision and Purpose

Some Causes of Poor Performance
- ☐ Team members are undisciplined and disorganized
- ☐ Team members don't manage time well
- ☐ Team doesn't plan
- ☐ Team doesn't manage and measure work
- ☐ Team has one or more lagging performers
- ☐ Individual team members do not agree with the priorities
- ☐ Team isn't customer focused
- ☐ Team doesn't have enough direct interaction with customers
- ☐ Team is in constant crisis mode
- ☐ Team has no goals

15

The Map

Finite resources. Multiple demands. Better get used to it. Most individuals, teams, and organizations face more demands on their time and skills than they have to give. The key is to separate the mission-critical few from the trivial many. High-performing teams identify early which activities are key to achieving their objectives. That's where the best teams focus their energy. Focus with laser precision. A focus that effectively blocks out the noise and distractions that can derail priorities. The best teams focus without becoming rigid. As business demands shift, high-functioning teams need to be nimble. If a team's focus is too intense, it's hard to change course. On the other hand, without focus, teams run the risk of spreading resources too thin, performing the wrong tasks, and jeopardizing team effectiveness and morale. If there is little or no focus, the team will have a hard time defining what's important, and team leaders will have nothing tangible to get the team to rally behind. Unfocused teams can get caught up in activity without purpose, be in a constant reactive or crisis mode, and be vulnerable to the whims of any stakeholder with a need. Any good manager, any successful team leader understands the importance of focusing team efforts on the mission-critical few. Be both focused and agile. Don't get distracted. Match resources with what you can and must deliver.

Some Remedies

☐ **1. Set specific, clear, and measurable goals.** Goal setting is more complex than telling people to do their best. It's about providing direction and setting performance expectations to guide behavior. Armed with specific goals, team members are able to prioritize which tasks they should focus on in their daily work. Clear goals reduce uncertainty and ambiguity. Everyone knows exactly what to do. Goals that have quantifiable measures let team members know what success will look like and how their efforts will be evaluated. Goals like the ones described here are especially important in a virtual team environment. For team members that don't physically sit together, it is easier to get distracted by outside-the-team work demands. Having clear and measurable goals helps these team members stay focused on team objectives, regardless of physical proximity. Post team goals in the workplace and on any other media that is viewable by the entire team.

☐ **2. Align the team's efforts with the organization's strategy, vision, and goals.** Team goals need to be aligned with the organizational goals and translated into the team's priorities. The clearer the line of sight, the easier it is for the team to stay aligned. A clear line of sight is especially critical

15

for virtual teams since they are more at risk to drift from the team focus and become fragmented. Here are some steps to align team goals with organizational goals:

- Get a clear understanding of the organization-wide vision, mission, strategies, and goals. Invite someone from the organization who is familiar with the vision, mission, strategies, and goals to present them to the team. Encourage the team to ask lots of clarifying questions. Ask about the assumptions that were used to create the vision. Ask about the risks and unknowns. Ask about any future scenarios that may affect the vision. Ask what the organization expects from this specific team.

- In a team meeting, solicit suggestions about what parts of the organization-wide vision, mission, strategies, and goals this team can add value to and support. Whether it's increased market penetration, better cost management, opening new territories, or being the leader in customer service, most teams will find pieces and parts of the organization-wide thrust they can become part of.

- With as much precision as possible, have the team outline the specific subgoals and tactics that support the organization thrust.

- Put all of the goals and tactics together into one plan to see if they are attainable, given the resources of the team.

- Set measures ahead of time that will help the team track its performance against team goals.

- Present the plan back to the person or function who presented the organization thrust to find out if they see the plan as aligned and on target.

- Make any adjustments that might be necessary and execute the plan.

☐ **3. Prioritize team work efforts.** The reality is that organizations have more opportunities than they can possibly address with their resources. Priorities help to leverage scarce resources in the team. What needs to be accomplished? What is the time frame? What resources will be needed? Does the team have a resource allocation plan? Using team goals, separate what the team needs to do into mission critical, important to get done, nice if there is time left over, and not central to what the team is trying to achieve. When faced with choices or multiple things to do, apply this scale and always choose the highest priority. Keep in mind that picking a few critical priorities means rejecting or delaying others. Each rejected priority has one or more customers. Many times teams do not have as much of a problem rank ordering priorities as they do saying no to stakeholders of tasks not selected. Make the team's prioritization process transparent so that everyone involved has an understanding of criteria used.

☐ **4. Meet periodically to reassess priorities.** The team's priorities will likely change. This might occur as a result of the larger organization changing its strategy or structure, customer requirements shifting, marketplace trends, or even a change in team membership and leadership. The team's activities and priorities need to be examined on a regular basis to reinforce shared understanding and direction, especially for virtual teams that are highly susceptible to focus drift. The team should keep its priorities and goals posted in the workplace and on the virtual space so team members see them every day. Use team meetings to review the work priorities of the group and of each individual. Help team members prioritize the work they have on their plates by keeping all good ideas on the list, but moving them up or down so the team can focus on its top priorities.

☐ **5. Start with the customer and do a value chain analysis.** One way to set priorities is to perform a value chain analysis. The process starts with what the customer wants, needs, will pay for, or has requested. Then the planning process unfolds backwards. In order to get customers what they want, we would need to be able to do...? In order to do that, we would need to be able to...? And so on. Then each step is resourced. What resources are needed to accomplish the right process outcomes for each step? Who is going to be responsible for making sure that step is accomplished in sequence, on time, and at or under budget? Focusing on what customers need and want will ensure that resources—people, knowledge, technology, and facilities—are deployed effectively.

☐ **6. Install a trend/change scanning process.** Things change. New competitors emerge. Markets close, others open. New technology appears. Regulatory controls tighten. Customer needs change. Teams can lose time and waste resources during change. Instead of waiting for something to happen, teams need to anticipate and plan for change. Teams that adopt a proactive approach to change explore possibilities that might cause priorities to shift. When the team initially sets its priorities, extend the discussion to include what the team would do if things change. Do a change analysis, listing likely change inside the team, to the organization in which the team resides, to the customers of the team, to the resources, and to the world outside the organization. Do change-scenario planning to predetermine how the team would change if anticipated change occurs. Have each member report periodically to the rest of the team, suggesting the most likely changes. Have the team play out the change in terms of what the team would need to do to adjust. Sometimes change planning isn't enough. In these cases, teams can still be proactive by having a scanning discipline to detect internal and external change. When the early signs of change are detected, assemble the team and modify and adjust the plan.

15

□ **7. Solicit feedback from customers.** If the team is going to succeed, everyone on the team must intimately understand customer requirements. If the team wants its members to demonstrate extraordinary service, individuals should be able to easily identify customer needs and expectations. If you want to find out what customers want, you need to ask them. There are several ways to do this:

  – Direct contact with customers. Direct contact with customers can be very informative for team members, especially if the organization is in the type of business where most employees may not normally have routine customer contact. Use focus groups or customer forums and have team members ask customers how the team is doing as the provider of a product or service. Ask detailed questions such as: What do we do best? What could we do better? What would you like to see us do differently?

  – Survey your customers. Most companies survey their employees annually. Why not survey your customers too? The goal is to gather more detailed data on key customer requirements. These include things like quality, accuracy, timeliness, value, comparison to the competition, and likelihood to become a repeat customer. Gather this data and communicate the findings to the wider organization so resources can be aligned to respond to the customer feedback.

  – Assign team members to specific customer groups—geographic or, better yet, by industry. Team members can become the team's subject-matter experts for their assigned customer group, building relationships and learning about their customer's business, even their customer's competitors.

□ **8. Plan the work and then work the plan.** There are really two parts to the equation of focusing on team objectives. The first is to develop a plan that, if executed, will accomplish the objectives. The second is executing the plan. There won't be traction for execution unless the plan is readily visible and understood. Ensure that team members truly grasp the plan details. Engage all in planning and prioritizing work activities. Research has found that one of the best ways to get people engaged and committed is to ask for their input, especially when the work is taking shape. Make sure that all team members understand and agree with the plan. Try to reduce the overall work plan to individual plans so each member has a clear template of what he/she needs to do. Throughout the year, keep referring back to the plan for guidance.

□ **9. Stay on track.** Be diligent. Even with a solid plan, teams sometimes are distracted by situations perceived as crises or by activities that are seen as more enjoyable. Enthusiastic, high-energy teams can have a tendency

15

to jump into too many things at once. Any of these team behaviors can result in the team heading off course, potentially missing goals, frustrating members, and lowering productivity. If the team starts to get off track, consider some of the following tips:

- Pace the team efforts. Make sure team members aren't starting on the work before the plan is solid and resources have been properly allocated.

- Verify that all team work activities support the team plan and goals. If not, is the plan still valid? Or are the activities underway not the most important things for the team to be working on now?

- Maintain an eye on process. Is the team being slowed down by inefficient workflows?

☐ **10. Watch out for too much focus on work.** Sometimes there is a fine line between a passion for work and an obsession with it. By placing too much focus on work, team members' lives can get out of whack. If one or more members of the team seem significantly out of balance, spending too much time at work, analyze the cause. Is the team understaffed? Are the objectives unrealistic? Are some members not carrying their fair share of the load? Do some processes run inefficiently and require long hours? Work with the team leader to identify possible solutions and intervene with team members who are crossing the line.

15

Suggested Readings

Atkinson, P. (2003). Shaping a vision – Living the values. *Management Services, 47*(2), 8-11.

Brake, T. (2006). Leading global virtual teams. *Industrial & Commercial Training, 38*(3), 116-121.

Duarte, D. L., & Snyder, N. T. (2006). *Mastering virtual teams: Strategies, tools, and techniques that succeed* (3rd ed.). San Francisco: Jossey-Bass.

Garton, C., & Wegryn, K. (2006). *Managing without walls: Maximize success with virtual, global, and cross-cultural teams.* Lewisville, TX: MC Press.

Hackman, J. R. (2002). *Leading teams: Setting the stage for great performances.* Boston: Harvard Business School Press.

Hunsaker, P. L., & Hunsaker, J. S. (2008). Virtual teams: A leader's guide. *Team Performance Management, 14*(1/2), 86-101.

Jones, S. D., & Schilling, D. J. (2000). *Measuring team performance: A step-by-step, customizable approach for managers, facilitators, and team leaders.* San Francisco: Jossey-Bass.

Katzenbach, J. R., & Smith, D. K. (2005). The discipline of teams. *Harvard Business Review, 83*(7/8), 162-171.

LaFasto, F., & Larson, C. (2001). *When teams work best.* Thousand Oaks, CA: Sage.

Lawler, E. E., III. (2000). *From the ground up: Six principles for building the new logic corporation.* San Francisco: Jossey-Bass.

Thompson, L. L. (2004). *Making the team: A guide for managers* (2nd ed.). Upper Saddle River, NJ: Pearson.

15

Translation to the Leadership Architect® Competency Library

In order for a team or individuals on a team to perform well in this area, these are the competencies that would most likely be in play. Aside from a team improvement plan where everybody works on the same thing, some individual team members may need to work on some of these competencies. A critical number (but not necessarily all) of team members would have to be good at:

Mission Critical:	**Important:**	**Nice to Have:**
15. Customer Focus	5. Business Acumen	35. Managing and
50. Priority Setting	46. Perspective	Measuring Work
	47. Planning	58. Strategic Agility
	53. *Drive for* Results	65. *Managing* Vision and
		Purpose

In addition to the 10 tips listed for this dimension, there are additional tips that may apply from *FYI For Your Improvement™*. Below are the four items from the Team Architect® that make up this dimension. The item number appears to the left of each item. Immediately below the text of each item are competency and tip numbers from *FYI*. The competency is listed first (from 1 to 67), followed by the tip number (1 to 10). For example, 33-4 refers to competency 33 (Listening), tip number 4. The tips are generally written for individual development, so some adaptation might be needed in the team context.

15. The team focuses more on its customers than on itself.
    15-1,3,4,5,8,9; 46-1; 53-1; 63-1,6

33. The team's strategies are insightful and successful.
    2-1,5; 5-6; 15-3; 46-3,9; 58-3; 65-10; 101-2,6

51. The team's tactics and annual plans are on target.
    5-6; 15-1,4; 16-2,3; 46-3; 47-1,3,7; 50-3

69. The team focuses on the critical-few priorities; it is not easily diverted.
    16-3; 35-1,7; 43-1,2; 50-2,3,6; 53-3,4

Dimension 16
Assignment Flexibility

Definition:
Team members are assigned work flexibly, have sufficient autonomy over their work, and share and balance workloads.

Addresses the question:
Do team members pitch in and help others get their work done?

A Dimension in the TASK SKILLS Factor
The effort necessary to execute successfully.

> *Light is the task where many share the toil.*
> Homer (8th century BCE) – Greek poet

Items
16. The team assigns work flexibly to team members.
34. Team members pitch in and share the load.
52. Team members have the autonomy needed to do their work.
70. The team uses cross-training so team members can fill in for one another.

Unskilled
☐ Team rigidly assigns certain work to certain members
☐ Some team members carry greater workloads than others
☐ Team does not give members developmental assignments outside their areas of expertise
☐ Team members don't do more than the minimum assigned workload
☐ Team members don't help each other
☐ Team members don't cross-train to cover one another
☐ Team members are micromanaged
☐ Some team members act like martyrs when asked to pitch in and help others
☐ Team members act as lone individuals rather than team players
☐ Each team member stays so busy that there is no time left for anything else
☐ Jobs are narrow in scope and have boundaries that are too defined and rigid
☐ Team members are not acknowledged or rewarded for helping each other

Skilled

- ☐ Primary roles are clear in the team
- ☐ Team members show interest in what other team members are doing
- ☐ Team members volunteer their help before they have to be asked
- ☐ The team sets aside time for learning from others inside the team
- ☐ Jobs are designed so that everybody does a little bit of everything
- ☐ Team members know each other's expertise, skills, knowledge, and abilities
- ☐ Team members are given considerable freedom and discretion in deciding how to carry out their tasks
- ☐ Team members willingly step out of their areas of specialization to assist the team
- ☐ Team members learn from each other so that they can fill in for one another
- ☐ Team members are rewarded for sharing and balancing the work
- ☐ The team naturally looks for ways to build skills; cross-training and other developmental opportunities are the norm

Overused

- ☐ Team is too loose in the way it distributes work
- ☐ Team members are jacks-of-all-trades and masters of none
- ☐ Team members spend so much time helping one another that they don't get their individual assignments completed on time
- ☐ Team carries one or more lagging performers whose work is done by others
- ☐ It's hard for people outside the team to know whom to go to on an issue
- ☐ Team has trouble focusing on the critical-few tasks it needs to do
- ☐ Team members expect so much variety that they have trouble getting their routine core tasks accomplished
- ☐ Team members spend too much time looking for new things to learn and do
- ☐ New team members have difficulty adjusting to the extent of assignment flexibility
- ☐ Team members have trouble when they move on to other teams with less internal flexibility

Note on overused strengths: Overused skills and disproportionately used strengths tend to have the negative effects listed above. To decrease those negative consequences, you have two alternatives. You can scale down or use the strength less, or you can compensate for it with another skill or

behavior. In practice, it is very difficult to get an individual or a team to use a strength less. In most cases, the best path is to develop compensators. Team Architect® Dimensions that can compensate for overusing this dimension and compensating skills from the Leadership Architect® Library's 67 Competencies are listed below.

(Note: Team Dimension numbers are listed in parentheses. Competencies are listed in numerical order by competency number.)

Compensating Team Dimensions:

☐ Talent Allocation and Deployment (8)
☐ Managing Process (14)
☐ Focusing (15)
☐ Delivering the Goods (18)
☐ Team Leader Fit (20)

Compensating Competencies:

☐ 13. Confronting Direct Reports
☐ 39. Organizing
☐ 50. Priority Setting
☐ 53. *Drive for* Results

Some Causes of Poor Performance

☐ The work of the team doesn't lend itself to cross-training; the work is too specialized
☐ Some team members have a fear of failing when they work outside their areas of specialty
☐ Some team members can't deal with the ambiguity of flexible work assignments
☐ Team prefers organization and task structure
☐ Team is rigid, inflexible
☐ Team leader is poor at delegating
☐ Team members are too specialized for cross-training to be practical
☐ Some team members overdo work/life balance
☐ Some team members are workaholics
☐ Team is not made up of learners
☐ Team members prefer to work on their own and at their own pace
☐ Team members are comfortable in their specialties

The Map

Teamwork. A term that gets tossed around a lot, sometimes excessively. At its core, though, teamwork is each member doing a part of the work. The emphasis is not on personal glory but rather the effectiveness of the whole. How that work is assigned and monitored can make the difference between a dysfunctional and highly effective team. In a team, each member brings a unique set of skills and talents. Successful teams know the talents of fellow members. They leverage those talents as needed. High-functioning teams understand that it's impractical for one or a few to carry an outsized share of the burden for more than the briefest of times without the team suffering. Overall balance of the workload is critical. The key question is how to achieve that balance. Build flexibility into work assignments. Make sure that there is opportunity to enhance the skills of team members on critical tasks so that when the inevitable fire drill heads the team's way, there is no shortage of talent to handle it. Cross-training is one of those one-plus-one equals three (or more) equations. Besides providing relief to the lone subject-matter expert, cross-training provides developmental opportunities for members and creates a deeper level of expertise in the team. When it comes to monitoring the work, team leaders need to exercise some balance and flexibility as well. A micromanaged team moves slower than one that's given autonomy over assignments. Set clear expectations, then give up tight control so team members can complete the work with a sense of ownership. Everyone will benefit.

Some Remedies

☐ 1. **Analyze what portion of each job might be general enough to be shared by others on the team.** Most jobs have general and specific parts to them. Some parts of the job can be performed by those with rudimentary knowledge; other parts require specialized skills. Line up all of the jobs. Do a task analysis. List the 10 main duties or tasks that make up each job. Which tasks require a high degree of specialization? Which are more general and more easily shared across the team? List the 10 in order from the most specialized to the most general. Have other team members review the tasks and put their names next to the ones they think they can do. This approach provides a system for sharing and balancing the work. You also can assign multiple people to each job: one as lead and the others as backups based upon what each member of the team puts down.

☐ **2. Design jobs so that task sharing is more possible.** Some jobs are designed so that only people with very specialized skills can do them. Others are designed so that each job has a little bit of everything in it. Most fall somewhere in the middle. For assignment flexibility to take hold in the team, it's important to try to design jobs so tasks can be evenly balanced across the team. Identify those tasks that don't require a highly specialized skill set and can therefore be more evenly distributed across the team. An added benefit to identifying general skill tasks is that it expands options for bringing talent into the team. It's easier to find someone who is skilled in the general area of the team's business than to hunt down a specialist in a particular area. Distribute the work to achieve an equal workload when possible, but be realistic. Don't sacrifice the quality and productivity of the team's output for the sake of balance. Some tasks always will be specialized due to their technical nature and the deep level of expertise needed to perform them. You don't want to have a wide, shallow pool of expertise. Look for a mix of depth and breadth when designing jobs in the team.

☐ **3. Prioritize cross-training.** The days of single-function, single-task jobs are just about gone. Instead, most people who work in teams now are required to learn a variety of roles to support their team's daily activities. Cross-training provides several benefits:
- It allows for more seamless service to customers without the hassle of being transferred or passed off to a number of people to answer questions or get results.
- It allows for cost efficiencies in the organization. Since cross-training can eliminate many process steps and handoffs, it can increase productivity and, at times, decrease the number of employees needed to provide a service or complete a task.
- It provides increased job satisfaction. Employees who are given task variety and opportunities to develop skills tend to be more engaged.

To make cross-training effective, first, identify and plan for the skills that are necessary for the team to be successful. Involve all team members in this process. Identify the time requirements that will be involved for cross-training so that productivity and service do not slip. Enlist other resources to help cover the time when the team is cross-training. Then assess each team member against the skills noted as important for the cross-training effort. Identify the largest skill gaps. Prioritize the most critical skills and people to be trained. Finally—and this is critical—follow through to maintain credibility and buy-in to the process. Remember that cross-training requires discipline. It also requires time. Too often, we make

16

excuses to not develop ourselves. We're too busy, other things are more important. Make the time. No excuses.

☐ **4. Avoid cross-training derailments.** If previous cross-training efforts have failed, determine whether training requests/needs are based on *skill* deficiencies (people don't know how) or *will* deficiencies (people don't want to) before you decide to invest more time and money in training. If lack of skill is the issue, review the skill-gap analysis. Was the gap too large, the learning curve too steep for the person to succeed? If so, consider a different cross-training opportunity for that person. If lack of motivation is derailing cross-training efforts, consider this: team members will likely be more motivated to learn a new task when they've had some input on what they are going to learn and whom they are going to learn it from. Therefore, solicit input from team members on the jobs or tasks they are interested in learning. A few things to consider:

- Ensure people meet entry-level job requirements before providing cross-training. These requirements might encompass health, safety, technical, or educational qualifications, among other things.
- Determine if the technical requirements for cross-training a particular skill create such a steep learning curve that there is an impractical time horizon for development.
- Allow people to make mistakes; create a learning environment.
- Identify technical skills that are used so infrequently that there is little need to have more than one person with the expertise on the team.
- Be mindful of the time it takes to cross-train.
- Recognize that people learn differently and at different speeds.
- Don't allow people to cross-train on too many things at once.

☐ **5. Develop the performance capability of others.** What happens if a member on the team is struggling with performance? Does it frustrate other team members? How do they respond? Do they complain about that person to the other team members or to the boss? Do they shun that person because of it? High-functioning teams have a vested interest in every member's success. These teams know that the team rises or falls on the shoulders of not one, but all, members. Help those members who are struggling. Instead of being frustrated, team members who recognize a performance gap help the underperforming team member find a path to recovery. Developing others in this way also helps avoid situations where the few do the work of many. Avoid rewarding poor performers by decreasing their workload. Increase the performance capability of underperforming team members and the result will be an overall higher-performing team with higher morale.

☐ **6. Roll up your sleeves and pitch in.** Team players on high-functioning, interdependent teams are willing to lose some of their individualism. They don't seek individual credit for accomplishments. They understand that their work isn't done until everyone's work is done. They know the meaning of team effort. Good team members monitor their own work as well as those around them. They offer to help when they see a team member overloaded or when a team member has a more pressing priority than their own. Team members shouldn't have to be told to help out others on the team. It should come naturally from their commitment to the team goals and their commitment to one another. *More help? See Chapter 3 – Thrust Commitment, and Chapter 6 – Trust Inside the Team, in this book.*

☐ **7. Set up a reward system for helping others.** If the team needs some extrinsic incentive to help fellow members, implement a recognition program. People like to be rewarded differently based on what motivates them: time off, a parking place, an e-mail or personal call from an executive, or recognition from peers. The rewards used in teams should acknowledge behavior that is consistent with its overall strategy. Actively helping each other to achieve goals is behavior that should be valued in all teams. Some teams might have a rotating trophy or symbol that has special meaning to the team. When there is lack of face-to-face interaction, as with virtual teams, it's important to reinforce that virtual help is valued. Design the recognition program so that virtual tools like the team Web site, audio- or videoconference calls, and electronic bulletin boards are leveraged to show virtual team members that their efforts matter. Acknowledge teamwork and togetherness when it is displayed at its finest. It will create pride and a sense of spirit within the team.

☐ **8. Give team members ownership of their work.** Leaders of high-performing teams realize that it's important to select the best talent for the team and then let them do their jobs. These leaders trust their team's skills. They communicate, set time frames and goals, and then get out of the way. If there's a problem, the leader chips in to help. Monitoring of the work is done at time-definite checkpoints either by calendar or assignment progress points, like completion of a first draft. This approach is a must for virtual teams. Because of their geographic dispersion, virtual team members need to work independently in order to be productive. Time zone differences and other barriers make it difficult for leaders to monitor virtual team members' work, so working with a high degree of autonomy is critical to meet objectives. Keep in mind that providing too much autonomy and independence does not shape an effective team. In order to be a team, all team members must work collaboratively and communicate sufficiently with the leader.

□ **9. Balance the load across multiple resources.** Often, it seems that one or a few team members are swamped and others are less busy. Load balancing is used in computing and basically addresses balancing a workload among multiple computer devices. This same concept can be applied in the workloads of teams. Load balancing enables less busy team members to help those that are overloaded until the deadline or pressure has passed. Ideally, when the tides shift, those that benefited from being helped will reciprocate. Research indicates that engagement, morale, and enthusiasm in load-balanced teams are generally higher than in teams where a few do all the work. Set up a system for load balancing. Have the team determine the criteria and process for signaling for help. Set up a system where asking is shameless and blameless and help is freely given and rewarded. Don't limit resources to inside the team. There may be times when the whole team is at capacity and calling for outside help is the best solution. Whatever process is developed, make sure it is understood by everyone to decrease friction between team members.

□ **10. Make each team member's expertise and skills known to all.** Create an online directory that includes each team member's photo, expertise and experience, and current role and responsibilities. Frequently, virtual team members have few or no opportunities to meet face-to-face. Collaboration between virtual team members starts once they know more about each other's backgrounds and skills. Inventory each team member's expertise. Define each other's roles and responsibilities clearly and publish them on the Web space. Keep the directory updated as new skills are acquired through cross-training or the addition of new team members. A robust directory also helps team members know whom to contact when they need help or when they need to determine how to assign tasks. A detailed listing of the team's skills also sends a powerful message both inside and outside the team that there is a lot of talent to be found within the team's ranks.

Suggested Readings

Barner, R. W. (2000). *Team troubleshooter.* Palo Alto, CA: Davies-Black.

Blackburn, R., Furst, S., & Rosen, B. (2003). Building a winning virtual team: KSAs, selection, training, and evaluation. In C. B. Gibson & S. G. Cohen (Eds.), *Virtual teams that work: Creating conditions for virtual team effectiveness* (pp. 95-120). San Francisco: Jossey-Bass.

Chinowsky, P. S., & Rojas, E. M. (2003). Virtual teams: Guide to successful implementation. *Journal of Management in Engineering, 19*(3), 98-106.

Duarte, D. L., & Snyder, N. T. (2006). *Mastering virtual teams: Strategies, tools, and techniques that succeed* (3rd ed.). San Francisco: Jossey-Bass.

Hunsaker, P. L., & Hunsaker, J. S. (2008). Virtual teams: A leader's guide. *Team Performance Management, 14*(1/2), 86-101.

Kanaga, K., & Kossler, M. E. (2007). *How to form a team: Five keys to high performance* (Rev. ed.). Greensboro, NC: Center for Creative Leadership.

Katzenbach, J. R., & Smith, D. K. (1993). *The wisdom of teams.* New York: HarperCollins.

Kirkman, B. L., & Rosen, B. (1999). Beyond self-management: Antecedents and consequences of team empowerment. *Academy of Management Journal, 42*(1), 58-74.

Langfred, C. W. (2007). The downside of self-management: A longitudinal study of the effects of conflict on trust, autonomy, and task interdependence in self-managing teams. *Academy of Management Journal, 50*(4), 885-900.

Parker, G. M. (2008). *Team players and teamwork: New strategies for developing successful collaboration* (2nd ed.). San Francisco: Jossey-Bass.

Ruyle, K. R., Eichinger, R. W., & De Meuse, K. P. (2009). *FYI for Talent Engagement™: Drivers of best practice.* Minneapolis, MN: Lominger International: A Korn/Ferry Company.

FACTOR V: TASK SKILLS

16

Translation to the Leadership Architect® Competency Library

In order for a team or individuals on a team to perform well in this area, these are the competencies that would most likely be in play. Aside from a team improvement plan where everybody works on the same thing, some individual team members may need to work on some of these competencies. A critical number (but not necessarily all) of team members would have to be good at:

Mission Critical:	Important:	Nice to Have:
18. Delegation	2. *Dealing with*	37. Negotiating
27. Informing	*Ambiguity*	45. Personal Learning
56. Sizing Up People	19. Developing Direct	54. Self-Development
60. *Building Effective*	Reports and Others	55. Self-Knowledge
Teams	36. Motivating Others	
	42. Peer Relationships	
	62. Time Management	

In addition to the 10 tips listed for this dimension, there are additional tips that may apply from *FYI For Your Improvement*™. Below are the four items from the Team Architect® that make up this dimension. The item number appears to the left of each item. Immediately below the text of each item are competency and tip numbers from *FYI*. The competency is listed first (from 1 to 67), followed by the tip number (1 to 10). For example, 33-4 refers to competency 33 (Listening), tip number 4. The tips are generally written for individual development, so some adaptation might be needed in the team context.

16. The team assigns work flexibly to team members.
    18-2,3,5,9; 27-2; 36-10; 37-4; 56-3,5; 110-5

34. Team members pitch in and share the load.
    36-3; 60-1,3,5,6,7,8; 62-2; 65-2; 110-4

52. Team members have the autonomy needed to do their work.
    18-1,2,3,8,9; 27-2,3; 35-1,7; 36-1

70. The team uses cross-training so team members can fill in for one another.
    5-7; 19-1,2,3,4,6,8; 31-5; 46-9; 56-3

Dimension 17
Measurement

Definition:
Team uses a performance measurement system to track results; members understand success measures and use feedback to improve team performance.

Addresses the question:
Does the team have adequate process and outcome measures to guide its work?

A Dimension in the TASK SKILLS Factor
The effort necessary to execute successfully.

> *Measure what is measurable, and make measurable what is not so.*
> Galileo Galilei (1564-1642) – Italian philosopher, astronomer, and mathematician

Items
17. The team regularly tracks measures of its performance.
35. Performance improvement feedback to one another is common on this team.
53. Success measurements are open and known to all on the team.
71. This team is effective at creating process measures to keep itself on track and get early warning.

Unskilled
☐ Team does not have a process in place to measure its performance
☐ Team does not have well-defined outcome metrics
☐ Team does not have well-defined process metrics
☐ Team members do not give one another feedback regarding their performance
☐ Team does not debrief successes and failures as a group
☐ Team metrics are not aligned with organizational priorities
☐ Metrics are only known by the leader or a few select team members
☐ Team members are unclear about who is responsible for what
☐ Team has metrics but they don't measure the right things

☐ Team members are distrustful of measures; they fear they might be used to assign blame

☐ Team leader does not use metrics to hold members accountable for performance

☐ Team has metrics but they are cumbersome and too complex

☐ Team members are not committed to the goals or performance metrics

Skilled

☐ Team measures are aligned with vision and strategy

☐ The team creates clear measures for key processes, tasks, and outcomes

☐ Metrics are robust and measure both internally and externally, including the customer

☐ All team members can explain the measurement system to someone outside the team

☐ The team believes that measurement is positive and constructive, not punitive

☐ Mistakes are treated as learning opportunities on the team

☐ Team members buy into and are committed to team metrics

☐ Performance metrics clearly assess performance against team objectives and goals

☐ The team debriefs its successes and failures as a group

☐ The metrics used are reliable and valid

☐ Performance metrics indicate the team's strengths and weaknesses

☐ Team has a method for publishing progress on performance criteria

☐ Team members take the measurement results seriously and take specific actions that lead to improvement

Overused

☐ Team spends too much time on measurement at the expense of productivity

☐ Measurement becomes a goal and a pursuit of its own

☐ Team members are too direct with each other; feedback is harmful

☐ Team is too aggressive in its pursuit of measures

☐ Team does a disservice to the soft issues, the "people stuff," because it is so focused on numbers and hard data

☐ Team members are always looking over one another's shoulders and inspecting each other's work

☐ Team agonizes over every measurement, leading to analysis paralysis

☐ New team members have a hard time getting up to speed in a measurement-rich environment

Note on overused strengths: Overused skills and disproportionately used strengths tend to have the negative effects listed above. To decrease those negative consequences, you have two alternatives. You can scale down or use the strength less, or you can compensate for it with another skill or behavior. In practice, it is very difficult to get an individual or a team to use a strength less. In most cases, the best path is to develop compensators. Team Architect® Dimensions that can compensate for overusing this dimension and compensating skills from the Leadership Architect® Library's 67 Competencies are listed below.

> (Note: Team Dimension numbers are listed in parentheses. Competencies are listed in numerical order by competency number.)

Compensating Team Dimensions:

- ☐ Thrust Management (1)
- ☐ Thrust Clarity (2)
- ☐ Delivering the Goods (18)
- ☐ Team Leader Fit (20)

Compensating Competencies:

- ☐ 36. Motivating Others
- ☐ 50. Priority Setting
- ☐ 53. *Drive for* Results
- ☐ 60. *Building Effective* Teams

Some Causes of Poor Performance

- ☐ Team is too busy to take the time to develop metrics
- ☐ Team is too busy to review performance against metrics
- ☐ Team members are disorganized
- ☐ Team members are inexperienced
- ☐ Team members do not manage time well
- ☐ Team members avoid conflict associated with giving feedback on performance goals
- ☐ Team members are unmotivated
- ☐ Team doesn't have access to measurement technologies
- ☐ Team leader permits performance to slip; ignores missed performance goals
- ☐ Organization has a weak performance culture
- ☐ Senior leaders or sponsors aren't asking for the measures
- ☐ Team members may think performance measures are inaccurate

The Map

The old adage is true: don't expect what you don't inspect. Inspection means comparison to a standard. It means measurement. It focuses attention and resources on whatever's being measured. Measurement helps people decide where to allocate their time and effort. Measurement guides decision making. Measurement lets everyone know where they stand. Measurement that is visible and applied to everyone levels the playing field because everyone participates in the scrutiny. Measurement allows a corrective feedback loop to help team members correct their efforts as quickly as possible. Measurement helps direct equitable rewards. Measurement ensures that team efforts are aligned with the grander vision and plan. Measurement enables the team to pursue a path of continuous improvement. Measurement makes team discussions and problem-solving activities more on point and less on opinion. It highlights mission-critical tasks. Measurement creates a culture of accountability. For most, measurement is motivating. Bottom line: the time it takes to design, apply, and track processes, tasks, and outcomes will pay huge dividends in the more effective use of team resources and increased team results.

Some Remedies

□ **1. Measure the right things.** How do we know we're doing well? How do we measure success? Determining what is important to measure can be a daunting task for any team. In most teams, there is likely a wide array of things that can be measured. The challenge is in finding the right things. It's natural for teams to get sidetracked measuring what is readily accessible or easily quantifiable. To ensure that the team is using meaningful measures of performance, the team's first duty is to establish its key performance indicators (KPIs). KPIs are a set of progress indicators to measure data against, a sort of team success gauge. They help the team assess progress toward declared goals. Indicators can be financial or non-financial, short-term or long-term, and will vary from team to team. For a call center, a KPI might be average hold times. A human resource team may consider employee engagement rates or turnover important success measures. Sales teams look at lead conversion. When determining what are the right KPIs for your team, use the following criteria: (a) the measure must reflect the team and organization's goals, (b) be key to team success, and (c) they must be measurable. Reduce the volume of possible measures down to the critical few and focus on analyzing those thoroughly and consistently.

□ **2. Use the right combination of measures to get a complete picture of team performance.** Measuring outcomes is generally easiest for a team.

Outcomes are usually very visible products and/or services everyone can see and readily measure. Most teams can easily get their attention wrapped around outcomes. Yet outcomes don't happen in a vacuum. To ensure the outcome measures are valid, clarity around the tasks and processes that lead to those outcomes is critical. Start with the end in mind and work backwards. Determine the critical tasks needed to achieve the outcome and how to measure for effectiveness. Then identify the processes employed to complete those tasks and monitor for continuous improvement as needed. Some things to keep in mind about the different levels and types of activities to measure include:

– Outcome measures quantify the end product or output of processes and tasks performed by the team. They are generally viewed as the primary products or services of the team and are most closely associated with the team's results. The prime judge of outcome metrics is the customer. Was it what the customer wanted and needed or ordered? Was it on time? Was it delivered in a customer-friendly way? Did it work? Did it last?

– Task measures assess the extent to which the bulk of the work associated with meeting customer needs and fulfilling business requirements is effective. Teams have to decide which tasks are the most important ones to measure. Tasks to measure should be those identified as having the most value in moving the strategy forward. Without this kind of prioritization, the team can get overloaded with measuring minutia.

– Process metrics evaluate the collection of steps to complete tasks. The starting point for identifying process metrics is to identify those processes linked to the team's primary services or desired team results. What process steps are necessary to produce the tasks and outcomes above? These steps can be identified by flowcharting a team's process. There are several flowcharting software packages available. Important to see are the number of steps, how long they take, how much each costs, and how much each adds value to producing the outcomes. Real fine-tuning occurs at the process step level.

Outcome, task, and process metrics should each be considered equally when determining what constitutes superior performance. The key for implementation is to put them together into a measurement process that is participative, well supported, and monitored for success.

☐ **3. Avoid common measurement pitfalls.** Team studies have tracked both successful and unsuccessful measurement systems. Understanding why team measures often fail can help build perspective when developing

17

team measurement systems from scratch. Following are some common measurement pitfalls:

- Metrics that are too complex to understand.
- Measures that take up too much time to complete.
- Measures of things that really don't make much of a difference to team success.
- Measurement systems with no consequences.
- Metrics that are only of interest to managers.
- Measures that the team cannot improve upon.
- Metrics that only measure outcomes, not the path to get there.
- Metrics that only measure process, not the outcomes.
- Metrics that chill initiative and creativity.

Once the team has created a draft of their measures, do a check against these pitfalls. Re-work as needed.

☐ **4. Build a sense of ownership for team measures.** The most direct way for team members to feel a sense of personal ownership over performance metrics is to be included in the development of those metrics. Team members are more likely to accept and be committed to the metrics when they are part of the process. The more a decision impacts team members, the more they should be involved. For team members to readily accept accountability for the metrics, they need to buy into them. Be able to explain the system to a visitor, customer, or business partner. Teams that really understand and own their measurement system willingly go over their feedback or measurement reports in detail. They want to know where they stand at any point in time. Teams that don't understand or buy into metrics skim over the information or avoid it entirely. Engaging team members in the development of team metrics builds clarity. Clarity on metrics should be as important as clarity on thrust or the team's goals. Make sure the measurement system models how team members think about their collective work.

☐ **5. Create a clear line of sight between individual members' work and team/organizational success measures.** A sense of ownership begins when team members can see that their work directly affects the organization. When they see that their contributions are important, why the work of the team matters, how the team fits into the value chain. Creating a line of sight is about translating strategy into job-specific tasks. About linking individual work to team and organizational objectives. When the work is aligned, individual measures of success are rolled up to team measures of success and help move the organization forward. An effective measurement system draws a clear line of sight between the business strategies, the customer needs, and the team's strategy for accomplishing its portion of business objectives. Connecting these elements gets the team and the business to work together, creates mutual buy-in and support for goals, and ultimately synchronizes performance. A proven method to connect individual, team, and organizational performance is through the balanced scorecard approach. A balanced scorecard is a widely used performance measurement that provides a mechanism for translating organization-wide success measures down to, first, business units, then to support units or departments, and finally to teams or individuals. When determining team performance measures, a team can use the general scorecard categories of customer perspective, business processes, learning and growth, and financials as a guideline. Include customers' perspectives so the team looks outward. If the organization is pushing for streamlined processes, team business process measures can be built around continuous improvement. And so on. The end result of using a balanced scorecard approach should be consistent focus across all levels of the organization.

☐ **6. Learn to measure the unmeasurables.** Output. Goods. Services. Things with a number attached to them. Things that are quantifiable. When we seek to measure, we instinctively gravitate toward those things that are more readily quantifiable. How many widgets were produced? Were they quality widgets? Did they come in under budget? Some things are just easier to measure than others. In a knowledge-based work world, developing and tracking hard measures is, well, hard. Hard-to-measure teams are a reality. Many times these are teams in support functions, staff functions that support the line business. Areas like research and development, marketing, human resources, finance. Rather than hard-to-measure teams throwing up their collective hands in defeat, find ways to quantify the seemingly unquantifiable. Identify the products or services the team provides. Then do a functional analysis. Break down team functions into tasks, identify the expertise needed to perform them, and the output created. Define expectations for what constitutes success using standard measurement criteria like quantity, quality, timeliness, and cost. When selecting measures, make sure they are ones that are sensitive to team performance. Try to combine with other or existing measures for less effort, but be sure that it's possible to isolate team impact. If this seems too ambitious to start, use benchmarking as a way to begin quantifying performance. Find out who is the best at a comparable function and study them. Ultimately, to show value to the organization, teams need to be able to provide a ready answer to the question: What evidence exists that the team has performed in a way that benefits the organization?

17

☐ **7. Measure the "what" as well as the "how" of team performance.** Call center hold times decreasing by 30% based on team sponsored initiative. Quality errors down 10% due to process redundancies uncovered by the team. Sales increasing $2 million year-over-year because of the team's push for a consultative selling methodology. KPIs. Quantity, quality, timeliness, and cost measures. All focus on external business results. All focus on what the team delivers. But what's delivered is driven by how the team functions. How it operates. How it behaves. The deliverables won't be there if the team doesn't function. Implement process metrics to assess how it operates, to get at the "how" that drives the deliverables. Noise and friction in the team, whether caused by one or more members behaving badly or by pervasive lack of trust, chill collaboration and slow productivity. Teaming competencies are drivers of team effectiveness. Competencies such as priority setting, peer relationships, dealing with ambiguity, and listening. If team members lack skill in these areas, team results will suffer. Look at the competencies needed individually and then in aggregate across the team. Measure the gaps. Does the team succeed because of or despite members' participation? How is the team perceived outside? Political land mines abound for teams that don't play nice with others. As part of measurement, assess how the team is being perceived. Use 360° feedback as a measure of team performance on the "how." Include this kind of measure in team key performance indicators.

☐ **8. Review existing measures regularly.** Measurement should be a prominent topic at regular team meetings, whether face-to-face or via conference calls and Webcasts. The whole reason for having teams is to improve organizational performance. If a team's charter and measurement system are appropriately aligned, members will talk about measures as if they were running their own business. Consider using a technique where each team member is responsible for monitoring a measure and facilitating discussion of the measure, progress, barriers, etc. at the team meetings. This approach will help to teach team members to keep an eye on the measurement system and instill accountability. Use the sessions to stimulate problem solving that leads to improved performance. Also, use the sessions to make sure the measurements are really adding value to the team and to ensure the method or tool used for measurement is still effective.

☐ **9. Encourage the use of constructive feedback.** Teams that trust each other are transparent. They are high on integrity. Tell it like it is. When people know they are valued and respected, they have broad shoulders and can more easily take criticism because they know it's offered with the best intentions, to help the individual and the team do better. At the outset, establish a high-candor-feedback protocol in the team—between members and between the leader and the team. Make feedback the norm, a constant in team interactions. In that way, when the team analyzes performance measures and debriefs either successes or failures, it looks forward as well as backward. The team should ask individually and collectively: What could I/we have done better/differently to bring about a more positive result? And, for successes, feedback is equally important. Actions and behaviors that enable success should be surfaced and cataloged to leverage in the future. Without an atmosphere of transparency, team feedback goes underground. Members become frustrated with underperforming members and may demonstrate passive-aggressive behaviors. In that atmosphere, trust erodes. Transparent feedback, on the other hand, helps team members adjust what they are doing along the way and make midcourse corrections that will bring about a positive outcome.

☐ **10. Use technology to harness the information to be measured.** To reap the full benefit of measurement, it's important to automate and use technology when possible. Technological applications allow for a deeper, more comprehensive tracking of data. Reports that slice and dice data in a myriad of ways can yield valuable information for the team. Automating measurement also frees up team resources for other, more valuable, duties. Some KPIs, like tracking customer satisfaction survey results, can be measured with something as simple as a spreadsheet. Others, like account penetration, business unit sales revenues, or speed to answer, may require a more sophisticated business intelligence (BI) application. BI applications provide historical, current, and predictive views of business operations, most often using data that have been organized in a data warehouse. Measurement technology such as Gartner's Business Activity Monitoring works best for real-time measurement. This type of technology provides real-time information about the status and results of various operations, processes, and transactions. In a call center, for example, Business Activity Monitoring software can track how long a call has been in queue and route it to an alternate destination after a specified time frame. This type of measurement enables a team to make well-informed business decisions, quickly address problem areas, and take advantage of emerging opportunities.

17

Suggested Readings

Cascio, W. F. (2000). Managing a virtual workplace. *Academy of Management Executive, 14*(3), 81-90.

DeVita, M. A., Hillman, K., & Bellomo, R. (Eds.). (2006). *Medical emergency teams: Implementation and outcome measurement.* New York: Spring Science+Business.

Eichinger, R. W., Ruyle, K. E., & Lombardo, M. M. (2007). *FYI for Performance Management™: Universal dimensions for success.* Minneapolis, MN: Lominger International: A Korn/Ferry Company.

Gibson, C. B., & Cohen, S. G. (Eds.). (2003). *Virtual teams that work: Creating conditions for virtual team effectiveness.* San Francisco: Jossey-Bass.

Hunsaker, P. L., & Hunsaker, J. S. (2008). Virtual teams: A leader's guide. *Team Performance Management, 14*(1/2), 86-101.

Jones, S. D., & Schilling, D. J. (2000). *Measuring team performance: A step-by-step, customizable approach for managers, facilitators, and team leaders.* San Francisco: Jossey-Bass.

Katzenbach, J. R., & Smith, D. K. (1993). *The wisdom of teams.* New York: HarperCollins.

Marquardt, M. J., & Horvath, L. (2001). *Global teams: How top multinationals span boundaries and cultures with high-speed teamwork.* Mountain View, CA: Davies-Black.

Meyer, C. (1994). How the right measures help teams excel. *Harvard Business Review, 72*(3), 95-103.

Shane, S. L., & Von Glinow, M. A. (2008). *Organizational behavior: Emerging realities for the workplace revolution* (4th ed.). New York: McGraw-Hill.

Shaw, D. G., & Schneier, C. E. (1995). Team measurement and rewards: How some companies are getting it right. *Human Resource Planning, 18*(3), 34-49.

Translation to the Leadership Architect® Competency Library

In order for a team or individuals on a team to perform well in this area, these are the competencies that would most likely be in play. Aside from a team improvement plan where everybody works on the same thing, some individual team members may need to work on some of these competencies. A critical number (but not necessarily all) of team members would have to be good at:

Mission Critical:	Important:	Nice to Have:
35. Managing and Measuring Work	27. Informing	13. Confronting Direct Reports
52. Process Management	47. Planning	34. Managerial Courage
	50. Priority Setting	56. Sizing Up People
	53. *Drive for* Results	60. *Building Effective* Teams

In addition to the ten tips listed for this dimension, there are additional tips that may apply from *FYI For Your Improvement*™. Below are the four items from the Team Architect® that make up this dimension. The item number appears to the left of each item. Immediately below the text of each item are competency and tip numbers from *FYI*. The competency is listed first (from 1 to 67), followed by the tip number (1 to 10). For example, 33-4 refers to competency 33 (Listening), tip number 4. The tips are generally written for individual development, so some adaptation might be needed in the team context.

17. The team regularly tracks measures of its performance.
    29-6; 35-1,2,5,6,7; 50-2; 52-3,8; 53-3

35. Performance improvement feedback to one another is common on this team.
    13-2; 19-3; 27-2; 29-1,6; 34-3; 35-7; 56-4,7; 60-8

53. Success measurements are open and known to all on the team.
    27-2; 35-1,2,5,6,7; 50-2,3; 52-5; 56-4

71. This team is effective at creating process measures to keep itself on track and get early warning.
    32-2,3; 35-2,6,7; 52-3,5,8; 53-1,3

FACTOR V: TASK SKILLS

17

Dimension 18
Delivering the Goods

Definition:
Team utilizes resources sufficiently, and works collaboratively and diligently to accomplish mission-critical goals.

Addresses the question:
Does the team get the job done?

A Dimension in the TASK SKILLS Factor
The effort necessary to execute successfully.

> *The greater the loyalty of a group toward the group, the greater is the motivation*
> *among the members to achieve the goals of the group,*
> *and the greater the probability that the group will achieve its goals.*
> Rensis Likert – American educator and psychologist

Items
18. The team is effective in finding the resources it needs to get its work done.
36. The team makes no excuses for not meeting performance goals; it identifies and attacks the causes of missing the mark and fixes them.
54. The team consistently meets or exceeds its goals.
72. This team is a role model for others on getting things done.

Unskilled
- ☐ The team gets easily distracted from its mission-critical priorities
- ☐ Team's poor relationships with others in the organization interfere with getting the cooperation necessary to achieve results
- ☐ The team is inconsistent in execution
- ☐ Team talent is not in balance; a few do all the work
- ☐ Team members don't work well as a team
- ☐ The team wants to do everything itself; it does not ask for help
- ☐ The team doesn't clarify priorities well
- ☐ Team has spotty performance results
- ☐ Team gives up in face of obstacles; doesn't persevere

☐ Team does not analyze performance breakdowns
☐ The team does not have the necessary talent to accomplish its mission
☐ There is little accountability for missed team goals

Skilled

☐ The team is willing to go outside to get help and resources
☐ Team is perceived by others as both hardworking and high performing
☐ There are few bumps in the road or surprises the team has not prepared for ahead of time
☐ Everyone on the team works hard and contributes
☐ The team always finds a way to get things done despite difficulties or obstacles
☐ The team plans its work and then methodically works its plan
☐ The team focuses on solving problems rather than placing blame when things don't go right
☐ The team looks for ways to innovate and continuously improve
☐ The team has the necessary talent to accomplish its goals
☐ Team members work collaboratively as a team by sharing the workload and helping each other
☐ The team regularly reviews performance against measures
☐ The team members and leader hold each other accountable for performance goals

Overused

☐ The team always wins the prize for performance but doesn't have much fun; the pressure to perform is too great
☐ Team asks for help so much that it has exhausted its resources
☐ The team's sharp task focus chills creativity and innovation
☐ Team takes so many risks that there is too much collateral damage to justify the results
☐ The team gets unduly upset when something happens to sidetrack the plan
☐ The team is so engaged in its own performance that it doesn't help other teams out when they need it
☐ Expectations for new team members to perform immediately are unrealistic
☐ The team is arrogant; others are tired of hearing about them and their achievements
☐ The team may be too hard on itself when performance goals are missed

18

Note on overused strengths: Overused skills and disproportionately used strengths tend to have the negative effects listed above. To decrease those negative consequences, you have two alternatives. You can scale down or use the strength less, or you can compensate for it with another skill or behavior. In practice, it is very difficult to get an individual or a team to use a strength less. In most cases, the best path is to develop compensators. Team Architect® Dimensions that can compensate for overusing this dimension and compensating skills from the Leadership Architect® Library's 67 Competencies are listed below.

(Note: Team Dimension numbers are listed in parentheses. Competencies are listed in numerical order by competency number.)

Compensating Team Dimensions:
☐ Team Atmosphere (13)
☐ Team Support from the Organization (19)
☐ Team Leader Fit (20)

Compensating Competencies:
☐ 2. *Dealing with* Ambiguity
☐ 21. *Managing* Diversity
☐ 28. Innovation Management
☐ 31. Interpersonal Savvy
☐ 38. Organizational Agility
☐ 42. Peer Relationships
☐ 60. *Building Effective* Teams

Some Causes of Poor Performance
☐ Members are uncomfortable asking for help
☐ Members see outreach for resources as a sign of weakness
☐ The team has burned bridges in the organization
☐ The team is not ambitious
☐ Team work habits are not strong
☐ There is a lot of noise and tension in the team
☐ Team isn't comfortable with ambiguity
☐ Team doesn't learn from past performance
☐ Team is resistant to change
☐ Team doesn't do a good enough job setting priorities
☐ Team members are unskilled
☐ Team leaders do not recognize or reward performance

18

The Map

At the end of the day, it's performance that counts. Consistent performance counts even more. Even marginal teams can get lucky and perform well once in a while. Results-driven, effective teams always perform well. They get the mission-critical products and services produced on or ahead of schedule, at or under budget, at a high level of quality. Results-driven teams have clear goals and maintain an unswerving focus on meeting or beating them. For these teams, the finish line is never truly crossed. Exceeded goals? These teams celebrate and then turn to the future. High-performing teams hunger for the next challenge. Missed the mark? These teams never make excuses. They don't resort to blaming circumstances or each other. High-performing teams are ever on the alert for emerging problems and quickly hone in on root causes for performance breakdowns. These teams have a work ethic that is the standard bearer in the organization. No martyrs to be found. Nothing is for show. The work of the team is seen as valuable by others, integrated into the organizational strategy. All this makes others more willing to share resources when needed. On a high-performing team, individual members blend well. Competition is focused outward, not inward. The team is balanced. All hands are engaged. The strength of this team is greater than the sum of its parts.

Some Remedies

☐ **1. Envision success.** Results-driven teams focus their eyes on the prize. In order to do that, the team needs to know what the prize is, what it's striving toward. Walk the team through a visioning exercise. Ask them to envision the team completing its work and reaching its goals successfully. How will customers feel? How will each member feel? What's in it for the team? What kinds of rewards and consequences will there be? Will all of the above be motivating or satisfying for the team? Then work backwards with the visioning. Why was the team successful? What did it do well? What did it avoid doing? Challenge the team to think through how they will have to function to achieve the vision. To what extent will all of the above be possible because the team operates as a team and not just as a collection of individuals? If this exercise does not produce excitement in the team, then you need to rethink the goals or lower your expectations.

☐ **2. Set the right goals, then excel at execution.** Research on high-performance work teams indicates that aggressive or stretch goals almost always lead to better results. Further, goals that are aligned with the overall business strategy help teams to prioritize their work. Aligned goals make it easier for the team to face downstream decisions and choices. Will

18

176

the decision or choice move the goals forward? If not, it likely won't get airtime in the team. While setting these types of goals is important, it's execution that makes or breaks performance. Execution is not just the tactical components of the team's work. Execution is a discipline, a set of behaviors that enables the team to perform well. Teams that excel at execution focus on how. When goals are set, an execution-oriented team asks: How will we achieve them? What processes need to be in place? What resources will we need? How will we measure our progress? Many teams and team leaders put a lot of effort and resources into planning but stop there. If a team is full of idea generators but no one can execute, it's highly unlikely team objectives will be met. Move beyond planning and concentrate on execution.

☐ **3. Reach across boundaries for resources.** Results-driven teams aren't afraid to ask for help. Teams should identify what resources are necessary (time, money, people, equipment), determine what is missing, and then figure out where to go to make the request. Teams whose members are skilled influencers have more success than others at obtaining resources. Influencers don't just ask for things. They find some common ground. Create a compelling case to inspire the resource providers. Paint a vivid picture of what results these resources will bring. When influencing others in this way, think about what your team is working on and how it affects others' results. Are the team's results important to others? Go into these relationships with a trading mentality, not a handout mentality. Be a role-model team with enviable resources, and others will want to trade with you.

☐ **4. Know how to navigate the organizational maze.** High-performing teams are resourceful. They are able to figure out how to get more done with less, find the path of least resistance. These teams know how to get things done both through formal channels and informal networks. They work the organization network to get things done for the team. These teams avoid political traps and dead ends. They know whom to rely on for expediting things. They know the major gatekeepers who control the flow of resources, information, and decisions. These teams recognize that the best path to get something done may not be direct. The formal organization works only some of the time. Much of the time, the informal organization runs the show. For teams to be successful, they have to know how to work the maze. And to be patient with process. Things sometimes take time. Maybe the best way to approach someone is through someone else. When is the right time to approach someone for a decision or an action? Learn the informal organization. Identify the key players, especially the gatekeepers and the traffic controllers.

18

☐ **5. Get the right people on board.** It is vital to have team members with the right skills, abilities, and knowledge to achieve the team goals. It also includes having team members with good interpersonal skills that fit well in the team. Research suggests that the most effective teams have a balance of skills and abilities. Successful teams realize that having balance does not mean equal use of all skills at all times. Balance means having the capability to use various skills when required. A team's need for particular skills is situational, driven by team objectives and business demands. Beware of stacking the deck too much in favor of certain skills. Successful teams also use workarounds to compensate for skill deficiencies. People workarounds reposition individuals in roles so their skills complement the skills of others. For instance, a team member who is skilled at analysis but unable to speak in front of a group to save his/her life might call on another teammate to present the data to senior leaders. Task workarounds reposition or restructure tasks to take advantage of the complementary skills of individuals. A high-performing team knows when and where to combine and leverage member skills most efficiently.

☐ **6. Develop a calculated-risk orientation as a team.** Results-driven teams don't play it safe. These teams know that operating the same year after year is going to yield the same results. And for teams that are looking for ever-increasing results—for exceptional results—running in place is the same as moving backwards. Playing it safe is not a path to innovation and continuous improvement. Neither is being reckless. Find the balance that promotes calculated risk taking. Develop methods for risk analysis and define risk thresholds based on the impact of the decision, good or bad. Train team members to assess risks and set confidence levels that are factored into decisions. Team leaders should publicly support the team's decisions which are well-thought-out and stand behind them as they experiment with new things. Remember that pushing the envelope and taking chances will likely lead to more misfires and mistakes. Taking chances may also lead to better results. When things go wrong, high-performing teams persevere. Take a collective breath. Depersonalize, drop the defense scripts, and just fix it. Treat mistakes or failures as a chance to learn. As a team leader, send a clear message that there is amnesty for reasonable, calculated risks that don't pan out. Sometimes the greatest leaps forward in innovation come from learning what not to do.

☐ **7. Take the time to find root causes of performance problems.** A common side effect of high-performing, results-oriented teams is impatience. Since these teams move fast, they typically do not take the time to define problems. Rather, they tend to take the first seemingly viable solution that comes along. When performance goals are not achieved, it is essential to find out why and what can be done together as a team to prevent the performance breakdown from reoccurring. No teams are immune to errors and problems. In general, the sooner you address a performance problem in the team, the easier it is to solve. Conduct during- and after-action review meetings to discuss performance problems. Go beyond listing what went well, what didn't, and what to do differently. Probe to find the root cause(s) of the performance problem. Here are some ideas to get to the root of complex problems:

- Ask more questions. In one study of problem solving, 7% of comments were questions and about half were answers. We jump to solutions based on what has worked in the past.
- Complex problems are hard to visualize. They tend to be either oversimplified or too complex to solve unless they are put in a visual format. Cut problems up into their component pieces. Examine the pieces to see if a different order would help, or how you could combine three pieces into one.
- Construct a pictorial chart or storyboard where a problem is illustrated by its components being depicted as pictures.
- Tell stories that illustrate the pluses and minuses of a problem, then flowchart those according to what's working and not working.
- Do scenario planning. Think through every possible condition, every worst case the team can think of. Scenario planning like this sometimes suggests a different solution. Taking the present state of affairs and projecting into the future may indicate how and where the system will break down.
- Do certain members of the team avoid making the tough points? In almost any group, there are topics so hot they can't be mentioned, let alone discussed. A technique pioneered by Chris Argyris can bubble root causes to the surface. Everyone takes three index cards and writes down three undiscussables. (Names are not used; the assumption is that the position has an effect on behavior, and even if people think the issue is personal, they are asked to see it in system or group terms.) The cards are then shuffled and each person receives a different three back. The cards are read, charted, and themes are arrayed for discussion.

☐ 8. Regularly reevaluate team goals. A high-performing team is a goal-oriented team. These teams keep a laser focus on team goals. But that focus has to be balanced with flexibility. Business demands are constantly in flux. Economic trends, market forces, technology upgrades, customer demographics—all these factors make it crucial to periodically review and reassess team goals. Being too rigid in a fast-changing environment may be disabling to team performance. The team needs to be open to change. And the goals should be too. When creating goals, build in flexibility. Don't paint the team into a corner by crafting goals that are so specific that any changes in business demands nullify their effectiveness. Once goals are established, the team should constantly scan the business landscape. Keep monitoring and evaluating the relevance of the goals and plans related to the business environment. Encourage team members to actively question the continued value of goals and do a gut check: Will accomplishing this goal achieve the business results we're looking for? If a goal appears obsolete or won't move the business forward, adapt it or eliminate it.

☐ **9. Foster collaboration on achieving results.** A high-performing team is likely made up of high-performing individuals. Many times making the leap from individual performance to team performance can be difficult. The behaviors that distinguish individuals may be counterproductive to team performance. Most successful individual performers are smart, action oriented, results driven, and know their subject matter well. The magic of building a high-performing team is in channeling those individual talents into a cohesive whole. In a team setting, individual talents are cataloged, leveraged, and celebrated, but primarily in the context of how that person contributes to the collective. Pool the smarts of team members and distribute the work so that the respective subject-matter expertise of all members is optimized. Balance action orientation with interpersonal skills like patience and listening to ensure the team moves fast, but not so fast that all members aren't heard. Build reward systems that harness drive for results and competitiveness toward meeting team— not individual—objectives. High-performing teams operate as one. These teams collaborate to achieve goals. When one or more team members are struggling, the others happily lend a hand. Members recognize that the success or failure of one affects the team overall. On a high-performing team, there are no go-it-alone types.

☐ **10. Celebrate team wins.** Results-driven, high-performing teams are challenged by the hunt. The hunt to reach a mark no one has reached before. To overcome an obstacle seen by others as insurmountable. To try something for the first time and have it succeed. At the end of the hunt, these teams want to be recognized. Rewarded for their achievements. To keep these teams motivated, celebrate wins. Often. Incremental wins and grand finale wins. Rewarding results keeps energy levels and motivation high in the team. Recognition and rewards can be given formally or informally. Design a recognition system that motivates team behavior but is flexible enough to accommodate individual preferences. For example, some team members will be ecstatic when offered a half-day off as a

18

reward for long hours they put in to meet a critical business objective. Other team members wouldn't respond so positively; they might even view it as a punishing consequence of their good performance. In a virtual environment, it can be tougher to recognize the work of virtual team members. When there is lack of face-to-face interaction, it is crucial to reinforce the perception that virtual work is valued. Use Web-based technology, such as team Web site, audio- or videoconference calls, and electronic bulletin boards, to promote team successes and performance. Call out how the work of one or a few virtual members was instrumental to the success of the team overall. Since many times virtual team members don't have the same opportunities to interact with senior executives as more centrally located members do, ask senior leaders to make phone calls or send personal notes congratulating these members on a job well done. Bottom line: reward the behavior you want repeated.

Suggested Readings

Beyerlein, M. M., Freedman, S., McGee, C., & Moran, L. (2003). *Beyond teams: Building the collaborative organization.* San Francisco: Jossey-Bass/Pfeiffer.

Bossidy, L., Charan, R., & Burck, C. (2002). *Execution: The discipline of getting things done.* New York: Crown Business.

Duarte, D. L., & Snyder, N. T. (2006). *Mastering virtual teams: Strategies, tools, and techniques that succeed* (3rd ed.). San Francisco: Jossey-Bass.

Gibson, C. B., & Cohen, S. G. (Eds.). (2003). *Virtual teams that work: Creating conditions for virtual team effectiveness.* San Francisco: Jossey-Bass.

Hackman, J. R. (2002). *Leading teams: Setting the stage for great performances.* Boston: Harvard Business School Press.

Herrenkohl, R. C. (2004). *Becoming a team, achieving a goal.* Mason, OH: South-Western.

Jenewein, W., & Morhart, F. (2008). Navigating toward team success. *Team Performance Management, 14*(1/2), 102-108.

Katzenbach, J. R., & Smith, D. K. (1993). *The wisdom of teams.* New York: HarperCollins.

Kaye, B., & Jordan-Evans, S. (2008). *Love 'em or lose 'em. Getting good people to stay* (4th ed.). San Francisco: Berrett-Koehler Publishers.

LaFasto, F., & Larson, C. (2001). *When teams work best.* Thousand Oaks, CA: Sage.

Lombardo, M. M., & Eichinger, R. W. (2004). *The leadership machine: Architecture to develop leaders for any future.* Minneapolis, MN: Lominger International: A Korn/Ferry Company.

Massey, T. (2005). *Ten commitments for building high performance teams.* Bandon, OR: Robert D. Reed.

Nemiro, J., Beyerlein, M. M., Bradley, L., & Beyerlein, S. (Eds.). (2008). *The handbook of high-performance virtual teams: A toolkit for collaborating across boundaries.* San Francisco: Jossey-Bass.

Parker, G. M. (2008). *Team players and teamwork: New strategies for developing successful collaboration* (2nd ed.). San Francisco: Jossey-Bass.

Robbins, H., & Finley, M. (2000). *The new why teams don't work: What goes wrong and how to make it right.* San Francisco: Berrett-Koehler Publishers.

Ruyle, K. R., Eichinger, R. W., & De Meuse, K. P. (2009). *FYI for Talent Engagement™: Drivers of best practice.* Minneapolis, MN: Lominger International: A Korn/Ferry Company.

Treffinger, D. (2006). *Creative problem solving: An introduction* (4th ed.). Waco, TX: Prufrock Press.

Wheelan, S. A. (2005). *Creating effective teams: A guide for members and leaders* (2nd ed.). Thousand Oaks, CA: Sage.

18

Translation to the Leadership Architect® Competency Library

In order for a team or individuals on a team to perform well in this area, these are the competencies that would most likely be in play. Aside from a team improvement plan where everybody works on the same thing, some individual team members may need to work on some of these competencies. A critical number (but not necessarily all) of team members would have to be good at:

Mission Critical:	Important:	Nice to Have:
39. Organizing	1. Action Oriented	16. *Timely* Decision
43. Perseverance	35. Managing and	Making
50. Priority Setting	Measuring Work	37. Negotiating
51. Problem Solving	52. Process Management	47. Planning
53. *Drive for* Results		62. Time Management

In addition to the 10 tips listed for this dimension, there are additional tips that may apply from *FYI For Your Improvement*™. Below are the four items from the Team Architect® that make up this dimension. The item number appears to the left of each item. Immediately below the text of each item are competency and tip numbers from *FYI*. The competency is listed first (from 1 to 67), followed by the tip number (1 to 10). For example, 33-4 refers to competency 33 (Listening), tip number 4. The tips are generally written for individual development, so some adaptation might be needed in the team context.

18. The team is effective in finding the resources it needs to get its work done.
    4-1; 37-1,4; 38-4,10; 39-2; 42-1; 43-1,2,8

36. The team makes no excuses for not meeting performance goals; it identifies and attacks the causes of missing the mark and fixes them.
    16-2,3; 32-2,3; 43-1; 51-1,8; 52-3,8; 53-3

54. The team consistently meets or exceeds its goals.
    1-1,5; 36-3,10; 43-1,8; 50-2,3; 53-3; 60-1

72. This team is a role model for others on getting things done.
    1-1; 9-1,5; 35-1,2,7; 39-2; 43-1,8,9

18

Dimension 19
Team Support from the Organization

Definition:
Organization sets clear objectives, provides team with access to resources, information and training; empowers the team to make decisions and rewards team performance.

Addresses the question:
Does the team get all of the organizational support it needs to perform its job?

A Dimension in the TEAM SUPPORT FROM THE ORGANIZATION Factor
How well the leadership of the organization enables the team to perform.

In order for your team to meet its goals, you must secure organizational support.
– Center for Creative Leadership

Items
73. The leadership of the organization sets clear and challenging strategies, goals, and measures for teams to rely on and plan against.
74. The leadership of the organization gives the team easy access to the resources, information, and training it needs to get the job done.
75. The leadership of the organization gives the team the authority to make its own decisions and the organization expedites making decisions that impact the team.
76. The leadership of the organization uses a reward system that encourages team performance.

Unskilled
☐ The organization does not have a clear vision, mission, or strategic business proposition for teams to plan against
☐ The organization does not have aligned performance measures in place
☐ The organization does not make accommodations to support virtual teams
☐ Organizational politics get in the way of the team having access to needed people, information, and resources
☐ The organization has not widely communicated the charter of teams

19

☐ Decisions critical to team success frequently get stalled somewhere in the organizational pipeline

☐ The organization does not respond to requests for resources from the team in a timely manner

☐ Leaders of this organization do not reward teams directly

☐ Performance measures are much more focused on individuals than on teams

☐ The leaders of this organization do not model effective team behaviors

☐ The leaders of this organization are not good at staffing teams with balanced and appropriate talent

☐ Organization does not give teams autonomy to perform; team activities are micromanaged

Skilled

☐ The leadership of the organization provides the ongoing support needed to keep teams on pace

☐ The leadership of the organization recognizes and supports team goals that are aligned with the business and cultural capabilities of the organization

☐ The rewards system in the organization is designed to include rewards for team accomplishments

☐ The organization communicates its strategy, direction, and goals to the team

☐ The leadership of the organization celebrates the achievements of winning teams publicly and loudly

☐ When a team's performance is meeting expectations, the organization gets out of the way and lets the team run

☐ The leadership of the organization is skilled at identifying talent and assembling the right teams for the jobs to be done

☐ The leadership of the organization is actively involved in the talent management moves throughout the organization

☐ The leadership of the organization actively listens to and values team recommendations

☐ The organization has a process in place that supports skill acquisition and knowledge expansion in teams

☐ The culture of the organization values teams; team membership is seen as an attractive career path

☐ The structure of the organization enables teams to thrive; silos and other barriers are kept to a minimum

Overused

☐ The organization overemphasizes teams beyond what is objectively needed by the business proposition

☐ The leadership of the organization does too much for teams

19

☐ The leadership of the organization overprescribes the goals and measures of the team, leaving little for the team to identify on its own

☐ The leadership of the organization provides too many answers for the team, leaving little for the team to do on its own

☐ The leadership of the organization gives the team so much autonomy that the business suffers before there is intervention to correct poor team performance

☐ The leaders are so team oriented that the organization loses significant talent due to the lack of individual rewards and recognition

☐ The leaders are so team oriented that the development of key individual talent is inadequate to staff the future

☐ The organization is so team oriented that individuals do not develop sufficiently to staff top leadership jobs; resulting lack of bench strength requires key jobs to be filled with outside talent

Note on overused strengths: Overused skills and disproportionately used strengths tend to have the negative effects listed above. To decrease those negative consequences, you have two alternatives. You can scale down or use the strength less, or you can compensate for it with another skill or behavior. In practice, it is very difficult to get an individual or a team to use a strength less. In most cases, the best path is to develop compensators. Team Architect® Dimensions that can compensate for overusing this dimension and compensating skills from the Leadership Architect® Library's 67 Competencies are listed below.

(Note: Team Dimension numbers are listed in parentheses. Competencies are listed in numerical order by competency number.)

Compensating Team Dimensions:

☐ Thrust Management (1)
☐ Thrust Commitment (3)
☐ Talent Acquisition and Enhancement (7)
☐ Talent Allocation and Deployment (8)
☐ Resource Management (9)
☐ Team Learning (10)
☐ Decision Making (11)
☐ Conflict Resolution (12)
☐ Managing Process (14)
☐ Focusing (15)
☐ Measurement (17)

19

Compensating Competencies:

- ☐ 5. Business Acumen
- ☐ 36. Motivating Others
- ☐ 56. Sizing Up People
- ☐ 58. Strategic Agility
- ☐ 60. *Building Effective* Teams

Some Causes of Poor Performance

- ☐ Organization leaders are unskilled at visioning and strategic planning
- ☐ Organization leaders are unskilled communicators
- ☐ Organization leaders delegate ineffectively
- ☐ Organization leaders are poor talent managers
- ☐ Organization leaders mostly function as individual performers; they do not work well within their own top management team
- ☐ Organization leaders are not timely decision makers
- ☐ Organization leaders have no experience in forming and sustaining a virtual workforce
- ☐ Organization leaders do not understand teams
- ☐ Organization leaders are poor motivators
- ☐ Organization is constricted by hierarchical design
- ☐ Organization is hampered by command and control mind-set
- ☐ Organizational culture rewards in-person face time
- ☐ Organization leaders do not value teams; their entire focus is on individual behaviors and performance

The Map

Without strong support from the organization, even great teams are likely to falter and fail to live up to their potential. The organization provides resources—money, materials, time, talent. The organization provides direction—vision, strategy, goals. Without these things, a team cannot hope to function at maximum effectiveness. For the most part, this element of team effectiveness is outside the direct control of individual teams. Organizations have to create and maintain a comprehensive support system and be team oriented to enable high-performing teams. Organizations that excel at providing support to teams have a viable and energizing business proposition and communicate it to them. These organizations measure progress and outcomes so that teams can plan and track against results. Supportive organizations know that teams have to be given space to perform. Leaders of these organizations freely delegate to and dependably provide resources for teams. They don't micromanage.

19

They don't ignore. Teams are heard in these organizations. Critical decisions aren't held up in committee. The organization's structure enables, rather than chills, teaming. Organizations that enable team effectiveness knock down silos, demand a free flow of information, and encourage cross-functional collaboration. The organization's leaders pay a great deal of attention to talent management. They identify and distribute the right talent to ensure team success. They promote the value of team assignments and link it to career progress. These organizations know that high-performing teams are interdependent, have mutual accountability. And they build a rewards system that recognizes this type of collaborative accomplishment.

Some Remedies

☐ 1. **Set the business proposition.** A compelling organizational mission and vision set the tone for how teams will operate. Where the team will focus efforts. How team objectives will take shape. An effective mission gives the organization an identity and reason for existing. Organizations with a powerful mission statement have a good story to tell. A story told with vivid language. Usually one that starts with the customer and clearly describes how the organization serves the customer better than the competition. If a mission is about who the organization is, then a vision is about looking to the future. Crafting an organizational vision answers questions like: What will be different in the future? The same? Be specific. Get people together and take time to discuss the vision. Pull out varying perspectives. Keep in mind that mission and vision will be set against the backdrop of the organization's values. Value statements put into words what it is the organization cares about. Which attributes will be recognized and rewarded in leaders, in the workforce, and in teams. Identify only the values that the organization really will exemplify, reward, and promote at every opportunity. They should be few in number. And everyone should be easily linked to the mission and vision. Show the value of teams by spotlighting their importance through the values statement. Be clear in illustrating how integral teams are to the mission and vision, how the focus on teaming will enable the organization to realize its vision.

☐ 2. **Create a compelling business strategy with teams at the core.** Once solidified, the mission, vision, and value statements set the context for business strategy. The strategy is the organization's road map for making the vision a reality. Like mission, vision, and values, a compelling business strategy takes the long view. Emphasizes what actions will enhance long-term owner and customer value. It puts meat on the bones of the mission statement. A compelling strategy starkly contrasts the organization with the competition. It is easily understood. It engages all stakeholders—

customers, investors, and the workforce. It defines what it is that the organization will do better than any other—like focusing on teams as a means of sustaining competitive advantage. It clearly spells out the value proposition. In an organization that values teams, the strategy becomes the road map for using teams to achieve results. The business strategy should be something that provides guidance and focus for team effort, resource allocation, decision making, and behaviors. A clear, teams-based strategy is one that charts a course, energizes teams, and promotes a sense of common purpose.

☐ **3. Promote a common mind-set by getting the message out.** Clearly communicate the strategy, vision, mission, and values to teams. Create a shared vocabulary that is used consistently in all messages around strategy, mission, vision, and values. Reinforce the message and vocabulary at every opportunity. A common language is critical to arriving at a shared understanding in the organization. In an organization that sees teams as central to its business proposition, it's nearly impossible to overcommunicate about the importance of teams in achieving strategy, mission, vision, and values. Communicating clearly and often promotes buy-in, commitment, and involvement around a teams-based business strategy. Craft the message by carefully considering the audience and purpose. What important information do teams need to understand the strategy? To align their efforts to the strategy? To accomplish their objectives effectively? Engage an internal or external PR staff member to help create key messages. Use as many media and channels as practical to communicate. Provide equal opportunity for all team members—virtual or collocated—to get the message. Leverage technology to reach all team members. Videos. Postings on team Web sites. Special forums for information sharing. Information lunches. Newsletters. Hold all leaders accountable for teaching, for explaining, for modeling, and rewarding the behaviors that support teaming, and watch as teams and the organization flourish.

☐ **4. Drive team alignment by measuring the right things.** How do we know we're doing well? How do we measure success? Determining what is important to measure can be a daunting task for an organization. No doubt there is a wide array of things that can be measured. The challenge is in finding the right things. It's too easy to get sidetracked measuring what is easily accessible, easily quantifiable. To ensure that the organization is using meaningful measures of performance, tie the measures to the business strategy. Establish key performance indicators, or KPIs, so that teams can track progress executing on the strategy. When measures are aligned, individual measures of success, rolled up to team measures of success, help move the organization forward. Indicators can be financial or non-financial and will vary, depending on the team responsible for the output. If a tenet of the business strategy is to grow market share, a sales team's KPI could be sales revenues or lead conversions in that market. Track KPIs using a balanced scorecard approach. A balanced scorecard helps illustrate alignment up and down the chain. Shows how the efforts of teams impact the organization overall. The end result of using a balanced scorecard approach should be consistent focus across all levels of the organization. Outcome, task, and process measures should each be considered equally when determining what constitutes superior performance. Reduce the volume of possible measures down to the critical few and focus on analyzing those thoroughly and consistently.

☐ **5. Evaluate organization design to support team performance.** All teams exist in a structure. Some organization structures are more conducive to high-performing teams than others. At a basic level, highly centralized command-and-control structures make it difficult for all but single-function teams to perform at peak capacity. In contrast, decentralized, flatter structures can't exist without a widespread and institutionalized team mind-set. Matrixed organizations function because multi-functional teams are formed to meet business demands. In a global marketplace, teams are becoming increasingly virtual. Structures that enable virtual team success are adaptive, technically advanced, and non-hierarchical. Take a hard look at the existing design and structure. How many layers are there? Can a team gain quick access to the very top of the organization? Does the organization have communications systems that enhance rapid exchanges of needs and information? Can the team requisition the resources it needs with minimum friction and noise? Is the bureaucracy kept to a minimum? Knock down silos that don't add value, that block collaboration across groups. Give teams the autonomy they need to perform. Give them resources and the authority to decide and act. Be on call to help when needed. Make timely decisions so teams can move on with their work. Provide a framework and support system that empowers teams to excel.

☐ **6. Focus on the competencies that make high-performing teams.** Identifying the technical skills needed to make a high-performing team is usually pretty straightforward. Will the team be implementing a new computer system? Creating a new product? Reengineering a process? All these deliverables require straightforward, specific functional skills. In addition, there are other skills—essential competencies—that determine how the deliverables are created. Teams improve performance by developing competencies. Research suggests that the most effective teams share a meaningful challenge and a focus on performance. Competencies like a healthy drive for results—supported by setting priorities, planning, and organizing—enable this kind of team performance mind-set. High-performing teams need to be skilled at informing so members have the information needed to do their work. Conflict in a team can be constructive or destructive, depending on how it's handled. So, a balance of standing up for oneself and managing conflict effectively is important. Teams can't maximize performance by stepping over everyone in their path. So, interpersonal skills need to be a focus as well. Competencies that play into this dynamic are listening, the ability to motivate, and managing peer relationships. Staff teams with these competencies in mind. If these skills are in short supply in the organization, team assignments can be a powerful means to help build these competencies. Research strongly indicates that people develop the most through on-the-job assignments. Participation in a team that's addressing real, meaningful business problems can be a very effective proving ground and accelerant for building competencies.

☐ 7. **Ensure that talent management practices support teams.** Lack of talent management has caught some organizations asleep at the wheel with dwindling bench strength and no system to prepare the next leaders for key positions. Talent management, done right, is a disciplined process. Organizations that follow the principles are reaping the rewards. It's tough for organizations to execute talent management well because it takes time, patience, and involvement from senior leaders. Organizations that are good at talent management are proactive with recruiting, development, and placement of talent. They know the difference between high performers and high potentials. They hire high performers for the technical jobs. They hire for potential in other key jobs. They give high potentials opportunities to do things that make them stretch early in their careers. To make a strong statement about the importance of teams in the organization, make teams a focal point of the talent management system. They put high potentials on high-profile teams working on high-stakes projects so they have an opportunity to learn a ton about the business, the culture, and the expertise of their teammates. Spotlight teams and team accomplishments through rewards and recognition. Demonstrate that team membership and teaming behaviors are valued, expected, and rewarded in the organization. Weed out mavericks whose only focus is on how team assignments further their own careers. Design the system so that the talent in the organization sees team involvement as an attractive career choice. Successful organizations develop team players who are put on teams to learn something powerful, to have an impact on the organization, and who then move on to bigger and better things.

19

☐ **8. Unlock the potential of virtual teams.** In a global marketplace, virtual teams are on the rise. These teams can take many shapes. Some teams are wholly virtual—no two members physically sit together within the same four walls. Others are a combination of collocated and dispersed members. Whatever the composition of a virtual team, this growing trend is a potential boon for organizations who are able to manage the virtual team dynamic effectively. Teams bring diversity to the work at hand. Diversity of experience, opinions, and insights. Virtual teams have these same qualities and more. When members are from different parts of the world, they bring the varied perspective of different cultures. This type of diversity spurs innovative thought. Avoids the pitfalls of groupthink. A virtual team model can bring efficiencies as well as increased innovation. Virtual team communication relies on technology with less frequent face-to-face interactions. This reduces the cost of coordinating work efforts and collaboration. To maximize virtual team effectiveness, integration into the overall organization is critical. When team members are geographically dispersed, it is common for the prevailing culture, structure, policies, and norms of the physical location to dominate in the team member's mind. Working relationships can be inhibited by difference between locations in things as basic as simple meeting protocols or decision-making processes. A strong, overriding culture that spans the entire organization, establishes shared norms, and integrates and actively supports teams—including virtual teams—will be most effective. In that kind of culture, team members will prioritize the total organization culture, including norms and policies, over those of their home location. Make sure virtual team members have equal access to leadership, resources, and technology. Find ways for virtual team members to get exposure to senior leaders. Recognize their contributions equally. Organizations that do these things well enjoy a significant return on investing in virtual teams.

☐ **9. Reward both individual and team performance.** Finding the right balance between individual and team incentives isn't easy. Surveys of both American and European companies show that organizations struggle with basing compensation for individuals on team performance. Yet, research clearly shows that organizations that consistently reward individuals *and* teams for performance outperform those that don't. Business is a team sport. Consider how to reward teams in addition to individual rewards. Organizations need to get comfortable with having different types of compensation systems: those that reward business unit results, team results, individual results, and sometimes a combination of results. The simplest way to reward the team is to pay them based on whether they accomplish their team goals or not. The key is to make sure the rewards

19

system isn't set up so that an individual or team can win by making another individual or team within the organization lose. Don't tempt individuals to do the wrong thing for the team in order to get a bigger deposit in their bank account. In teams, individual performance still matters, but it is looked at through a dual lens: what the individual member contributes and how that performance contributes to the team's success.

☐ **10. Create a culture that teams trust.** Teams expect the organization and its leaders to deliver on promises. Teams need a clear understanding of their performance objectives and associated constraints or limitations. Probably nothing chills trust more than when the organization says one thing and ends up doing something else. Trust in the organization and its leaders is built when actions match words. When the organization lives up to its commitments. When it provides adequate resources to the team. Uses fair performance and process measures. Compensates team accomplishments fairly. Leaders in the organization must be willing to listen to what the team needs and recommends and then do something about it on a timely basis. Even when the answer is no, timely and direct communication is critical. Don't lead teams into thinking their opinions about a decision really affect the outcome when it doesn't. Teams know when they are being jerked around. Don't ask for team input when a decision has already been made. If a decision requires a leader to use his/her authority without discussion, just say so. Some organizations use teams as a guise for getting employees to commit to a preconceived solution. A team submits one suggestion after another and encounters rejection at every turn until, finally, they get the thumbs-up only to find out it's for the decision the organization wanted all along. This may work well once, but after that, teams won't play the game. Therefore, investments in team recommendations need to be as hefty as the recommendation to fund the team's existence to start with.

19

Suggested Readings

Beyerlein, M. M., Freedman, S., McGee, C., & Moran, L. (2003). *Beyond teams: Building the collaborative organization.* San Francisco: Jossey-Bass/Pfeiffer.

Cascio, W. F. (2000). Managing a virtual workplace. *Academy of Management Executive, 14*(3), 81-90.

Duarte, D. L., & Snyder, N. T. (2006). *Mastering virtual teams: Strategies, tools, and techniques that succeed* (3rd ed.). San Francisco: Jossey-Bass.

Dyer, W. G., Dyer, W. G., Jr., & Dyer, J. H. (2007). *Team building: Proven strategies for improving team performance* (4th ed.). San Francisco: Jossey-Bass.

Gibson, C. B., & Cohen, S. G. (Eds.). (2003). *Virtual teams that work: Creating conditions for virtual team effectiveness.* San Francisco: Jossey-Bass.

Hackman, J. R. (2002). *Leading teams: Setting the stage for great performances.* Boston: Harvard Business School Press.

Hoefling, T. (2003). *Working virtually: Managing people for successful virtual teams and organizations.* Sterling, VA: Stylus.

Kaplan, R. S., & Norton, D. P. (1996). *The balanced scorecard.* Boston: Harvard Business School Press.

Katzenbach, J. R., & Smith, D. K. (1993). *The wisdom of teams.* New York: HarperCollins.

Lawler, E. E., III. (2000). *From the ground up: Six principles for building the new logic corporation.* San Francisco: Jossey-Bass.

Lombardo, M. M., & Eichinger, R. W. (2004). *The leadership machine: Architecture to develop leaders for any future.* Minneapolis, MN: Lominger International: A Korn/Ferry Company.

Ruyle, K. R., Eichinger, R. W., & De Meuse, K. P. (2009). *FYI for Talent Engagement™: Drivers of best practice.* Minneapolis, MN: Lominger International: A Korn/Ferry Company.

Wheelan, S. A. (2005). *Creating effective teams: A guide for members and leaders* (2nd ed.). Thousand Oaks, CA: Sage.

19

Translation to the Leadership Architect® Competency Library

In order for an organization's leadership to perform well in this area, these are the competencies that would most likely be in play. Aside from an organization improvement plan where all leaders work on the same thing, some individual leaders may need to work on some of these competencies. A critical number (but not necessarily all) of organization leaders would have to be good at:

Mission Critical:	Important:	Nice to Have:
18. Delegation	47. Planning	36. Motivating Others
20. Directing Others	50. Priority Setting	38. Organizational Agility
27. Informing	52. Process Management	53. *Drive for* Results
35. Managing and Measuring Work	60. *Building Effective* Teams	56. Sizing Up People
65. *Managing* Vision and Purpose		58. Strategic Agility

In addition to the 10 tips listed for this dimension, there are additional tips that may apply from *FYI For Your Improvement*™. Below are the four items from the Team Architect® that make up this dimension. The item number appears to the left of each item. Immediately below the text of each item are competency and tip numbers from *FYI*. The competency is listed first (from 1 to 67), followed by the tip number (1 to 10). For example, 33-4 refers to competency 33 (Listening), tip number 4. The tips are generally written for individual development, so some adaptation might be needed in the team context.

73. The leadership of the organization sets clear and challenging strategies, goals, and measures for teams to rely on and plan against.
27-2,7; 35-1,6,7; 50-3; 58-2,8; 63-3; 65-1,2

74. The leadership of the organization gives the team easy access to the resources, information, and training it needs to get the job done.
18-2,3; 27-2,7; 38-4,10; 39-2; 50-2,3; 63-6

75. The leadership of the organization gives the team the authority to make decisions or at least get one made immediately.
1-2; 18-2,4,8,9; 27-1,5; 35-1,2; 110-1

76. The leadership of the organization uses a reward system that encourages team performance.
35-1,2,3,6; 110-1,4,6,7,8,9

Dimension 20
Team Leader Fit

Definition:
Team leader aligns the team to the organization's vision and strategy and champions the team to the organization; empowers, motivates, and develops team members to achieve goals.

Addresses the question:
Does the team have the right leader?

A Dimension in the TEAM LEADER FIT Factor
How well-matched the team leader is with the needs of the team.

> *If anything goes bad, I did it. If anything goes semi–good, then we did it.*
> *If anything goes really good, then you did it.*
> Paul "Bear" Bryant – American football coach

Items
77. The leader of this team has the necessary skills, perspective, and style (manages in a team way) to lead this team to excel.
78. The leader of this team has sufficient strategic and tactical planning skills to set a clear and challenging direction for and with the team.
79. The leader of this team lets people work on their own, recognizes and rewards good performance, challenges and coaches the team when it needs to perform better, and critiques the team when it has performed poorly.
80. The leader of this team runs interference outside the team, is politically astute in helping and protecting the team, seeks information and resources not readily available, and gets external buy-in for team initiatives.

Unskilled
☐ The team leader lacks key skills required for the team's mission
☐ The team leader fails to motivate the team to excel
☐ The team leader does not align the work of the team to the vision and strategy of the organization

20

- ☐ The team leader does not empower individuals or the team to make decisions or perform
- ☐ The team leader does not provide feedback to the team or individual members
- ☐ The team leader fails to coach or does so ineffectively
- ☐ The team leader does not set clear expectations around performance
- ☐ The team leader places inadequate emphasis on team performance
- ☐ The team leader does not engage virtual team members
- ☐ The team leader does not effectively run interference for the team in the rest of the organization
- ☐ The team leader is not well connected to others in the organization, including key sponsors
- ☐ The team leader doesn't build rapport and a sense of mutual accountability in the team

Skilled

- ☐ The leader of the team is a strong, effective communicator
- ☐ The leader of the team is sensitive to the varying needs of each individual on the team
- ☐ The team leader models exemplary teaming behavior
- ☐ The team leader advocates for the team in the organization
- ☐ The team leader seeks feedback on performance; is self-aware and has a catalog of strengths and weaknesses
- ☐ The team leader builds a sense of camaraderie in the team
- ☐ The team leader trusts the team to get the job done; empowers team to perform with minimal support
- ☐ The team leader monitors the team's performance and coaches team members to improve performance when needed
- ☐ The team leader sets priorities that are aligned with the organization's objectives and vision
- ☐ The team leader communicates expectations and gains buy-in from team members
- ☐ The team leader provides developmental opportunities and assignments
- ☐ The team leader ensures that virtual team members have equal exposure and recognition for team accomplishments

Overused

- ☐ The team leader is a one-trick pony; skills are so specialized that they may be good for this team and for this situation, but not good in other situations

20

☐ The team leader is a team advocate at the expense of advocacy for the broader organization

☐ The team leader prioritizes virtual team member engagement to the point that local members feel neglected

☐ The team leader is so focused on teaming behavior that results may suffer

☐ The team leader builds such a strong sense of team identity that it is hard for new members to break in and get up to speed

Note on overused strengths: Overused skills and disproportionately used strengths tend to have the negative effects listed above. To decrease those negative consequences, you have two alternatives. You can scale down or use the strength less, or you can compensate for it with another skill or behavior. In practice, it is very difficult to get an individual or a team to use a strength less. In most cases, the best path is to develop compensators. Team Architect® Dimensions that can compensate for overusing this dimension and compensating skills from the Leadership Architect® Library's 67 Competencies are listed below.

(Note: Competencies are listed in numerical order by competency number.)

Compensating Team Dimensions

All dimensions may apply. The team will have to perform under little or no constructive leadership.

Compensating Competencies:

☐   2. *Dealing with* Ambiguity
☐ 19. Developing Direct Reports and Others
☐ 28. Innovation Management
☐ 50. Priority Setting
☐ 51. Problem Solving

Some Causes of Poor Performance

☐ The team leader's skills are not aligned with the mission of the team

☐ The team leader is not self-aware and doesn't know his/her strengths and weaknesses

☐ The team leader is uncomfortable giving up power or authority

☐ The team leader has a tactical, narrow perspective

☐ The team leader is not politically or organizationally agile

☐ The team leader does not have enough of the universal skills of a good manager and leader

20

☐ The team leader does not adapt well to change

☐ The team leader avoids open conflict

The Map

Teams come in many shapes and sizes. Cross-functional and specific to a business unit. Permanent and temporary. Stable or fluid team membership. Virtual and collocated in close physical proximity. Self-directed versus managed decision making. Executive, management, non-management, or a mix of all. With the wide array of team types out there, it's no wonder that finding the right leader to enable a team to be successful can be a challenge. What defines an effective team leader will, to some extent, vary depending on the type of team being led. Certain kinds of skills work with certain kinds of teams and team tasks. Self-directed teams typically need a light leadership touch—guidance on strategic priorities, air cover in the organization, and access to resources the team needs to get the job done. Conventionally managed teams typically require a more hands-on leadership approach—clear direction, regular monitoring, and inspiration to rally around shared objectives. Senior or executive teams bring together strong, opinionated individuals who are used to leading, to being in charge. The leader of a team of forceful individual executives has to manage those big personalities to get results. Virtual team leaders have to overcome time, technology, and sometimes cultural barriers in order to lead their teams effectively. The best team leaders can serve either multiple teams or can shift gears with the same team over time. Bottom line: effective team leaders are adaptable and flex to fit the team's needs. That's not to say every team has a unique set of leadership requirements. In fact, there are some universal interpersonal competencies that are helpful when leading almost any team in almost any situation. Those competencies enable leaders to provide challenges, set up chances to learn and grow, and provide autonomy. Effective team leaders know themselves, seek feedback on their performance, and hold their teams to the same high standards to which they hold themselves. They create a strong sense of cohesion. They trust the team to perform, and the team, in turn, trusts its leader to provide support and coaching to help it be successful.

Some Remedies

☐ 1. **Audit the current state of team leader fit.** Does the team have the right leader? Does the leader have the right skills? Are the leader's perceptions of team effectiveness in sync with those of the team members? Sometimes the best way to answer questions like this is by gathering the data through an assessment. The leader and the team can separately weigh in on areas such as shared purpose and objectives, trust in the team, collective team talent, and operating skills. The goal is to determine not only how well a team is working together, but to surface any misalignments between the team and its leader. Some themes will likely emerge. Leaders may overestimate how much strategic direction they are giving the team or underestimate the level of trust members have in each other and the team's chances for success. Identifying areas that are out of sync will provide focus for development of the team leader and/or the team. Any audit of team effectiveness should also include team leader fit. Have the team evaluate its leader on things like communicating strategy, coaching and development, empowerment, garnering resources, and running interference in the organization. Guarantee safe harbor for the team when evaluating the leader; otherwise, results won't be valid. This type of feedback exercise helps the team feel valued and helps the leader increase his/her effectiveness.

☐ **2. Drive alignment messages.** Team leaders play multiple roles, depending on the makeup and charter of the team. They can be doers who contribute directly to team work output, managers who direct and monitor the work done by team members, or both. The team leader many times also plays the role of chief translator for organizational mission and strategy. Translating organizational priorities into team priorities creates a sense of purpose and generates energy as the team senses they're pulling in the same direction. Team leaders who do this well communicate frequently to ensure the team knows what the organization is doing and why at all times. These leaders know that being kept in the loop helps team members feel valued and more likely to work toward collective goals, act in concert with greater efficiency and effectiveness. It's practically impossible to overcommunicate in this area. Every team member should be able to clearly explain the team's strategy and how it aligns with the organization's strategy. They should be able to explain how their individual and team efforts contribute to achieving organizational objectives.

☐ **3. Build relationships to motivate the team.** Effective team leaders create a climate in which team members want to do their best, are energized about the direction of the team, and confident in their ability to execute. Effective leaders use language to paint pictures that illustrate the importance of team objectives. They celebrate successes when the team hits the mark. They understand that motivation is highly personal and adjust their messages accordingly. They learn what motivates the team—as a whole and individually. They take cultural norms into consideration when determining what motivates virtual team members. Create connections.

20

Individual team members who feel connected at some level to their leader tend to be more engaged in their work. Building this connection isn't hard. Learn three non-work things about everyone on the team—their interests and hobbies or their children or something you can chat about. Being the team leader doesn't always ensure closeness with the team. Some team leaders are better at bonding with their teams than others. It can be especially difficult if the team leader is brought into a long-standing team that has a lot of history. Suggest some formal team building and include face-to-face time with virtual team members if at all possible. Uncover common interests. Create situations where everyone's skills get discovered and where no one has an advantage because of rank, tenure, or technical expertise. Make time for activities that promote team camaraderie.

☐ 4. Be the team's champion in the organization. Advocating for the team in the organization is one of the most powerful ways for a leader to gain the team's trust. For teams to stay as productive as possible, they need to have confidence in their abilities and know that their leader trusts them to perform and will provide support when needed. These teams have leaders who are willing to take the heat and shield the team from organizational politics that might get in the way of the team's work. Championing the team in the organization means more than running interference. It means knowing how to work the maze, get needed resources, knock down bureaucracy if it is impeding productivity. Organizationally savvy leaders work the internal network to get things done for the team. They avoid political traps and dead ends. They can reliably expedite requests. They have relationships with the major gatekeepers who control the flow of resources, information, and decisions. And they know the most effective pathway to get answers. Team leader champions are skilled at influencing others. They don't just ask for things. They find some common ground. Create a compelling case to inspire the resource providers. Paint a vivid picture of what results these resources will bring. They share best practices with other groups. They're not afraid to ask for resources but adopt a trading mentality rather than a handout mentality. Being a strong advocate for the team in the organization doesn't mean the leader won't hold the team to high expectations. Accountability is critical in a high-performing team. The leader has to expect it and call it out when results aren't there. A strong team advocate gives the team confidence that the leader is looking out for their shared interests and will provide the appropriate amount of air cover in the organization for decisions and actions the team undertakes.

☐ 5. Let the team work the plan. In all but the most tightly managed, command-and-control team dynamics, performance flourishes most when teams are given enough elbow room to perform. Autonomy.

20

202

Empowerment. Shared decision making. All these increase engagement and, ultimately, productivity. The more a decision impacts the team, the more they should be involved. Sharing in decisions is also on-the-job training for developing skills like problem solving, decision quality, and conflict management. Moving decision-making authority to the front lines of the team can be a risky business. Giving the team autonomy over the work can lead to both positive strides forward and a couple of steps back. Publicly support team decisions that are well-thought-out and stand behind team members as they experiment with new things. Nothing stifles initiative more than continually being second-guessed. Send a clear message that there is amnesty for reasonable, calculated risks that don't pan out. Sometimes the greatest leaps forward in innovation come from learning what not to do. Figure out ways to give team members as much control over their work as possible. Minimize bureaucratic control. Give them as much latitude to make decisions as is reasonable. As much autonomy as possible. Discretion. Flexibility. Try to establish the habit of cooperatively setting goals, schedules and due dates, and identifying the resources needed for the task. And, very importantly, let the team figure out how to get the work accomplished.

☐ **6. Keep a focus on team performance.** There's no getting around it, even in a team. Performance counts. In a team, ownership and accountability for wins and losses are shared by all, yet the leader does carry a heavier burden in that regard. The leader is ultimately accountable. The best team leaders are driven to achieve results and pass on that drive to the team members. When the performance is there, the leader needs to crow about it, loudly and often. Find accomplishments and outcomes that warrant celebration. If the team misses the mark, it can't be swept under the rug. Team leaders need to work with their team to figure out what's going wrong or getting in the way of the team performing. Is the team getting bogged down in minutiae? Set clear priorities so that the team stays focused on what's mission critical to their success. Missing needed resources? Identify what the team needs and teach team members how to negotiate, bargain, and influence to get what they need. Is there wasted motion? Follow best practices for streamlining team work processes for maximum efficiency. Lack of interdependence among team members? Arrange for team members to leave their comfort zones and depend on one another. Use exercises where individual performance means nothing if the team's performance doesn't prevail. Make sure the exercises focus on team outcomes, not individual success. To drive performance in the team, be crystal clear that outcomes are the responsibility of each team member as well as the leader.

20

☐ **7. Give the gift of feedback.** Teams that consistently perform well and continuously improve are those that have a high-candor feedback protocol. Team leaders need to establish this protocol at team formation so it becomes one of the team's norms. Set the tone so that it is understood that the purpose of feedback is to help guide and support team members to be successful in their work. Establishing expectations around feedback in this way communicates positive intent and helps remove tension. Remember that effective feedback shouldn't be one way. The leader delivers feedback to the team and individual members, sure; but, the leader should also ask for regular feedback from the team. And team members should freely give feedback to each other. In teams that have created a culture steeped in candor and straight talk, giving and receiving feedback is as natural as breathing. Feedback is given frequently, usually in real time during and immediately following performance. The feedback is tied to goals. Performance goals. Developmental goals. Feedback on performance helps the team adjust what they are doing along the way and make midcourse corrections. Developmental and career feedback shows individual team members that what they are doing is important and that the leader is there to help them grow and progress with the organization. Start viewing the giving—and receiving—of feedback as a gift, not a burden.

☐ **8. Master leading virtual teams.** If leading a team that works in close physical proximity is tough, the challenges facing leaders of virtual teams can be especially daunting. Building and maintaining focus in a virtual team often falls on the shoulders of the leader. They may feel like they're the glue that holds a virtual team together. One virtual team manager put it this way: "How can I build a team when there are 30 people dispersed across several countries and time zones?" Time zone constraints are a reality that can slow teams down. Someone is bound to be inconvenienced: a 6:00 a.m. teleconference on the east coast of the United States means 8:00 p.m. in Asia. Team leader rapport-building opportunities are usually limited to a virtual setting. Research on communication indicates that more than 50% of communication power is lost when not done face-to-face. We lose body language, voice-tone subtleties, facial expressions. Team leaders who overcome these roadblocks take a proactive stance. These leaders communicate with virtual members—a lot. They give adequate work direction, check in frequently, and provide feedback on performance. Feedback to virtual team members is especially vital since they often feel isolated from the overall team. These leaders leverage technology to streamline communication. Alternative methods like instant messaging, desktop videoconferencing, and team Web site postings. This focus on technology is critical in virtual team leadership. The baseline expectation

20

204

is that technology will be an aid to the team's work. When technology is a barrier, it's especially demotivating to virtual teams. Stay current on collaboration technologies. Make sure that differences in hardware or software configurations don't get in the way of team productivity. When leading virtual teams across different cultures, be careful not to impose one culture over another. Instead, find "third ways" to collaborate—less a compromise between two or more disparate ways of doing things and more a creation of new norms unique to the team. Virtual members sometimes fear that their careers will suffer, that they will be overlooked. Recognize virtual team member contributions equally. Play an active role in career planning; emphasize virtual team membership as an attractive developmental and career path, not a dead end.

☐ **9. Focus on building competencies that make good team leaders.** Skills that help a person excel as an individual contributor—being smart, technically proficient, and results driven—are not necessarily the skills that make a good team leader. Effective team leaders have strong interpersonal skills, know how to develop people, and have a knack for getting work done through others as much as or more than doing it themselves. Research is clear that lack of core interpersonal skills is a fatal flaw for team leaders that stumble. Outside of these general skills, when deciding the right fit between a potential leader and the team, consider the following:

– What skills are needed, given the team's priorities and responsibilities?
– What style will work best with the team dynamics?
– What developmental and work experiences will add the most value?
– What values will best fit?
– What technical or functional skills will be needed?

Armed with this information, summarize and prioritize the competencies that are mission critical to all of the above. Which are nice to have and which are most important? If the team leader were to derail due to competency gaps, which ones would be the most likely culprits? These can vary by the culture of the organization, charter of the team, makeup of the team, and customer demands. Minimize risk by staffing the team with a leader who possesses the right skills to enable the team to be successful.

☐ **10. Invest in a personal coach/mentor for team leader development.** Team leaders have a lot on their plates. They are constantly juggling multiple roles. As agents of the organization, team leaders facilitate policies and influence how they are applied to team members. As leaders, they are pivotal partners in the psychological contract that affects team member commitment. This doesn't even count the pressure to "make the numbers." To help team leaders be most effective, invest in a coach or advisor. One skilled in human and team behavior who can observe, provide non-threatening feedback, and create a development plan for the leader to be successful. This is generally an external resource. A personal coach should gather feedback on the team leader from team members, peers, boss, customers, and others (via 360° or interviewing) and use it to understand how the team leader is perceived. The coach should also do some firsthand observing to test for accuracy and validity of the feedback. This can be done in team meetings, everyday team activities, and even social settings. The coach may have the team leader complete some standardized psychological questionnaires to dig deeper. The key is for the coach to be able to present to the leader the most accurate and complete picture possible. After that, the coach will help the leader devise a development plan that is made up primarily (70%) of on-the-job development activities to improve his/her performance. A smaller portion will also include learning from other key people (20%), and finally, perhaps some training or books (10%) to close other gaps that may be lacking. The coach and the leader should meet regularly if there are serious performance/leadership gaps.

20

Suggested Readings

Duarte, D. L., & Snyder, N. T. (2006). *Mastering virtual teams: Strategies, tools, and techniques that succeed* (3rd ed.). San Francisco: Jossey-Bass.

Gibson, C. B., & Cohen, S. G. (Eds.). (2003). *Virtual teams that work: Creating conditions for virtual team effectiveness*. San Francisco: Jossey-Bass.

Hackman, J. R. (2002). *Leading teams: Setting the stage for great performances*. Boston: Harvard Business School Press.

Harkins, P. (2006). High-impact team leaders. *Leadership Excellence, 23*(10), 3-4.

Hunsaker, P. L., & Hunsaker, J. S. (2008). Virtual teams: A leader's guide. *Team Performance Management, 14*(1/2), 86-101.

Jenewein, W., & Morhart, F. (2008). Navigating toward team success. *Team Performance Management, 14*(1/2), 102-108.

Katzenbach, J. R., & Smith, D. K. (1993). *The wisdom of teams*. New York: HarperCollins.

LaFasto, F., & Larson, C. (2001). *When teams work best*. Thousand Oaks, CA: Sage.

Parker, G. M. (2008). *Team players and teamwork: New strategies for developing successful collaboration* (2nd ed.). San Francisco: Jossey-Bass.

Wheelan, S. A. (2005). *Creating effective teams: A guide for members and leaders* (2nd ed.). Thousand Oaks, CA: Sage.

20

Translation to the Leadership Architect® Competency Library

In order for the leader of a team to perform well, these are the competencies that would most likely be in play. Individual team leaders may need to work on some or all of these competencies to improve his/her performance as a leader:

Mission Critical:	Important:	Nice to Have:
18. Delegation	9. Command Skills	8. Comfort Around
20. Directing Others	33. Listening	Higher Management
27. Informing	56. Sizing Up People	12. Conflict Management
35. Managing and	65. *Managing* Vision and	36. Motivating Others
Measuring Work	Purpose	47. Planning
45. Personal Learning		50. Priority Setting
60. *Building Effective*		
Teams		

In addition to the ten tips listed for this dimension, there are additional tips that may apply from *FYI For Your Improvement™*. Below are the four items from the Team Architect® that make up this dimension. The item number appears to the left of each item. Immediately below the text of each item are competency and tip numbers from *FYI*. The competency is listed first (from 1 to 67), followed by the tip number (1 to 10). For example, 33-4 refers to competency 33 (Listening), tip number 4.

77. The leader of this team has the necessary skills, perspective, and style (manages in a team way) to lead this team to excel.
5-6; 9-8; 18-10; 27-1; 32-1; 35-1,2; 56-3; 110-1,4

78. The leader of this team has sufficient strategic and tactical planning skills to set a clear and challenging direction for and with the team.
27-2,3; 35-2,3; 47-1,7; 58-3,4; 65-1,2

79. The leader of this team lets people work on their own, recognizes and rewards good performance, challenges and coaches the team when it needs to perform better, and critiques the team when it has performed poorly.
13-2,5; 18-8; 27-2; 35-7,9; 110-3,5,8,10

80. The leader of this team runs interference outside the team, is politically astute in helping and protecting the team, seeks information and resources not readily available, and gets external buy-in for team initiatives.
2-5; 8-6; 9-1; 37-1,2; 38-4,10; 42-5; 43-8; 48-2

Appendix A
General Plan

The following is a general development plan for any competency or behavior that is not directly contained under the 20 dimensions of the team model. This general plan works for individual team member plans or for the entire team in general.

☐ **1. Detail the need.** In order to make sure the individual or team is working on the right things, get more detailed and behavioral feedback on the need. Most of the time, people or teams are weak in some aspect of a competency. It's almost never all aspects of interpersonal skills, for example. It's usually something specific—relationship skills with upper management under the pressure of tough questions from two of the seven on the management committee on topics the team cares deeply about. To find out more about what the need is specifically, go to a few people who might know and who will tell you if you ask. Accept that the team has a need. Don't be defensive or try to rationalize away the need. Say that the team is concerned about the need and has requested more detailed information so they can focus on an efficient plan for growth and development. Ask the person for specific examples. What? When? Where? With whom? In what settings? Under what conditions? How many times? What signs and signals are they reading? Might anyone they know be of help? Get as specific as you can. Listen, don't rebut. Take notes. Thank them for the input.

☐ **2. Read the "bible" on this need.** Every skill or competency has had one or more books written about it: How to negotiate to win. How to get along with bad bosses. How to win friends. How to be more creative. Go to a business bookstore or go out to the Internet and buy at least two books for each team member covering the need. Have each member scan the first book. Have them just read the first sentence of every paragraph. Don't read to learn. Just read to see the structure of the book. Have a team meeting and debrief the first book. What did members take away from that book? How do people chunk the need? How is it structured? How many aspects of the need are there? Then have everyone read the second book thoroughly. This time to learn. The books may reference or lead to other books or articles on the skill. Have a second team meeting and debrief the second book. Try to answer the following questions: What's the research on the skill? What are the aspects of the skill? What are the 10 how-to's all the experts would agree to? How is this skill best learned? What are some

A-1

action steps the team could take to build the skill? Combine these learnings with Step 1 to either confirm or modify the specifics of the need.

☐ **3. Study legendary (either successful or not) teams.** Try to find books or articles about teams that have the skill you are trying to build or teams that didn't have it and stumbled. The Boeing 777 team. The research team that created Nylon. The Iacocca team that created the first minivan. The GE team. The Mars Lander team. *BusinessWeek* and other publications regularly run articles on successful and not-so-successful teams. Try to see how they wove the skill the team is working on into their fabric of skills. Was there a point when the team wasn't good at this skill? What was the turning point? Add these learnings to the definition of the need.

☐ **4. Learn from a course.** Find the best course the team has access to on the need. It might be offered in your organization, or more likely, it will be a public program. Find one that is taught by the author of a book or a series of articles on this need. Be sure to give it enough time. It usually takes three to five days to learn about any skill or competency. One- to two-day courses are usually not long enough. You can either send one or a few members who bring back the learning, or the entire team can attend. Or you can bring the teacher to the team. Find a course where the team can learn the theory and have a lot of practice with the skill. Find one that videotapes if the skill lends itself to the lens. Team members should become immersed in the course. No phone calls. Don't take any work. No sightseeing. Just do the course. Be the best student in the course and learn the most. Seldom will a course alone be sufficient to address a need. A course always has to be combined with the other remedies in this general development plan, especially stretching tasks, so the team can perform against the need under pressure.

☐ **5. Create the plan.** With all of the detailed data created in Steps 1–4, it's time to put together a plan. There are four kinds of action plans. The team needs to know what to:

- Stop doing. Since the team has a need in this area (the team doesn't do this well), it needs to stop some things that aren't working.
- Start doing. The team needs to start doing some things it either doesn't like doing, hasn't ever done, or doesn't even know about. Even if the team is bad at something, there are things it does in this area that it is probably good at.
- Keep doing. Even in an area of need or a weakness, there are probably things that the team can keep doing with no problem.
- Keep doing but modify. There are things the team can keep doing, but they need slight to moderate modifications to work better.

Ask a number of people who would be willing to help the team work on this skill. Tell them the team has discovered and taken ownership of this need and wants to do something about it. List the specific need the team has decided to work on in Step 1, and ask the person to tell you the things the team should stop doing, start doing, keep doing, and keep doing but modify.

☐ **6. Learn from others.** Research shows that we learn best from others when we:

- Pick multiple models, each of which excels at one thing, rather than looking for the whole package in one person or one team. Think more broadly than the current setting for models; add some off-work models.

- Ask team members to take both the student role and the teacher role. As students, study other people and other teams—don't just admire or dislike what they do. One key to learning from others is to reduce what they do or don't do to a set of principles or rules of thumb to integrate into the team's behavior. As teachers, it's one of the best ways to learn something because it forces team members to think it through and be concise in their explanations.

- Rely on multiple methods of learning—interview people and teams, observe them without speaking with them, study remote models by reading books or watching films, get someone to tutor the team, or use a contrast strategy. Sometimes it's hard for team members to see the effects of their behavior because they are too close to the problem. Pick two people or teams—one who is much better than the team at the need and one who is much worse. Copy what the good model does that leads to good outcomes. Get rid of the behaviors that match what the bad model does.

☐ **7. Get a learning partner.** Sometimes it's easier for a team to build a new skill if they have someone to work with. If they can find another person or team working on the same need, they can share learnings and support each other. Take turns teaching each other some to-dos—one of the best ways to cement learning. Share books they've found. Courses they've attended. Models they've observed. They can give each other progress feedback. Have the other person or team agree to observe and give feedback against the learning objectives.

☐ **8. Try some stretching tasks, but start small.** Seventy percent of skill development happens on the job. As you and your team talk with others while building this skill, get the other person or team to brainstorm tasks and activities your team can try. Write down five tasks team members will commit to doing, tasks like:

- Initiate three conversations with team partners.
- Make peace with someone they've had problems with.
- Write a business plan for the team.
- Negotiate a purchase.
- Make a speech.
- Find something to fix.

Team members can try tasks off the job as well: teach someone to read, be a volunteer, join a study group, take up a new hobby—whatever will help them practice the need in a fairly low-risk way. After each task, ask team members to write down the positive and constructive aspects of their performance and note things they will try to do better or differently next time.

☐ **9. Track progress.** The team is going to need some extra motivation to get through this. The team needs to be able to reward itself for progress it has made. Others may not notice the subtle changes for a while. Set progress goals and benchmarks against them. Keep a log. Make a chart. Celebrate incremental progress. Make sure all team members have access to the progress information.

☐ **10. Get periodic progress feedback.** Teams can get feedback from three kinds of sources. The team can self-assess progress. This probably would be the least accurate. Teams can ask the same set of people who helped them detail the need in the first place. That's a good strategy, but remember that the other person or team will have a blended view—the team as it was before and the team now. Sometimes it's hard for someone who observed the need at its worst to be convinced much progress has been made. Best is to ask a group of people who haven't known the team before or for long. They don't have a history of seeing the team not doing well in this skill over a long period of time. Their feedback would be the most useful.

Team Development Plan

The following pages provide you with a Development Plan template where you can record your team's development need and action plan. There are two examples (Unskilled and Overused) to help you get started. For more details, refer to the Introduction in this book.

PERMISSION TO COPY DEVELOPMENT PLAN: *This confirms that Lominger International: A Korn/Ferry Company is granting you the right to make copies of the Team Development Plan on pages A-6 through A-11 of FYI for Teams™ appendix. Such copies are for the internal use of your organization only. All copies must retain the copyright notice located on the bottom of each page.*

Sample Team Development Plan (Unskilled):

Team Development Need: 14 Managing Process

TEAM MEMBER NAME:
TO BE COMPLETED BY:

TEAM "BEFORE" DESCRIPTION *(Unskilled)*	SOME CAUSES FOR THE TEAM
Team members do not anticipate problems or roadblocks.	Team members may not be process oriented; not systems oriented.

TEAM LEARNINGS FROM "THE MAP"

Most processes start with the end in mind and design the process backwards. The methods include a measurement element so the team can monitor results and a continuous improvement component.

QUOTES THAT INSPIRE THE TEAM

"It is a fact that in the right formation, the lifting power of many wings can achieve twice the distance of any bird flying alone." – Author Unknown

TEAM ACTION PLAN
(Development Remedies)

14.4 – Recognize common process breakdowns: Look for trends where high-frequency and high-impact problems occur with the processes.

14.6 – Make process measures open and visible: Use signs or technology to post team goals, processes, data, and progress toward accomplishment.

14.9 – Do roadblock scenario planning: By thinking about all of the things that could go wrong, the team can design checks and balances.

(Related individual competency)
51.4 Problem Solving – Get out of your comfort zone: Beware of "I have always…" or "Usually I.…" Ask yourself if this is really like problems you have solved in the past.

TEAM "AFTER" DESCRIPTION
(Skilled)

The team anticipates problems and makes process adjustments to overcome problems and roadblocks.

The team has measurement systems that provide early warnings on broken processes.

SUGGESTED READINGS

Measuring team performance: A step-by-step, customizable approach for managers, facilitators, and team leaders (2000) by S. D. Jones and D. J. Schilling.

Sample Team Development Plan (Overused):

Team Development Need: 13 Team Atmosphere

TEAM MEMBER NAME:

TO BE COMPLETED BY:

TEAM "BEFORE" DESCRIPTION (Overused)	SOME CAUSES FOR THE TEAM
Team is perceived as too tight a clique. It's extremely difficult for a new team member to fit in because the team is so close.	Team members may not have had enough time to bond.

TEAM LEARNINGS FROM "THE MAP"

People are more productive being part of a team where members trust, respect, and basically like being around each other. They want to work in an environment that's positive and energizing. They want to enjoy and have pride in what they do.

QUOTES THAT INSPIRE THE TEAM

"If you can laugh together, you can work together." — Robert Orben, American magician and writer

TEAM ACTION PLAN
(Development Remedies and Compensators)

13.4 — Help new team members get on board: The team needs to roll their sleeves back up and spend some time re-forming. Create an orientation process, including team charter and goals, role clarity for the new member, a candid assessment of how the team is doing.

Compensator:

1.5 — Involve the whole team: Everyone needs to be on board with the goals for a team to reach peak performance.

(Related individual competency)
65.2 Managing Vision and Purpose — Build a common mind-set: Provide everyone with a road map on how they are going to be part of something grand and exciting. Help people see how their efforts fit in.

TEAM "AFTER" DESCRIPTION
(Skilled)

Openings on this team are easy to fill.

The whole team celebrates its successes.

SUGGESTED READINGS

Team players and teamwork: New strategies for developing successful collaboration (2nd ed.) (2008) by G. M. Parker.

Team Development Plan:

....

....

....

TEAM MEMBER NAME: ....

TO BE COMPLETED BY: ....

TEAM "BEFORE" DESCRIPTION *(Unskilled or Overused)*	SOME CAUSES FOR THE TEAM

TEAM LEARNINGS FROM "THE MAP"

QUOTES THAT INSPIRE THE TEAM

....

TEAM ACTION PLAN
(Development Remedies or Compensators)
....

TEAM "AFTER" DESCRIPTION
(Skilled)
....

A

SUGGESTED READINGS

....

Appendix B
Team Architect® Sort Card Items by Factor and Dimension

Factor I. Thrust

DIMENSION 1 – THRUST MANAGEMENT
1. Disagreements on goals discussed
19. Scans environment
37. Constantly monitors accuracy
55. Sets challenging goals

DIMENSION 2 – THRUST CLARITY
2. Members understand goals
20. Clearly describes mission
38. Clearly states success measures
56. Goals align with work

DIMENSION 3 – THRUST COMMITMENT
3. Sense of commitment
21. Committed to goals
39. Responsible customer commitments
57. Shares values of organization

Factor II. Trust

DIMENSION 4 – TRUST IN TRUTHFUL COMMUNICATION
4. Says what's on minds
22. Understands differences
40. Open with one another
58. Improving process

DIMENSION 5 – TRUST IN ACTIONS
5. Backs each other up
23. Disagrees but still supports
41. Members "walk their talk"
59. Works well with other teams

DIMENSION 6 – TRUST INSIDE THE TEAM
6. Sacrifices for good of team
24. No internal competition
42. Effort into building team
60. Team members there to help

Factor III. Talent

DIMENSION 7 – TALENT ACQUISITION AND ENHANCEMENT
7. Systems to gain skills
25. Positive and negative feedback
43. Follows staffing process
61. Fills skill limitation gap

DIMENSION 8 – TALENT ALLOCATION AND DEPLOYMENT
8. Defers where one is more skilled
26. Talent viewed collectively
44. Strengths/weaknesses known
62. Talent is balanced

Factor IV. Teaming Skills

DIMENSION 9 – RESOURCE MANAGEMENT
9. Uses experience to strengthen
27. Team uses time well
45. Asks for outside help
63. Organizes and uses resources

DIMENSION 10 – TEAM LEARNING
10. Debriefs successes
28. Debriefs failures and mistakes
46. Practices improvement
64. Receptive to innovation

DIMENSION 11 – DECISION MAKING
11. Makes timely decisions
29. Some decisions delegated within team
47. Resists jumping to conclusions
65. Discusses problems objectively

DIMENSION 12 – CONFLICT RESOLUTION
12. Smooth internal communications
30. Takes on tough issues
48. Can reach a consensus
66. Calmly resolves conflict

DIMENSION 13 – TEAM ATMOSPHERE
13. Not just individuals
31. Members enjoy this team
49. Has a positive atmosphere
67. Team celebrates successes

DIMENSION 14 – MANAGING PROCESS
14. Spots problems early
32. Meetings are effective
50. Team is process-driven
68. Designs new processes

Factor V. Task Skills

DIMENSION 15 – FOCUSING
15. Focuses on customers
33. Strategies are successful
51. Tactics and plans on target
69. Focuses on critical priorities

DIMENSION 16 – ASSIGNMENT FLEXIBILITY
16. Assigns work flexibly
34. Members share load
52. Has needed autonomy
70. Uses cross-training

DIMENSION 17 – MEASUREMENT
17. Tracks performance measures
35. Performance improvement feedback
53. Known success measurements
71. Creates process measures

DIMENSION 18 – DELIVERING THE GOODS
18. Finds resources
36. Makes no excuses
54. Exceeds goals
72. Is role model

Factor VI. Team Support from the Organization

DIMENSION 19 – TEAM SUPPORT FROM THE ORGANIZATION
73. Leadership sets clear strategies
74. Easy access to resources
75. Authority to make decisions
76. Aligned reward system

Factor VII. Team Leader Fit

DIMENSION 20 – TEAM LEADER FIT
77. Necessary skills to lead
78. Planning skills to lead
79. Delegates; coaches; rewards performance
80. Runs interference outside team

Appendix C
Competency Summary

Competency Profile for a High-Performing Work Team

The following is a list of the 23 highest-related competencies for the first 18 dimensions (Dimensions 19 and 20 do not refer to competencies of the team). Competencies were weighted for each dimension: a mission-critical competency was given a weight of 3, important a 2, and nice to have a 1. This list should be a rough approximation of what the competencies of a high-performing work team should be if all dimensions are mission critical.

The competencies are listed in rank order from the most important (1st – *Drive for* Results #53) to the 23rd most important (*Managing* Vision and Purpose #65). A rank of 23rd doesn't mean it isn't important, because there are another 44 competencies that we didn't include.

These competencies are the most critical skills for a high-performing work team.

Rank Order	Competency	Rank Order	Competency
1st	*Drive for* Results (53)	13	Time Management (62)
2	Priority Setting (50)	14	Motivating Others (36)
3	Problem Solving (51)	15	Personal Disclosure (44)
4	*Building Effective* Teams (60)	16	Planning (47)
5	Informing (27)	17	Organizing (39)
6	Peer Relationships (42)	18	Delegation (18)
7	Conflict Management (12)	19	Managerial Courage (34)
8	Managing and Measuring Work (35)	20	Customer Focus (15)
		21	*Dealing with* Ambiguity (2)
9	Listening (33)	22	Business Acumen (5)
10	Process Management (52)	23	*Managing* Vision and Purpose (65)
11	Sizing Up People (56)		
12	Standing Alone (57)		

Mapping to the Leadership Architect® Competency Library

Since many teams don't emphasize all the dimensions for team effectiveness, the analysis below also lists the competency mapping results for each of the 20 dimensions. (Dimensions 1–18 list characteristics of the team; Dimension 19 lists characteristics of the organization; and Dimension 20 lists characteristics of the team leader). For example, for a team to be successful in Dimension 1 – Thrust Management, the competency Priority Setting (50) is mission critical. Problem Solving (51) is an important competency, and Process Management (52) is a nice to have competency.

Dimension 1 – Thrust Management

Mission Critical	**Important**	**Nice to Have**
2 *Dealing with* Ambiguity	5 Business Acumen	15 Customer Focus
35 Managing and Measuring Work	12 Conflict Management	32 Learning on the Fly
50 Priority Setting	51 Problem Solving	33 Listening
53 *Drive for* Results		34 Managerial Courage
57 Standing Alone		37 Negotiating
		46 Perspective
		52 Process Management
		58 Strategic Agility

Dimension 2 – Thrust Clarity

Mission Critical	**Important**	**Nice to Have**
27 Informing	5 Business Acumen	33 Listening
35 Managing and Measuring Work	15 Customer Focus	47 Planning
	46 Perspective	49 Presentation Skills
	65 *Managing* Vision and Purpose	50 Priority Setting
		52 Process Management
		58 Strategic Agility
		67 Written Communications

Dimension 3 – Thrust Commitment

Mission Critical	**Important**	**Nice to Have**
35 Managing and Measuring Work	36 Motivating Others	15 Customer Focus
53 *Drive for* Results	42 Peer Relationships	22 Ethics and Values
60 *Building Effective* Teams	50 Priority Setting	43 Perseverance
	65 *Managing* Vision and Purpose	

C-2

Dimension 4 – Trust in Truthful Communication

Mission Critical	**Important**	**Nice to Have**
12 Conflict Management	29 Integrity and Trust	21 *Managing* Diversity
33 Listening	42 Peer Relationships	22 Ethics and Values
34 Managerial Courage	60 *Building Effective*	45 Personal Learning
44 Personal Disclosure	Teams	56 Sizing Up People
57 Standing Alone		

Dimension 5 – Trust in Actions

Mission Critical	**Important**	**Nice to Have**
12 Conflict Management	18 Delegation	29 Integrity and Trust
22 Ethics and Values	27 Informing	31 Interpersonal Savvy
33 Listening	57 Standing Alone	36 Motivating Others
42 Peer Relationships		37 Negotiating
44 Personal Disclosure		40 *Dealing with* Paradox
60 *Building Effective* Teams		53 *Drive for* Results

Dimension 6 – Trust Inside the Team

Mission Critical	**Important**	**Nice to Have**
42 Peer Relationships	12 Conflict Management	7 Caring About Direct Reports
51 Problem Solving	27 Informing	15 Customer Focus
53 *Drive for* Results	45 Personal Learning	36 Motivating Others
60 *Building Effective* Teams	50 Priority Setting	57 Standing Alone
	62 Time Management	

Dimension 7 – Talent Acquisition and Enhancement

Mission Critical	**Important**	**Nice to Have**
25 Hiring and Staffing	19 Developing Direct Reports and Others	1 Action Oriented
27 Informing	39 Organizing	12 Conflict Management
50 Priority Setting	62 Time Management	17 Decision Quality
51 Problem Solving		18 Delegation
53 *Drive for* Results		29 Integrity and Trust
56 Sizing Up People		34 Managerial Courage

Dimension 8 – Talent Allocation and Deployment

Mission Critical	Important	Nice to Have
44 Personal Disclosure	12 Conflict Management	25 Hiring and Staffing
55 Self-Knowledge	18 Delegation	39 Organizing
56 Sizing Up People	53 *Drive for* Results	40 *Dealing with* Paradox
60 *Building Effective* Teams		42 Peer Relationships

Dimension 9 – Resource Management

Mission Critical	Important	Nice to Have
39 Organizing	47 Planning	37 Negotiating
50 Priority Setting	53 *Drive for* Results	38 Organizational Agility
51 Problem Solving	62 Time Management	63 Total Work Systems
52 Process Management		

Dimension 10 – Team Learning

Mission Critical	Important	Nice to Have
32 Learning on the Fly	2 *Dealing with* Ambiguity	28 Innovation Management
33 Listening	35 Managing and Measuring Work	54 Self-Development
51 Problem Solving	45 Personal Learning	61 Technical Learning
	50 Priority Setting	
	62 Time Management	

Dimension 11 – Decision Making

Mission Critical	Important	Nice to Have
16 *Timely* Decision Making	12 Conflict Management	1 Action Oriented
17 Decision Quality	33 Listening	2 *Dealing with* Ambiguity
51 Problem Solving	50 Priority Setting	11 Composure
	53 *Drive for* Results	18 Delegation
		42 Peer Relationships

Dimension 12 – Conflict Resolution

Mission Critical	Important	Nice to Have
11 Composure	27 Informing	37 Negotiating
12 Conflict Management	33 Listening	50 Priority Setting
34 Managerial Courage	51 Problem Solving	57 Standing Alone
42 Peer Relationships		

Dimension 13 – Team Atmosphere

Mission Critical	**Important**	**Nice to Have**
36 Motivating Others	26 Humor	29 Integrity and Trust
60 *Building Effective* Teams	27 Informing	65 *Managing* Vision and Purpose
	42 Peer Relationships	
	53 *Drive for* Results	

Dimension 14 – Managing Process

Mission Critical	**Important**	**Nice to Have**
51 Problem Solving	53 *Drive for* Results	1 Action Oriented
52 Process Management	63 Total Work Systems	16 *Timely* Decision Making
		32 Learning on the Fly
		47 Planning
		50 Priority Setting

Dimension 15 – Focusing

Mission Critical	**Important**	**Nice to Have**
15 Customer Focus	5 Business Acumen	35 Managing and Measuring Work
50 Priority Setting	46 Perspective	58 Strategic Agility
	47 Planning	65 *Managing* Vision and Purpose
	53 *Drive for* Results	

Dimension 16 – Assignment Flexibility

Mission Critical	**Important**	**Nice to Have**
18 Delegation	2 *Dealing with* Ambiguity	37 Negotiating
27 Informing	19 Developing Direct Reports and Others	45 Personal Learning
56 Sizing Up People	36 Motivating Others	54 Self-Development
60 *Building Effective* Teams	42 Peer Relationships	55 Self-Knowledge
	62 Time Management	

Dimension 17 – Measurement

Mission Critical	**Important**	**Nice to Have**
35 Managing and Measuring Work	27 Informing	13 Confronting Direct Reports
52 Process Management	47 Planning	34 Managerial Courage
	50 Priority Setting	56 Sizing Up People
	53 *Drive for* Results	60 *Building Effective* Teams

Dimension 18 – Delivering the Goods

Mission Critical	**Important**	**Nice to Have**
39 Organizing	1 Action Oriented	16 *Timely* Decision Making
43 Perseverance	35 Managing and	37 Negotiating
50 Priority Setting	Measuring Work	47 Planning
51 Problem Solving	52 Process Management	62 Time Management
53 *Drive for* Results		

Dimension 19 – Team Support from the Organization

Mission Critical	**Important**	**Nice to Have**
18 Delegation	47 Planning	36 Motivating Others
20 Directing Others	50 Priority Setting	38 Organizational Agility
27 Informing	52 Process Management	53 *Drive for* Results
35 Managing and	60 *Building Effective*	56 Sizing Up People
Measuring Work	Teams	58 Strategic Agility
65 *Managing* Vision and		
Purpose		

Dimension 20 – Team Leader Fit

Mission Critical	**Important**	**Nice to Have**
18 Delegation	9 Command Skills	8 Comfort Around Higher
20 Directing Others	33 Listening	Management
27 Informing	56 Sizing Up People	12 Conflict Management
35 Managing and	65 *Managing* Vision and	36 Motivating Others
Measuring Work	Purpose	47 Planning
45 Personal Learning		50 Priority Setting
60 *Building Effective*		
Teams		

Developmental Difficulty

Based on the mapping to the Leadership Architect® Competencies, the list below shows the relative developmental difficulty for Dimensions 1–18, from hardest to develop (Trust in Actions #5) to easiest to develop (Managing Process #14).

Rank Order*	Dimension	Rank Order*	Dimension
1st	Trust in Actions (5)	10	Delivering the Goods (18)
2	Thrust Management (1)	11	Thrust Commitment (3)
3	Talent Acquisition and Enhancement (7)	12	Decision Making (11)
4	Trust in Truthful Communication (4)	13	Resource Management (9)
5	Assignment Flexibility (16)	14	Thrust Clarity (2)
6	Trust Inside the Team (6)	15	Measurement (17)
7	Talent Allocation and Deployment (8)	16	Team Atmosphere (13)
8	Conflict Resolution (12)	17	Focusing (15)
9	Team Learning (10)	18	Managing Process (14)

(from hardest to easiest)

The 67 Leadership Architect® Competencies

1 Action Oriented
2 *Dealing with* Ambiguity
3 Approachability
4 Boss Relationships
5 Business Acumen
6 Career Ambition
7 Caring About Direct Reports
8 Comfort Around Higher Management
9 Command Skills
10 Compassion
11 Composure
12 Conflict Management
13 Confronting Direct Reports
14 Creativity
15 Customer Focus
16 *Timely* Decision Making
17 Decision Quality
18 Delegation
19 Developing Direct Reports and Others
20 Directing Others
21 *Managing* Diversity
22 Ethics and Values
23 Fairness to Direct Reports
24 Functional/Technical Skills
25 Hiring and Staffing
26 Humor
27 Informing
28 Innovation Management
29 Integrity and Trust
30 Intellectual Horsepower
31 Interpersonal Savvy
32 Learning on the Fly
33 Listening

34 Managerial Courage
35 Managing and Measuring Work
36 Motivating Others
37 Negotiating
38 Organizational Agility
39 Organizing
40 *Dealing with* Paradox
41 Patience
42 Peer Relationships
43 Perseverance
44 Personal Disclosure
45 Personal Learning
46 Perspective
47 Planning
48 Political Savvy
49 Presentation Skills
50 Priority Setting
51 Problem Solving
52 Process Management
53 *Drive for* Results
54 Self-Development
55 Self-Knowledge
56 Sizing Up People
57 Standing Alone
58 Strategic Agility
59 *Managing Through* Systems
60 *Building Effective* Teams
61 Technical Learning
62 Time Management
63 Total Work Systems
64 Understanding Others
65 *Managing* Vision and Purpose
66 Work/Life Balance
67 Written Communications

*Note: Italicized words are not alphabetized.